MERCEDES-BENZ
PRODUCTION MODELS BOOK • 1946–1983

Detailed descriptions, specifications, photos,
production data and prices of all
1946–83 passenger automobiles

by W. Robert Nitske

World-wide distribution by
Motorbooks International
Publishers & Wholesalers Inc
Osceola, Wisconsin 54020, USA

Books by W. Robert Nitske

The Amazing Porsche and Volkswagen Story was published in 1958.

The Complete Mercedes Story was first published by the Macmillan Company in 1955.

Rudolf Diesel, Pioneer of the Age of Power (with Charles M. Wilson) was published by the University of Okalahoma Press in 1965.

The Life of Wilhelm Conrad Röntgen, Discoverer of the X-Ray, was published by the University of Arizona Press in 1971.

Travels in North America, 1822–1824, a translation of the important exploration diary of Duke Paul Wilhelm of Württemberg, was published by the University of Oklahoma Press in 1973.

Mercedes-Benz 300SL was published by Motorbooks International in 1974.

The Zeppelin Story was published by A. S. Barnes & Company in 1977.

Mercedes-Benz Production Models 1946–1975 was published by Motorbooks International in 1977.

Mercedes-Benz: A History was published by Motorbooks International in 1978.

Mercedes-Benz: Diesel Automobiles was published by Motorbooks International in 1981.

Copyright © 1977, 1983 by W. Robert Nitske
All rights reserved
Printed in the United States of America

First Printing

All illustrations are from the archives of the Daimler-Benz A.G.

Printed by Shandling Lithographing Co., Inc.
Tucson, Arizona 85705

Library of Congress Cataloging in Publication Data

Nitske, W. Robert.
Mercedes-Benz production models book, 1946-1983.

1. Mercedes automobile.   I. Title.
TL215.M4N518   1983   629.2'222   83-8041
ISBN 0-87938-190-6

World-wide distribution by:

Motorbooks International
Osceola, Wisconsin, U.S.A.

Table of Contents

Models Index. 4
Production Eras. 5
1946–1983 Model Details. 11
Model Offerings. 204
Production Totals 205
United States Sales 205
Model Designations. 206
Conversions of Power 208
Engine and Chassis Codes 209
Total Production of Models. 210
Engine Designations 212
Engine Production Details. 213
Acknowledgments. 218

Models Index

(Listed in order of their manufacture.)

Model	Page	Model	Page	Model	Page
170V	12	230S	64	450SEL 6.9	138
170Va	12	250S	66	280SL	140
170Vb	12	250SE	68	280SLC	140
170S	14	300SE	70	200	142
170Sb	14	300SEL	70	200D	144
170S-V	14	300SEL 6.3	72	220D	146
170D	16	200	74	230	148
170Da	16	200D	76	230E	148
170Db	16	220	78	240D	150
170DS	16	220D	80	250	152
170S-D	16	230	82	280	154
220	18	230/6	82	280E	156
220a	18	250	84	300D	158
300	20	280S	86	240TD	160
300b	20	280SE/SEL	88	300TD	162
300c	20	300SEL	90	230T	164
300d	20	250C	92	230TE	164
300S	24	250CE	92	250T	166
300Sc	24	280SE 3.5	94	280TE	166
180	26	300SEL 3.5	96	450SLC 5.0	168
180a, b, c	26	250	98	300SD	170
180D	28	280SEL 3.5	100	280CE	172
180Db	28	280SE 3.5	100	280C	174
180Dc	28	350SL	102	230C	174
300SL coupe	30	350SLC	104	230CE	174
300SL roadster	30	280	106	300CD	176
190SL	32	280E	108	280S	178
190	34	280CE	108	280SE	180
190b	34	280C	110	280SEL	180
190c	34	280SE 4.5	112	380SE	182
219	36	280SEL 4.5	112	380SEL	182
220S	38	300SEL 4.5	114	500SE	184
220SE	40	450SL	116	500SEL	184
190D	42	450SLC	118	300TD	186
190Dc	42	280S	120	200T	188
220	44	280SE	122	380SL	190
220S	44	350SE	124	380SLC	192
220SEb	46	350SEL	124	500SL	194
300SE	48	230/4	126	500SLC	194
230SL	50	240D	128	300SD	196
250SL	52	280SEL	130	380SEC	198
280SL	54	450SE	132	500SEC	200
600	56	450SEL	134	190	202
200	58	240D 3.0	136	190E	202
200D	60	300D	136		
230	62				

Production Eras

It is appropriate to begin this book on Mercedes Models with the year 1946. That year marked the beginning of the post-war production period and the Nallinger era, followed in 1963 by the Scherenberg era.

In the long and distinguished history of Daimler and Benz, there was always a definite engineering direction in their products, reflecting the personality of its then current Chef-Konstrukteur. It all began in 1900 when Wilhelm Maybach created the "New Daimler," developed from the 28-horsepower Phönix model built under the direction of Gottlieb Daimler in 1899. With the resounding success of this new 35-horsepower machine in Nice, the "Mercedes" era was first introduced.

Daimler received his basic patent number 28,022 for the fast-turning light gasoline engine on December 16, 1883. In October of that year, Karl Benz had established his Gas Engine Factory in Mannheim to build engines according to his own design.

On August 29, 1885, Daimler received patent number 36,423 for his vehicle and on January 29, 1886, Benz received patent number 37,435 from the Kaiserliche Patentamt for his motorwagon.

Wilhelm Maybach remained with Daimler until 1907 and was the creator of the powerful Mercedes racing car which in 1903 developed as much as 90 horsepower and in 1906 an astounding 120 horsepower.

Paul Daimler took over the responsibility of the Chief Constructor in 1907 to stay with the company until 1922. He made his debut with the 140-horsepower racing cars which astonished the automotive world with the decisive victories in the prestigious French Grand Prix. In 1910 the Knight patents for their engines was used, culminating in the 16/50-horsepower four-cylinder automobile in 1916 with that engine construction and a shaft drive, first used in 1905.

The 1914 racing cars — again to confound all expert observers — beat all competitors in the French Grand Prix. But Daimler's best remembered models were those using a supercharger. The 1921 models of 1.5 liter (6/25/40 horsepower) and 2.6 liter (10/40/65 horsepower) and the 2.0-liter racing car of 125 horsepower were truly exciting machines.

Ferdinand Porsche took over the leadership of the construction bureau in 1923 and remained there for five years. He was quick to capitalize on the victorious supercharged model and developed the four-cylinder engine into the six- and eight-cylinder types. In 1923 and 1924 the 2-, 4-, and 6-liter engines were used in passenger cars; and in 1928 the 2.6-, 3.5-, and 4.6-liter six- and eight-cylinder engines were used without superchargers in the sedan models Stuttgart, Mannheim, and Nürnberg.

In 1924 it was decided to merge the interests of the Daimler and the Benz companies and to create a unified construction bureau.

As usual, however, the best-remembered Porsche creations were the powerful supercharged sports cars. Beginning with the K-model in 1927, with a 6.2-liter engine of 24/100/140 horsepower, and the S model with the 6.8-liter engine developing 26/120/180 horsepower, these six-cylinder cars were further developed to appear in 1928 as the 7.1-liter 170/225 horsepower touring models SS and SSK.

In 1929 Hans Nibel took over the position of Chief Construction Engineer of the recently formed Daimler-

Benz Vis-à-Vis 1894

Daimler Vis-à-Vis 1894

Daimler Phoenix racer 1899

Mercedes racer 1901

Mercedes racer 1906

Benz company. As early as 1908 he had startled everyone with his huge 200-horsepower Blitzen Benz, a fantastic car, which in 1909 established a world's record of 228.094 kilometers (141.7 miles) per hour in the United States to remain unbroken until 1924. With Max Wagner, Nibel was also responsible for the streamlined, rear-engined Benz Tropfenwagon of 1922. In the fall of 1926, Nibel joined the combined construction staff of the two merged firms, and was actively involved in the development details of the Porsche era models. (The SSK sports car of 1931 was a refinement of the touring car of 1928.)

In addition to the 1929 Nürnberg and Mannheim sedans, Nibel created the "Grosser Mercedes," a 7.7-liter limousine, with or without supercharger. A 1.7-liter six-cylinder sedan, the first car with swing axles, appeared in 1931, followed by similar 2-liter 200 models the following year. In 1934 the first rear-engined Mercedes, the 130 model, was built, and the 1.7-liter sedans using an X-shaped oval tubular chassis, 170V front-, and 170H rear-engined, attracted considerable comment. A 150H model followed soon.

Along with these many new construction models, Nibel also created in 1934 the first racing car for the 750-kilogram formula, the 3.3-liter 280-horsepower eight-cylinder machine; and from the eight-cylinder 380 model sports car with a supercharger of 1932 the 5-liter 100/160 horsepower 500K model sports car was developed.

After the sudden death of Nibel in 1934, Max Sailer — with Fritz Nallinger as deputy — took over the duties of the engineering division. Sailer, even more than most of his predecessors or successors, had been a successful racing competitor. In 1914 he had auspiciously participated in the French Grand Prix; in 1921 he won the Coppa Florio; and in 1923 he raced in the Memorial Day Classic at Indianapolis. He came to Untertürkheim from the position of manager of the Marienfelde plant. During the Sailer era, the first diesel-engined passenger car was marketed in 1935 — the 260D with the 2.6-liter 45-horsepower engine, utilizing the pre-chamber combustion system patented by Prosper L'Orange and developed originally at Mannheim in 1923. The advent of this diesel-engined sedan opened up an entirely new aspect in passenger automobile power.

But the racing cars developed by Sailer attracted the greatest admiration of automobile enthusiasts. These were: (1) in 1935 the 4- to 5.6-liter eight-cylinder cars to develop 600 horsepower, (2) the victorious 3-liter twelve-cylinder racing cars for the 1938-1939 formula, and (3) the spectacular 1.5-liter car of 1939 with the two-stage supercharger. There was also the 5.6-liter twelve-cylinder record car in 1936.

In addition, the six-cylinder sedans of 3.2 liters, developed from the 2.9-liter engines of 1932, were brought out in a 3.4-liter version as model 320. The 5.4-liter 115/180 horsepower eight-cylinder sports model 540K of 1937 was a further development of the 500K of 1934. And, of course, the 7.7-liter 155/230 horsepower eight-cylinder supercharged engine appeared in 1937 in a vastly improved Grosser Mercedes, using an oval tubular frame. In 1938 the 230 sedan model had the first all-steel body.

Throughout this brief resume of automobile development at Daimler-Benz, considerable emphasis has been given to the construction of racing cars. They were a most important part of the construction activity, and the valuable experience gathered in strong competition added immensely to the technical progress in automotive evolution. Especially in Mercedes automobiles was the influence of racing and sports engines and chassis noticable, perhaps more than in the products of any other passenger car manufacturer.

Wilhelm Maybach began this episode with the 30/35-

4.5-l. Mercedes racer 1914

Mercedes sports-and racing car 1921

1.5-l. Mercedes sports-and racing car 1922

1.5-l. Mercedes racer 1923

2-l. Mercedes racer 1924

horsepower four-cylinder Mercedes of 1901 which two years later developed 60 and 90 horsepower and in 1905 an even 100 horsepower. In 1906 the huge six-cylinder engine developed 120 horsepower. The last Maybach racing car (1907) had only 80 horsepower, but with many improvements in construction the car actually outperformed the earlier models.

During the Paul Daimler era, Otto Schilling was especially concerned with the further development of racing car construction. The 130-horsepower Mercedes created tremendous admiration by the automotive public when in 1908 Christian Lautenschlager won the French race over twenty-three competitors at an average speed of 111.1 kilometers per hour and Otto Salzer drove the record lap at 126.5 kilometers (78.56 miles) per hour. The 1914 Mercedes made history by repeating the victorious feat. And the supercharged four-cylinder racing cars of 1921 and 1922 with the 1.5-, 2.6-, and 2-liter engines of 40, 65, and 125 horsepower were amazing machines, and way ahead of their times.

During the Ferdinand Porsche regime, the experience with the 2-liter eight-cylinder car of 1923 with supercharger led to that treatment for the 1914 model Grand Prix machines. The further developed 2-liter cars competed successfully in the Sicilian Targa and Coppa Florio, driven by Werner, Lautenschlager, and Neubauer. However, the construction of the fantasic sports models, K, S, SS, and SSK, with their huge 6- and 7-liter six-cylinder engines and whining superchargers are much better remembered by the general public.

But in 1934 Hans Nibel constructed for the new formula a racing car with an eight-cylinder engine of 3.3-liter displacement and 280 horsepower. Only twenty-eight years before the Maybach six-cylinder 11-liter engine (140 millimeter bore and 120 millimeter stroke) had developed 120 horsepower. (Prior to this time the S series of sports cars had participated in racing events during the difficult economic times of the post-war era.) The Nibel racing car engines had steel cylinders with four valves each with spark plugs located between them, and two overhead camshafts; the crankshaft had roller bearings. With this car the golden epoch of racing began for Mercedes. Rudolf Caracciola and this 750-kilogram car seemed invincible. The work of Hans Nibel remained in the capable hands of his assistants Max Sailer, Max Wagner, Albert Hees, and Fritz Nallinger.

Under the leadership of Max Sailer, the construction bureau developed the 4- and 5-liter eight-cylinder racing cars of 350 to 600 horsepower for the 1935-37 period along with a twelve-cylinder record car of 5.6-liters in 1936. Out of ten Grand Prix, Mercedes won nine events. In 1937, seven out of twelve Grandes Epreuves went to the Mercedes drivers. For the 1938 formula, the 3-liter twelve-cylinder racing car developing 450 horsepower was built. Even with less power the car reached the same average speeds of the earlier machines. Once again, the Mercedes drivers Caracciola, von Brauchitsch, and Lang were overwhelmingly successful in international competition — in fact so much so, that the Italians decided to allow only 1.5-liter cars in the prominent Tripoli race in 1939. Sailer and Wagner created, in record time and complete secrecy, the two-stage supercharged V-8 cylinder machine which gave Mercedes a double victory over twenty-eight other competitors. Lang averaged 197.8 kilometers (122.9 miles) per hour and Caracciola 191.9 km, a truly magnificent accomplishment of superb engineering and masterful driving of an excellent product.

The Fritz Nallinger era, officially begun late in 1940 after the Max Sailer reign, had its real beginning with the 170 gasoline vehicles of the Nibel period. Nallinger developed the 170V then to such a high level that it proved to

Benz racer 1900

Benz racer 1908

1.5-l. Benz sports car 1922

Blitzen Benz 1911

2-l. Benz Tropfen racer 1922

be the best-selling Mercedes model for ten years. The diesel engine was also further developed into the 1.76-liter unit by Max Wagner when Nallinger interruped his activity from the fall of 1945 to May 1948.

Since the various models constructed during this period will be presented in detail, it will be superfluous to summarize the Nallinger era in this section, except for a brief mention of the racing activities.

Greatly encouraged by the splendid successes with their 300SL sports car in international competition in 1952, Nallinger and his able assistants designed a new formula I car. The 196 made its debut in 1954 at the French Grand Prix with a startling double victory and won five Grands Prix that year and five in 1955, driven by Juan Manuel Fangio (eight), Karl Kling (one), and Sterling Moss (one). The 2.5-liter eight-cylinder engine of 76 millimeter bore and 68.8 millimeter stroke developed about 280 horsepower. A sports racing car, the 300SLR, based on the formula car, had a 3-liter engine of 300 horsepower at 7,500 rpm. It won the championship for Mercedes in 1955.

When Fritz Nallinger retired from his position in 1963, Hans Scherenberg took over the helm. The various models brought out at first were still those in the development stage of his predecessor, but the New Generation models showed the distinct imprint of the new head of the construction department and can unquestionably be considered as falling into the Scherenberg era. With the introduction in 1972 of the S-class of cars the change was complete.

One of the extra curricular constructions, the C-111, created much comment when first shown at the Frankfurt Auto Show in 1969. It was a highly sophisticated engineering exercise and a purely experimental car, but speculation — and hopes for the availability of such a vehicle to the buyer — ran high. The small coupe had a 3-chamber Wankel rotary engine of 1.8-liter displacement, developing 330 horsepower at 7,000 revolutions per minute. It reached 0-60 miles per hour in 4.9 seconds and had a maximum speed of 162 miles per hour. The rotary engine weighed only 275 pounds (against the 495 pounds of the V-8 of 230 horsepower) and had only 950 parts (the V-8 had 1,750). A year later, a 4-chamber rotary engine was installed and even better performance figures were achieved (0-60 in 4.7 seconds; maximum speed 186 mph). However, the Wankel rotary engine was not yet considered to be ready for installation in regular passenger cars.

The experimental C-111 was used in 1976 to establish several world speed records in slightly modified form with aerodynamic headlight fairing and solid wheel covers, and with a 5-cylinder diesel engine installed.

The basic power unit was that of the current 300D passenger car, but equipped with a Garrett Airesearch turbo charger. The engine developed over 200 horsepower at 4,200 to 4,700 revolutions per minute and had 275 ft/lb. (38 mkg) torque at 3,600 rpm. The final drive ratio in fifth gear was 2.7. The fastest average speed achieved was 158.368 miles per hour (254.856 kilometers per hour) for one hour. World records for 5,000 miles at 156.928 mph (252.540 kmph), for 10,000 kilometers at 156.748 mph (252.249 kmph), and for 10,000 miles at 156.467 mph (251.798 kmph), and thirteen class records were established in less than sixty-four hours of driving on the test track at Nardo, Italy, by four factory drivers/engineers (Moch, Liebold, Waxenberger, and Kadon). The event indicated the importance of this reliable, economical, and fast diesel engine and signified a trend to turbocharging of this well-established and still highly promising power plant by the imaginative Mercedes-Benz engineering department.

Another highly important project executed under the leadership of Hans Scherenberg, head of the Research and

Mercedes-Benz Model K 1926

Mercedes-Benz Model S 1927

Mercedes-Benz Model SSK 1928

Mercedes-Benz Model SSKL 1931

Development Department, was the first of the special safety vehicles, the ESF (Experimentier-Sicherheits-Fahrzeug), constructed in 1971; even though passenger safety had always been a major consideration in the construction of Mercedes-Benz automobiles. This new safety vehicle included a vast number of outside and interior safety designs and devices and underwent extensive tests. Actually, more than a hundred safety elements had been developed and tested since 1946, and have been incorporated into the cars built. For instance, the cone type door lock was patented in 1949. In 1952 a patented body design, standard on all cars since 1959, was the safety body which upon impact would crush in front and rear but withstand exceptional forces in the extremely strong passenger compartment. Several ESF vehicles were built and exhaustively tested, and the ESF 24 looked startlingly similar to the production 450SE sedan.

Actually, the construction of safety cars was not new; in 1940 the experimental vehicle number 11 included the improved suspension system and such safety features as solid side protection and an extremely rigid floor and a three-part steering column. Design features over the years, adding to the safety of the cars built, were the complete independent wheel suspension in 1931, and the frame-floor construction and stressed chassis used since 1953. Engine features were the overhead camshaft design since 1952, the low-pivot single joint swing axle since 1954, power steering since 1959, air suspension system and automatic transmission since 1961, a dual circuit power braking with disc brakes for the entire passenger car line since 1963, a leveling adjustment device with coil springs available for all cars since 1965, the new diagonal-pivot swing axle from 1968 on, electronic fuel injection since 1969, and the interlocking brake system, optional on the S-class cars since 1978.

With the appearance in 1977 of the 450SLC 5.0 coupe, the new light-alloy engines were introduced. A reduction of 7 percent in weight over the 450SLC was achieved by the use of lighter metals. The turbo-charged 5-cylinder diesel was also shown at that time, but that S-class sedan was intended for the United States market only. And the entirely new line of station wagons, the T-range, with a choice of five different engines, made its initial appearance at that Auto Show.

Another record attempt, using the C-111 vehicle, but then modified with a rear stabilizing fin and some alterations to reduce wind resistance even further, was made in April 1978. Again, the Nardo track was chosen, but a thick fog curtailed the planned speed event. Records were established for from 100 to 1,000 kilometers, and miles, and up to 12 hours. The fastest run was 199.995 miles per hour for the 500 kilometers, and for 12 hours the average speed was 195.398 mph. Fuel consumption was a remarkable 14.7 miles per gallon, with speeds of the 2,295 cc turbo-charged diesel often exceeding 200 miles per hour.

Werner Breitschwerdt succeeded Hans Scherenberg as chief engineer, and introduced in 1979 the 380 and 500 lines of newly designed cars with the lighter engines. With less wind resistance than the previous models, these cars gave equal, or even superior, performance and used less fuel than those which they replaced — the 450s and 6.9.

That year, the cylinder cut-off system was demonstrated, promising a fuel saving of up to 32 percent. Work on that development had begun in 1974. Another innovation was the anti-knock control, whereby the compression could be raised to increase the thermal efficiency of the engine, thus allowing the use of a lower octane fuel.

With the introduction of the entirely new W-201 body style in late 1982, a small model automobile was again a vital part of the production program of Daimler-Benz.

Mercedes-Benz racer 1936

Mercedes-Benz racer 1938

Mercedes-Benz racer 1939

12-cyl. Mercedes-Benz record car 1936

From the dreary wartime charcoal-burning model (170)...

...to the handsome small sedans of more than thirty years later.

1946-1983 Model Details

In April 1945, the directors of the Daimler-Benz A.G. issued a statement to the effect that the company had "for all practical purposes ceased to exist." The devastation of their manufacturing facilities was appalling. The Untertürkheim automobile factory complex was 70 percent destroyed and the Sindelfingen plant about 85 percent. The truck facilities at Mannheim were 20 percent destroyed and those at Gaggenau about 80 percent. What remained of the Berlin Marienfelde factory was dismantled and shipped off by the victors.

Fortunately, the Untertürkheim, Sindelfingen, and Mannheim plants were in the same military occupational zone and they could be effectively managed after as many former employees and workers as possible were located. The slow and tedious task of cleaning up the rubble was begun and the reconstruction of manufacturing facilities made some progress.

Vehicle production could only be accomplished if the manufacture of previous models would be continued. It was the natural choice of the directors to put the 170 model into production as soon as possible. The other models, the larger 230 or the massive 540K or even the prestigious 770, were of course, never considered for manufacture at this critical time in 1945.

At first, repair maintenance work on existing cars and some assembly of the L 3500 model commercial vehicles occupied the small working force and cleared facilities. The first post-war four-cylinder engine for a 170V model was completed February 22, 1946, but entire cars were not produced until June; a total of 214 units were manufactured that year. In 1947 it was 1,045 inits, and the following year production reached 5,116 units. By that time the new currency reform had been instituted (on June 21, 1948) and the economy began to function properly. The financial paralysis ended with a sound governmental policy.

A Note on the U.S. Models

Prices quoted for the various models in the respective years are published merely as a matter of record. To compare those in Germany with their counterparts in the United States will only prove an exercise in frustration and drawing the obvious conclusions will be quite erroneous, at least for the models of recent years.

Because of the stricter emission and safety regulations, cars for the American market are equipped with many additional features. They also come furnished with many accessories generally available only optional at extra cost. For example, the United States 1976 price list enumerated 15 basic extra cost items for the 230 model and 6 for the 450SEL, while the German factory price list quoted actually 38 basic items for the 230.4 and 32 for the 450SEL as optional accessories. (A few were not available for U.S. cars.)

Nevertheless, despite the manifest futility, herewith are listed the exchange rates: In 1946 the U.S. dollar equalled about DM (German Mark) 2.50, but there was actually no official rate of exchange until 1948, when it was DM 3.33. In 1949 the rate was DM 4.20 which remained steady until 1961, when it was DM 3.98, and stayed that way until 1968. From 1969 the rate of exchange was slightly lower and dropped until it was in 1975 DM 2.49. The lowest point was reached in 1980 when it was DM 1.81. In 1981 the average exchange rate was DM 2.24, and in 1982 DM 2.51, to the U.S. dollar. (Pitfalls here are that the rate varied, sometimes hugely, during a given year.)

The 170V sedan, 1950

Prices and Production

The 170V four-door sedan sold for	DM 6,200
from July 1948	DM 8,180
from May 1949	DM 7,800
from January 1950	DM 7,380
The 170Va four-door sedan sold for	DM 7,400
The 170Vb four-door sedan sold for	DM 7,900
In New York the 170 sedan sold for	$ 2,850

Production of the 170V, 170Va, and 170Vb [Manufacturing designation 136 I-V] (from June 1946 until August 1953)

was in	1946	214 units
	1947	1,045 units
	1948	5,116 units
	1949	13,101 units
	1950	11,876 units
	1951	12,867 units
	1952	3,692 units
	1953	1,636 units
	total	49,367 units

Model 170V (1946-1953)

V (Vorn) = front

The four-cylinder engined 170V and 170H sedans had first been shown at the Berlin Auto Show in February 1936. Priced at 3,750 Reichsmark, this outstanding vehicle was thereafter available as a two-door and four-door sedan, open touring car, and even two- and four-door convertible, or cabriolet-limousine. And as a commercial vehicle, the 170 also came as an open or closed delivery van, ambulance, or police car.

The chassis was of oval tubes, and the three-bearing crankshaft engine was mounted on two rubber blocks for vibrationless operation. The independent rear suspension had coil springs, the front leaf springs. The chassis weighed 650 kilograms (1,433 pounds). With the 38-horsepower engine, the sedan reached a maximum speed of 100 kilometers (62 miles) per hour and used about 10 liters of fuel. By 1942 more than 90,000 units had been manufactured, providing impressive proof of the popularity of this model. Production of passengar car models was 71,973 units.

Announced as "ein Wagen, der Ihnen Freude macht," a car which brings joy to you, the 170V was welcomed as a vehicle incorporating the tested — and by over 100,000 owners admired — qualities of the earlier construction.

The 170V production in 1946 consisted almost exclusively of delivery trucks, ambulances, and police cruisers. This model remained practically unchanged until May 1950.

The 170Va, built from May 1950 until April 1952, had a larger engine (1,767 cubic centimeters) and greater horsepower (45), softer springing, telescopic shock absorbers and larger brakes, as well as other improvements.

The 170Vb, built from May 1952 until September 1953, had a wider track, hypoid rear axle, a larger windshield, and smoother hoodline.

Specifications

	170V	170Va / 170Vb
Engine type	4 cyl (M 136)	4 cyl (M 136)
Bore and Stroke	73.5 x 100mm (2.89 x 3.94 in)	75 x 100mm (2.95 x 3.94 in)
Displacement	1697 cc	1767 cc
Power output	38 hp (DIN) @ 3600 rpm	45 hp (DIN) @ 3600 rpm
Compression ratio	6:1 (from 1949: 6.5:1)	6.5:1
Torque	10 mkg @ 1800 rpm (72.35 ft/lb)	11 mkg @ 1800 rpm (79.59 ft/lb)
Carburetion	1 updraft carburetor Solex 30 BFLVS	
Engine speed at 100 km/hr	3300 rpm	3300 rpm
Gear ratios	I. 4.025:1 II. 2.280:1 III. 1.420:1 IV. 1.000:1	I. 4.025:1 II. 2.280:1 III. 1.420:1 IV. 1.000:1
Rear axle ratio	4.125:1	4.125:1
Chassis	X-shaped oval tubular	X-shaped oval tubular
Suspension	independent front, swing axle rear, with coil springs	
Brakes and area	drum, 564 cm² (87.4 sq in)	drum, 736 cm² (114 sq in)
Wheelbase	2845mm (112 in)	2845mm (112 in)
Track, front/rear	1310/1296mm (51.6/51.0 in)	Va: 1310/1342mm (51.6/52.8 in) Vb: 1310/1360mm (51.6/53.5 in)
Length	4285mm (168.7 in)	4285mm (168.7 in)
Width	1580mm (62.2 in)	1630mm (64.2 in)
Height	1610mm (63.4 in)	1610mm (63.4 in)
Ground clearance	185mm (7.3 in)	185mm (7.3 in)
Tires	5.50 x 16	5.50 x 16
Turning circle	11.5 meters (37.7 ft)	11.5 meters (37.7 ft)
Steering type and ratio	worm, 14.4:1	worm, 14.4:1
Weight	1160 kg (2552 lbs)	1185 kg (2607 lbs)
Maximum speed	108 km/hr (67 mph)	116 km/hr (72 mph)
Acceleration	36 sec 0-100 km	36 sec 0-100 km
Fuel consumption	11 liters/100 km (21 mpg)	10 liters (23.5 mpg)
Fuel tank capacity	42 liters (11.1 gallons)	42 liters (11.1 gallons)

The chassis of the 170V, 1946

Drawing of the 170Vb, 1953

The 170S sedan, 1949

Prices and Production

The 170S four-door sedan sold from 1949-1953 for....DM 10,100
    convertible B, two-door sedan – 1949-1951.......DM 12,850
    convertible A, 2-3 seats coupe – 1949-1951.......DM 15,800
The 170S-V four-door sedan sold from 1953-1955 for . .DM 8,300

Production of the 170S [136 IV] (from May 1949 until February 1952)

was in	1949	3,370 units
	1950	14,735 units
	1951	10,333 units
	1952	326 units
total		28,764 units

Production of the 170Sb [191] (from January 1952 until August 1953)

was in	1952	4,580 units
	1953	3,514 units
total		8,094 units

Production of the 170S [136 IV] convertible (from May 1949 until November 1951)

was in	1949	39 units
	1950	1,686 units
	1951	708 units
total		2,433 units

Production of the 170S-V [136 VIII] (from July 1953 until February 1955)

was in	1953	2,102 units
	1954	880 units
	1955	140 units
total		3,122 units

Model 170S (1949-1955)

S = Super

The 170S model, built from May 1949 to March 1952, was a further development of the V model sedan. The engine produced 52 horsepower. The valves were arranged side by side and a detachable light-alloy cylinder head was used. A downdraft Solex carburator was fitted with an air silencer and a wet-type air filter. The thermostat, set in the water circulation system, was so arranged that the heaviest work load in mountainous terrain would not cause any concern about water temperature. The drivability of the 170S showed a striking improvement, due to the more favorable weight distribution and center of gravity, with suitable track dimensions and the design of independent wheel suspension attached to the rigid cruciform frame of oval tube sections. Maximum speed was 120 kilometers (75 miles) per hour for this model which now had the larger body of the pre-war 230 model.

The car actually incorporated the newest scientific knowledge of modern automobile construction, coupled with the traditional qualities expected from the cars built by this company.

A convertible 170 model A was produced from May 1949 until February 1952, as was the model B, a convertible sedan.

The 170Sb, built from January 1952 until August 1953, had the gear shift lever attached to the steering wheel column, improved heating system, hypoid rear axle, wider track, and starting knob on the dashboard.

The 170S-V was to conclude the entire series. Built from July 1953 until February 1955, it incorporated the engine of the 170V, the chassis of the Sb with front axle of the V model, and the body of the S model.

Although no 170S models were sold in this country, an occasional one was brought back by tourists, and the editors of a magazine were able to test it. The 170S was found to be "one of the most interesting cars yet to pass through the hands of the test staff."

The 170S-V sedan, 1953

The 170S convertible A, 1949

The instrument panel of the 170S, 1949

Specifications

	170S / 170Sb	170S-V
Engine type	4 cyl (M 136)	4 cyl (M 136)
Bore and stroke	75 x 100mm (2.95 x 3.94 in)	75 x 100mm (2.95 x 3.94 in)
Displacement	1767 cc (107.7 cu in)	1767 cc (107.7 cu in)
Power output	52 hp (DIN) @ 4000 rpm	45 hp (DIN) @ 3600 rpm
Compression ratio	6.5:1	6.7:1
Torque	11.4 mkg @ 1800 rpm (82.5 ft/lb)	11 mkg @ 1800 rpm (79.6 ft/lb)
Carburetion	1 downdraft carburetor Solex 32 PBJ	1 updraft carburetor Solex 30 BFLVS
Engine speed at 100 hm/hr	3330 rpm	3330 rpm
Gear ratio	I. 4.025:1 II. 2.280:1 III. 1.420:1 IV. 1.000:1	I. 4.025:1 II. 2.280:1 III. 1.420:1 IV. 1.000:1
Rear axle ratio	S: 4.375:1 Sb: 4.44:1	4.125:1
Chassis	X-shaped oval tubular	X-shaped oval tubular
Suspension	independent front, swing axle rear, with coil springs	
Brakes and area	drum, 736 cm² (114 sq in)	drum, 736 cm² (114 sq in)
Wheelbase	2845mm (112 in)	2845mm (112 in)
Track, front/rear	S: 1315/1420mm (51.57/55.89 in) Sb: 1315/1435mm (51.57/56.49 in)	1310/1435mm (51.6/56.5 in)
Length	4455mm (175.4 in)	4450mm (175.2 in)
Width	1684mm (66.3 in)	1685mm (66.3 in)
Height	1610mm (63.4 in)	1590mm (62.6 in)
Ground clearance	185mm (7.3 in)	185mm (7.3 in)
Tires	6.40 x 15	5.50 x 16
Turning circle	12 meters (39.37 ft)	12 meters (39.37 ft)
Steering type and ratio	worm, 13.9:1	worm, 14.1:1
Weight	S: 1220 kg (2684 lbs) Sb: 1250 kg (2750 lbs)	1220 kg (2684 lbs)
Maximum speed	122 km/hr (76 mph)	115 km/hr (71 mph)
Acceleration	32 sec 0-100 km	39 sec 0-100 km
Fuel consumption	12 liters/100 km (19.5 mpg)	11.5 liters (20.4 mpg)
Fuel tank capacity	47 liters (12.4 gallons)	47 liters (12.4 gallons)

The 170D sedan, 1950

Model 170D (1949-1955)
D = Diesel

The introduction of the 170D in May 1949 indicated an increase in production facilities and further advancement in the passenger car program. This diesel-engined car was an even more economical automobile than the gasoline-powered model and was particularily well suited at that time of economic hardship in the country.

The experience gained in 1936 with the 2.6-liter diesel-engined passenger sedan (45 horsepower at 3,000 revolutions per minute) was utilized in the creation of this smaller displacement engine which had the good qualities and liveliness of a gasoline engine; in fact, in some respects was even superior. The pre-combustion chamber system engine developed 38 horsepower at 3,200 revolutions per minute. The torque curve was very steady over a wide range of engine speeds. Despite the unpleasant engine noise at idling speed, the exceptional qualities of this diesel model were readily recognized. Maximum speed was 100 kilometers (62 miles) per hour and climbing ability 29 percent in first gear. Fuel consumption was 6.4 liters for 100 kilometers of driving. And, as in all cars, the maximum speed was also the cruising speed of the vehicle.

Since there was no difference in the gasoline-engined 170 models and those equipped with the diesel engine, it was natural that the change-over in the two models coincided. The 170Da production was begun in May 1950, when the 170D model was discontinued, and ran until April 1952. At that time the 170Db appeared, to be built until October 1953.

The 170DS was built from January 1952 until August 1953 and the 170S-D from July 1953 until September 1955.

These inordinately sturdy and fantastically dependable diesel-engined cars were a most welcome addition to the previous gasoline models and represented the beginning of an unbelievable popularity of diesel models to come.

Prices and Production

The 170D four-door sedan sold from May 1949 for . . . .DM 9,200
and from January 1950 for . . . . .DM 8,620
The 170Da four-door sedan sold for . . . . .DM 8,900
The 170Db four-door sedan also sold for . . . . .DM 8,900
The 170DS four-door sedan sold for . . . . .DM 10,985
The 170S-D four-door sedan sold for. . . . . .DM 9,350

Production of the 170D, 170Da, and 170Db [136 I-VI] (from May 1949 to October 1953)

was in	1949	907 units
	1950	5,609 units
	1951	14,622 units
	1952	8,115 units
	1953	4,570 units
	total	33,823 untis

Production of the 170DS [191] (from January 1952 until August 1953)

was in	1952	6,734 units
	1953	6,251 units
	total	12,985 units

Production of the 170 S-D [136 VIII] (from July 1953 until September 1955)

was in	1953	6,494 units
	1954	5,992 units
	1955	2,401 units
	total	14,887 units

Specifications

	170D	170Da / 170Db	170DS	170S-D
Engine type	4 cyl diesel (OM 636)	4 cyl diesel (OM 636)	4 cyl diesel (OM 636)	4 cyl diesel (OM 636)
Bore and stroke	73.5 x 100mm (2.98 x 3.94 in)	75 x 100mm (2.95 x 3.94 in)	75 x 100mm (2.95 x 3.94 in)	75 x 100mm (2.95 x 3.94 in)
Displacement	1697 cc (103.5 cu in)	1767 cc (107.7 cu in)	1767 cc (107.7 cu in)	1767 cc (107.7 cu in)
Power output	38 hp (DIN) @ 3200 rpm	40 hp (DIN) @ 3200 rpm	40 hp (DIN) @ 3200 rpm	40 hp (DIN) @ 3200 rpm
Compression ratio	19:1	19:1	19:1	19:1
Torque	9.8 mkg @ 2000 rpm (70.9 ft/lb)	9.8 mkg @ 2000 rpm (70.9 ft/lb)	10.3 mkg @ 2000 rpm (74.5 ft/lb)	10.3 mkg @ 2000 rpm (74.5 ft/lb)
Carburetion	Bosch injection pump (pre-combustion chamber)		Bosch injection pump (pre-combustion chamber)	
Engine speed at 100 km/hr	3330 rpm	3330 rpm	3330 rpm	3330 rpm
Gear ratios	I. 4.025:1 II. 2.280:1 III. 1.420:1 IV. 1.000:1	I. 4.025:1 II. 2.280:1 III. 1.420:1 IV. 1.000:1	I. 4.025:1 II. 2.280:1 III. 1.420:1 IV. 1.000:1	I. 4.025:1 II. 2.280:1 III. 1.420:1 IV. 1.000:1
Rear axle ratio	4.125:1	4.125:1	4.125:1	4.125:1
Chassis	X-shaped oval tubular	X-shaped oval tubular	X-shaped oval tubular	X-shaped oval tubular
Suspension	independent front and rear swing axle with coil springs		independent front and rear swing axle with coil springs	
Brakes and area	drum, 564 cm² (87.4 sq in)	drum, 736 cm² (114 sq in)	drum, 736 cm² (114 sq in)	drum, 736 cm² (114 sq in)
Wheelbase	2845mm (112 in)	2845mm (112 in)	2845mm (112 in)	2845mm (112 in)
Track, front/rear	1310/1296mm (51.6/51.0in)	Da: 1310/1342mm (51.6/52.8 in) Db: 1310/1360mm (51.6/53.5 in)	1315/1435mm (51.6/56.5 in)	1310/1435mm (51.6/56.5 in)
Length	4285mm (168.7 in)	4285mm (168.7 in)	4455mm (175.4 in)	4450mm (175.2 in)
Width	1580mm (62.2 in)	1630mm (64.2 in)	1684mm (66.3 in)	1685mm (66.3 in)
Height	1610mm (63.4 in)	1616mm (63.4 in)	1610mm (63.4 in)	1590mm (62.6 in)
Ground clearance	185mm (7.3 in)	185mm (7.3 in)	185mm (7.3 in)	185mm (7.3 in)
Tires	5.50 x 16	5.50 x 16	5.50 x 16	5.50 x 16
Turning circle	11.5 meters (37.7 ft)	11.5 meters (37.7 ft)	12 meters (39.37 ft)	12 meters (39.37 ft)
Steering type and ratio	worm, 14.4:1	worm, 14.4:1	worm, 13.9:1	worm, 14.1:1
Weight	1250 kg (2750 lbs)	1250 kg (2750 lbs)	1275 kg (2805 lbs)	1300 kg (2860 lbs)
Maximum speed	100 km/hr (62 mph)	105 km/hr (65 mph)	105 km/hr (65 mph)	105 km/hr (65 mph)
Acceleration	58 sec 0-100 km	50 sec 0-100 km	56 sec 0-100 km	56 sec 0-100 km
Fuel consumption	7.5 liters/100 km (32 mpg)	7.5 liters/100 km (32 mpg)	8.5 liters/100 km (27.75 mpg)	8.5 liters/100 km (27.75 mpg)
Fuel tank capacity	37 liters (9.8 gallons)	37 liters (9.8 gallons)	47 liters (12.4 gallons)	47 liters (12.4 gallons)

The 220 sedan, 1951

Prices and Production

The 220 four-door sedan sold for . . . . .DM 11,925
The 220 two-door convertible sedan sold for . . . . .DM 15,160
The 220 2-3 seater convertible sold for . . . . .DM 18,860
The 220 2-3 seater coupe sold for . . . . .DM 20,850
The 220a four-door sedan sold for (in 1954) . . . . .DM 12,500
The 220 convertible sedan or coupe sold for . . . . .DM 21,500
 (The 1954 and 1955 models did not get the "a")

Production of the 220 [187] (from July 1951 to May 1954)
 was in 1951   3,453 units
      1952   9,165 units
      1953   3,322 units
      1954   214 units
    total 16,154 units

Production of the 220 convertible models, B and A [187] (from July 1951 to August 1955)
 was in 1951   368 units
      1952   1,178 units
      1953   403 units
      1954   259 units
      1955   152 units
    total   2,360 units

Production of the 220a model [180 I] (from March 1954 to April 1956)
 was in 1954   4,178 units
      1955 19,348 units
      1956   2,411 units
    total 25,937 units

Model 220 (1951-1956)

The 220 sedan was introduced at the Frankfurt Auto Show in April 1951. Regular production began in July of that year. In appearance this model closely resembled the proven 170S model, but the headlights were mounted in the fenders and the interior furnishings were more elegant. The good road-holding, soft suspension, and road safety were technically refined and superior in this six-cylinder automobile. The 2.2-liter overhead camshaft engine developed 80 horsepower at 4,600 revolutions per minute. The extremely quiet running short stroke engine had a specially balanced crankshaft and long water jackets to the cylinder parting line. The fully synchronized gear box was provided with a gear shift lever on the steering column. Special tuning of the suspension and a certain resilience of the front wheel suspension in a horizontal direction improved the suspension and achieved exceptional road-holding characteristics. The power-to-weight ratio of 16.5 kilograms (36.4 pounds) per horsepower was a considerable improvement over the 22.9 kilograms (50.5 pounds) of the 170S.

The 220 achieved 0 to 100 kilometers per hour in just 21 seconds and had a maximum and cruising speed of 140 kilometers (87 miles) per hour. With its elegant lines and fine interior, especially in the convertible sedan and convertible coupe, the 220 combined the qualities of a comfortable family car with those of a lively sports model.

The 220 sedan models were built from July 1951 to May 1954 and the convertible sedan types (B and A) from July 1951 to August 1955. A coupe model became available in May 1954; from 1954 on it came equipped with a curved windshield.

An improved 220a sedan with the new style body and the 85-horsepower engine was built in 1954. Introduced in March and produced from July, the model was built until April 1956.

The 220 sedan, 1954

The 220 convertible B, 1951

The 220 convertible A, 1951

Specifications

	220	220a
Engine type	6 cyl overhead camshaft (M180)	6 cyl overhead camshaft (M 180)
Bore and stroke	80 x 72.8mm (3.15 x 2.87 in)	80 x 72.8mm (3.15 x 2.87 in)
Displacement	2195 cc (133.9 cu in)	2195 cc (133.9 cu in)
Power output	80 hp (DIN) @ 4850 rpm	85 hp (DIN) @ 4800 rpm (92 hp SAE)
Compression ratio	6.5:1	7.6:1
Torque	14.5 mkg @ 2500 rpm (104.9 ft/lb)	16 mkg @ 2400 rpm (116 ft/lb @ 2500 rpm)
Carburetion	1 dual downdraft carburetor Solex 30 PAAJ	1 dual downdraft carburetor Solex 32 PAATJ
Engine speed at 100 km/hr	3470 rpm	3470 rpm
Gear ratios	I. 3.68:1 II. 2.25:1 III. 1.42:1 IV. 1.00:1	I. 3.40:1 later 3.52 II. 2.32:1 III. 1.52:1 IV. 1.00:1
Rear axle ratio	4.44	4.11 (37:9) finally 4.10 (41:10)
Chassis	X-shaped oval tubular	unit frame and body
Suspension	independent front, swing axle rear, with coil springs	independent front, single swing axle rear, with coil springs
Brakes and area	drum, 736 cm² (114 sq in)	drum, 1064 cm² (164.9 sq in)
Wheelbase	2845mm (112 in)	2820mm (111 in) convertible: 2700mm (106 in)
Track, front/rear	1315/1435mm (51.6/56.5 in)	1430/1470mm (56.3/57.7 in)
Length	4507mm (177.4 in) convertible A:4538mm (178.7 in)	4715mm (185.6 in) convertible: 4670mm (183.9 in)
Width	1685mm (66.3 in)	1740mm (68.5 in) convertible: 1760mm (69.3 in)
Height	1610mm (63.4 in) convertible A:1560mm (61.4 in)	1560mm (61.42 in) convertible: 1530mm (60.2 in)
Ground clearance	185mm (7.3 in)	185mm (7.3 in)
Tires	6.40 x 15	6.70 x 13
Turning circle	12 meters (39.37 ft)	11.7 meters (38.39 ft) convertible:11.4 meters (37.4 ft)
Steering type and ratio	worm, 13.9:1 (2.75 turns)	recirculating ball, 21.4:1 (4 turns)
Weight	1350 kg (2970 lbs) convertible: 1440 kg (3168 lbs)	1300 kg (2860 lbs) convertible: 1300 kg (2860 lbs)
Maximum speed	141 km/hr (87.5 mph) convertible B:140 km/hr convertible A:145 km/hr	150 km/hr (93 mph) convertible: 155 km/hr
Acceleration	21 sec 0-100 km	19 sec 0-100 km
Fuel consumption	14 liters/100 km (16.75 mpg) convertible A&B: 14.5 liters	13.5 liters/100 km (17.4 mpg) convertible: 14 liters
Fuel tank capacity	65 liters (17.2 gallons)	64 liters (16.9 gallons)

The 300 sedan, 1951

Model 300 (1951-1962)

The 300 model was also introduced to the public at the 1951 Frankfurt Show. It signified the return to the old custom of producing a truly outstanding luxury limousine of utmost comfort and superb roadability, capable of sustained high speed. It had a maximum and cruising speed of 160 kilometers (100 miles) per hour. The six-passenger sedan, with conservative lines, had a six-cylinder 3-liter overhead camshaft engine developing 115 horsepower. The short stroke engine with a special valve arrangement and combustion chamber design and thermostatically controlled water circulation and oil temperature, was most durable and extremely quiet running. It had a seven-bearing crankshaft. The chassis incorporated all of the features of the 170S plus a number of additional refinements such as a new steering mechanism design, electrical control of the auxiliary rear suspension which was adjustable from the driver's seat according to the load carried, hypoid bevel final drive, and dynamically balanced wheels. The car represented the ultimate in safety and riding comfort.

The 300 sedan was built from November 1951 until March 1954. It was also available in cabriolet form (pre-series production in April 1951 with regular production from March 1952). The type 300b, built from March 1954 until August 1955, had a more powerful engine (125 horsepower) and large dimension brakes, but the same body style. The 300c had standard transmission, two compound carburetors, higher compression and better axle ratio, and was built from September 1955 until July 1957. The cabriolet D was available until July 1956, when a special model with a wheelbase of 3,150 millimeters and overall length of 5,165 millimeters was built on individual order. Then followed the 300d with a slightly modernized body style and fuel injection engine. It was available until March 1962.

Prices

The 300 four-door sedan sold for	DM 19,900
The 300 four-door convertible sedan D sold for	DM 23,700
The 300b four-door sedan sold for	DM 22,000
The 300b four-door convertible sedan D sold for	DM 24,700
The 300c four-door sedan sold for	DM 22,000
The 300c four-door sedan "Automatic" sold for	DM 23,500
The 300c four-door convertible sedan D sold for	DM 24,700
The 300c four-door "Automatic" convertible sedan sold for	DM 26,200
The 300c four-door limousine with longer wheelbase was available at an additional	DM 3,000
The 300d four-door sedan hardtop sold for (available on special order only)	DM 27,000
The 300d four-door sedan, hardtop "Automatic"	DM 28,500
The price of the 300 sedan in the United States was	$ 6,980

Production

Production of the 300 and 300b sedans [186 II-III] (from November 1951 until August 1955)

was in	1951	47 units
	1952	2,659 units
	1953	1,776 units
	1954	1,185 units
	1955	547 units
	total	6,214 units

Production of the 300 and 300b convertible sedans [186 II-III] (from April 1951/March 1952 until July 1955)*

was in	1951	2 units
	1952	262 units
	1953	181 units
	1954	87 units
	1955	59 units
	total	591 units

Production of the 300c sedans [186 IV] (from September 1955 until June 1956)

was in	1955	330 units
	1956	885 units
	1957	217 units
	total	1,432 units

Production of the 300c convertible sedans [186 IV] (from September/December 1955 until June 1956)

was in	1955	3 units
	1956	48 units
	total	51 units

The 300d sedan, 1957

Production of the 300d sedans [189] (from August/November 1957 until March 1962)

was in	1957	144 units
	1958	1,165 units
	1959	607 units
	1960	581 units
	1961	535 units
	1962	45 units
	total	3,077 units

Production of the 300d convertible sedans [189] (from July 1958 until February 1962)

was in	1958	3 units
	1959	23 units
	1960	22 units
	1961	16 units
	1962	1 units
	total	65 units

*Note: When two different months are given as production figures, as in April 1951/March 1952, the first indicates the pre-production and the second the start of regular series production of the model.

The 300c sedan, 1955

Rear axle arrangement of 300 sedan, 1951

The 300c convertible D, 1955

Specifications

	300	300b	300c	300d
Engine type	6 cyl overhead camshaft (M 186)	6 cyl overhead camshaft (M 186)	6 cyl overhead camshaft (M 186)	6 cyl overhead camshaft (M 189)
Bore and stroke	85 x 88mm (3.35 x 3.46 in)	85 x 88mm (3.35 x 3.46 in)	85 x 88mm (3.35 x 3.46 in)	85 x 88mm (3.35 x 3.46 in)
Displacement	2996 cc (182.7 cu in)	2996 cc (182.7 cu in)	2996 cc (182.7 cu in)	2996 cc (182.7 cu in)
Power output	115 hp (DIN) @ 4600 rpm	125 hp (DIN) @ 4500 rpm (136 hp SAE)	125 hp (DIN) @ 4500 rpm (136 hp SAE)	160 hp (DIN) @ 5300 rpm (180 hp SAE)
Compression ratio	6.4:1	7.4-7.5:1	7.4-7.5:1	8.55:1
Torque	20 mkg @ 2500 rpm (114 ft/lb)	22.5 mkg @ 2600 rpm (163 ft/lb)	22.5 mkg @ 2600 rpm (163 ft/lb)	24.2 mkg @ 4200 rpm (175 ft/lb)
Carburetion	2 dual downdraft carburetors Solex 40 PBJC	2 dual downdraft carburetors Solex 32 PAJAT	2 dual downdraft carburetors	Bosch injection pump
Engine speed at 100 km/hr	3300 rpm	3300 rpm	3300 rpm (manual)	3300 rpm (automatic, 3-speed)
Gear ratios	I. 2.95:1 (later 3.30:1) II. 2.13:1 III. 1.46:1 IV. 1.00:1	I. 3.44:1 II. 2.30:1 III. 1.53:1 IV. 1.00:1	I. 3.44:1 II. 2.30:1 III. 1.53:1 IV. 1.00:1	I. 2.303:1 II. 1.435:1 III. 1.00:1
Rear axle ratio	4.44	4.67	4.67	4.67
Chassis	X-shaped oval tubular	X-shaped oval tubular	X-shaped oval tubular	X-shaped oval tubular
Suspension	independent front, swing axle rear, with coil springs		independent front, single swing axle rear, with coil springs	
Brakes and area	drum, 1270 cm² (197 sq in)	drum, 1470 cm² (228 sq in)	drum, 1470 cm² (227.9 sq in)	drum, 1470 cm² (227.9 sq in)
Wheelbase	3050mm (120 in)	3050mm (120 in)	3050mm (120 in)	3150mm (124 in)
Track, front/rear	1480/1525mm (58.2/60 in)	1480/1525mm (58.2/60 in)	1480/1525mm (58.3/60.0 in)	1480/1525mm (58.3/60.0 in)
Length	4950mm (194.9 in)	5065mm (199.4 in)	5065mm (199.4 in)	5190mm (204.3 in)
Width	1838mm (72.4 in)	1838 (72.4 in)	1838mm (72.4 in)	1860mm (73.2 in)
Height	1600mm (63.0 in)	1640mm (64.6 in)	1600mm (63.0 in)	1620mm (63.8 in)
Ground clearance	185mm (7.3 in)	185mm (7.3 in)	185mm (7.3 in)	185mm (7.3 in)
Tires	7.10 x 15 extra	7.10 x 15 extra	7.60 x 15 extra	7.60 x 15 extra
Turning circle	12.6-13.1 meters (41-43 ft)	12.6-13.1 meters (41-43 ft)	12.6-13.1 meters (41-43 ft)	12.8-13.3 meters (42-44 ft)
Steering type and ratio	worm, 17.9:1 (3.3 turns)	recirculating ball, 21.4:1 (3.75 turns)	recirculating ball, 21.4:1 (3.75 turns)	from Sept. '58 servo-assist, optional
Weight (automatic)	1780 kg (3916 lbs) convertible: 1830 kg (4026 lbs)		1860 kg (4092 lbs) convertible: 1910 kg (4202 lbs) 1910 kg (4202 lbs) convertible: 1960 kg (4312 lbs)	1950 kg (4290 lbs) 2000 kg (4400 lbs)
Maximum speed (automatic)	160 km/hr (99.5 mph)	163 km/hr (101 mph)	160 km/hr (99.5 mph) 155 km/hr (96.3 mph)	170 km/hr (105.6 mph) 165 km/hr (102.5 mph)
Acceleration (automatic)	18 sec 0-100 km	17 sec 0-100 km	17 sec 0-100 km 18 sec 0-100 km	17 sec 0-100 km 18 sec 0-100 km
Fuel consumption (automatic)	16.5 liters/100 km (14.2 mpg)	16 liters, super (14.7 mpg)	16 liters, super (14.7 mpg) 17 liters, super (13.7 mpg)	17 liters, super (13.7 mpg) 18 liters, super (13 mpg)
Fuel tank capacity	72 liters (19 gallons)	72 liters (19 gallons)	72 liters (19 gallons)	72 liters (19 gallons)

The 300Sc roadster, 1955

Prices and Production

The 300S coupe, convertible A, and roadster sold for DM 34,500. When in 1953 a new, modern showroom with excellent service facilities for Mercedes-Benz automobiles was opened at New York by the Hoffman Motor Company, importers for these cars in the United States, the 300S was priced at $12,500. The 300Sc coupe, convertible A, and open roadster sold for DM 36,500.

Production of the 300S model [188 I] (from September 1951/July 1952 until August 1955)

was in	1951	2 units
	1952	113 units
	1953	353 units
	1954	37 units
	1955	55 units
	total	560 units

Production of the 300Sc model [188 II] (from September/December 1955 to April 1958)

was in	1955	5 units
	1956	140 units
	1957	52 units
	1958	3 units
	total	200 units

# Model 300S (1951-1958)
S = Super

The 300S (super) model, first shown at the Paris Salon in October 1951 and produced in 1952, was created for the discriminating sports enthusiast driver. It was designed to carry on the tradition which had begun twenty-five years before with the 6-liter K model of 1927, followed by the superb S and SS models and finally the 540K model of 1936. With but half of the engine displacement, without supercharger, and weighing a ton less than its illustrious predecessor (and 450 pounds less than the 300 sedan), the 300S was actually faster, more responsive, safer, and more comfortable. (Karl Kling drove better times at the Nürburgring than with any other Mercedes since the SSK model.) The 540K had a 180-horsepower engine and weighed 5,735 pounds; the 300S had a 150 horsepower engine and weighed 3,880 pounds. Maximum speed was 109 miles per hour. The engine had a compression ratio of 7.5 to 1 and three downdraft carburetors. The wheelbase was 2,900 millimeters (114.2 inches) and overall length 4,700 millimeters (185 inches).

Two body styles were available, the coupe and convertible coupe or open roadster. The interior furnishings were of the finest material, real leather upholstery and rich wood matching the dash and the trim around the side and rear windows. The 300S was a joy to drive and to own, as this chronicler was fortunate to experience in ten years and a hundred thousand miles.

The 300Sc model was built from September 1955 until April 1958. That car had a fuel injection engine and single pivot swing axle, but was outwardly similar to the previous type, except that the rubber center piece in the bumpers was left off. A total of only 760 automobiles of both model types were produced.

The 300S line of cars was a truly "Super" range of models ever produced and was probably never exceeded in elegance. It was a joy to drive and for 10 years it was my pleasure and privilege to do so.

Specifications

	300S	300Sc
Engine type	6 cyl overhead camshaft (M 188)	6 cyl overhead camshaft (M 188)
Bore stroke	85 x 88mm (3.35 x 3.46 in)	85 x 88mm (3.35 x 3.46 in)
Displacement	2996 cc (182.7 cu in)	2996 cc (182.7 cu in)
Power output	150 hp (DIN) @ 5000 rpm	175 hp (DIN) @ 5400 rpm
Compression ratio	7.8:1	8.55:1
Torque	23.5 mkg @ 3800 rpm (170 ft/lb)	26 mkg @ 4300 rpm 188 ft/lb)
Carburetion	3 downdraft carburetors Solex 40 PBJC	Bosch injection pump
Engine speed at 100 km/hr	3260 rpm	3260 rpm
Gear ratios	I. 3.33:1 (later 3.68:1) II. 2.12:1 (later 2.25:1) III. 1.46:1 (later 1.42:1) IV. 1.00:1 (later 1.00:1)	I. 3.55:1 II. 2.30:1 III. 1.53:1 IV. 1.00:1
Rear axle ratio	4.125	4.44
Chassis	X-shaped oval tubular frame	X-shaped oval tubular frame
Suspension	independent front, swing axle rear, with coil springs	independent front, single pivot swing axle rear, with coil springs
Brakes and area	drum, 1270 cm² (197 sq in)	drum, 1470 cm² (228 sq in)
Wheelbase	2900mm (114.2 in)	2900mm (114.2 in)
Track, front/rear	1480/1525mm (58.2/60 in)	1480/1525mm (58.2/60 in)
Length	4700mm (185 in)	4700mm (185 in)
Width	1860mm (73.2 in)	1860mm (73.2 in)
Height	1510mm (59.4 in)	1510mm (59.4 in)
Ground clearance	180mm (7.1 in)	180mm (7.1 in)
Tires	6.70 x 15 extra	6.70 x 15 extra
Turning circle	12.2-12.7 meters (40-42 ft)	12.2-12.7 meters (40-42 ft)
Steering type and ratio	recirculating ball, 21.4:1 (3.75 turns)	recirculating ball, 21.4:1 (3.75 turns)
Weight	1760 kg (3880 lbs)	1780 kg (3924 lbs)
Maximum speed	176 km/hr (109 mph)	180 km/hr (112 mph)
Acceleration	15 sec 0-100 km	14 sec 0-100 km
Fuel consumption	17 liters, super/100 km (13.7 mpg)	
Fuel tank capacity	85 liters (22 gallons)	85 liters (22 gallons)

The 300S convertible, 1952

The 300S roadster, 1952

The 300S coupe, 1955; just like this writer owned for ten years

300S units built

	a,b	c
roadsters	141	53
convertibles	203	49
coupes	216	98

The 180 sedan, 1953

Prices

The 180 four-door sedan sold in 1953-1954 for. . . . . . .DM 9,950
(The U.S. price was $3,350 on the West coast)
in 1954-1956 . . . . .DM 9,450
in 1956-1961 . . . . .DM 8,700
from August 1961 .DM 8,950
from April 1962 . . . . .DM 9,350

For 180b and 180c power-assisted brakes were available at DM 300 extra cost.

The 180 sedan, 1953

Model 180 (1953-1962)

The 180 model, introduced in early 1953, featured a radically new type of chassis design, although the x-shaped oval tubular frame, used on the previous models, had proven thoroughly satisfactory. The most important element in this new design was that high sectional steel side members were united to the floor of the body to make a platform, greatly resistant to distortion. It actually doubled the rigidity of the assembly and considerably lessened noise.

The subframe which carried the entire power unit and transmission, as well as the steering and front wheel assembly, was anchored to the front part of the main chassis on rubber blocks on the three-point suspension system. This arrangement offered advantages in manufacture and maintenance. It was also the first example of a design where heavy components were readily detachable.

The double-joint swing axle was retained; and so was the four-cylinder, 1,767 cubic centimeter, 52-horsepower engine of the 170S model because of its ready availability and proven reliability. The external lines of the rather stubby-looking 180 model were in keeping with modern tendencies but retained the traditional radiator style. The radiator shell lifted up with the hood. The car was 22 percent roomier and more comfortable, more economical to operate, and allowed the driver an excellent view of the road. The window area was 40 percent greater than that of the 170S model. The smooth running and ideal road-holding properties were such that the driver was hardly aware of having reached its maximum speed of 125 kilometers (78 miles) per hour. The 180 model was built from September 1953 until August 1957. The 180a, built from September 1957 until July 1959, had the larger engine, 1,897 cubic centimeters and 65 horsepower. The 180b followed until August 1961. It had larger brakes, wider radiator, and no vertical bars on the bumpers. The 180c, with a changed valve gear was built from June 1961 until October 1962.

Production

Production of the 180 model [120 I] (from July 1953 until June 1957)

was in 1953	4,362 units
1954	20,306 units
1955	17,704 units
1956	8,464 units
1957	1,350 units
total	52,186 units

Production of the 180a model [120 II] from June 1957 until July 1959)

was in 1957	4,656 units
1958	15,967 units
1959	6,730 units
total	27,353 units

Production of the 180b model [120 III] (from July 1959 until August 1961)

was in 1959	7,314 units
1960	14,384 units
1961	7,717 units
total	29,415 units

Production of the 180c model [120 IV] (from June 1961 until October 1962)

was in 1961	4,980 units
1962	4,300 units
total	9,280 units

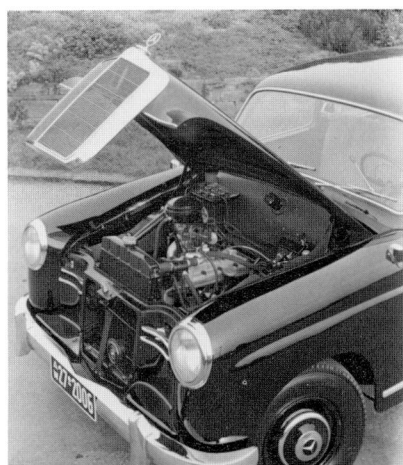

The engine compartment of the 180 sedan, 1953

Specifications

	180	180a, b, c
Engine type	4 cyl (M 136)	4 cyl (M 136)
Bore and stroke	75 x 100mm (2.96 x 3.94 in)	85 x 83.6mm (3.35 x 3.29 in)
Displacement	1767 cc (107.7 cu in)	1897 cc (115.7 cu in)
Power output	52 hp (DIN) @ 4000 rpm	65 hp (DIN) @ 4500 rpm b: 68 hp (DIN) @ 4400 rpm
Compression ratio	6.8:1	6.8:1 b: 7:1
Torque	11.4 mkg @ 1800 rpm (82.5 ft/lb)	13 mkg @ 2200 rpm (94 ft/lb) b: 13.2 mkg @ 2500 rpm (96/4 ft/lb)
Carburetion	1 downdraft carburetor Solex 32 PICB	1 downdraft carburetor Solex 32 PICB b: Solex 34 PICB
Engine speed at 100 km/hr	3390 rpm	3390 rpm
Gear ratios	I. 4.05:1 II. 2.38:1 III. 1.53:1 IV. 1.00:1	I. 4.05:1 II. 2.38:1 III. 1.53:1 IV. 1.00:1
Rear axle ratio	3.89 (35:9)	3.90 (39:10)
Chassis	unit frame and body	unit frame and body
Suspension	independent front, swing axle rear, with coil springs from Sept '55: single swing axle	
Brakes and area	drum 816 cm² (126.5 sq in)	b: drum, 1064 cm² (164.9 sq in) servo optional
Wheelbase	2650mm (104.3 in)	2650mm (104.3 in)
Track, front/rear	1420/1475mm (55.9/58.1 in)	1420/1475mm (55.9/58.1 in)
Length	4480mm (176.4 in)	4480mm (176.4 in)
Width	1740mm (68.5 in)	1740mm (68.5 in)
Height	1560mm (61.4 in)	1560mm (61.4 in)
Ground clearance	185mm (7.3 in)	185mm (7.3 in)
Tires	6.40 x 13	6.40 x 13
Turning circle	11.5 meters (38 ft)	11.5 meters (38 ft)
Steering type and ratio	recirculating ball, 18.5:1	recirculating ball, 18.5:1
Weight	1180 kg (2596 lbs) from Sept: 1200 kg (2640 lbs)	1210 kg (2662 lbs)
Maximum speed	126 km/hr (78.4 mph)	136 km/hr (84 mph)
Acceleration	31 sec 0-100 km	21 sec 0-100 km
Fuel consumption	11.5 liters/100 km (20.4 mpg)	10.5 liters (22.4 mpg)
Fuel tank capacity	56 liters (14.8 gallons)	56 liters (14.8 gallons)

The 180D sedan, 1954

Model 180D (1953-1962)

D = Diesel

The 180D was introduced after the 180 gasoline-engined sedan. Early production of this diesel-engined model was in October 1953 and regular production began in February 1954.

Again, in all respects, body and chassis of these two models were identical. The new unit frame construction and redesigned front end of this recently introduced four-door sedan was shared by both types. The 180D diesel engine was identical to that of the 170Db, but the rear axle ratio had been reduced and in September 1955 the engine output was raised to 43 horsepower. In April 1958 wind wings were placed on the front door windows, but otherwise the body remained the same as previously used.

The 180Db model production began in July 1959 and was to continue until August 1961. Larger diameter brakes, a wider radiator shell, and no vertical bumper bars were the only alterations.

The 180Dc, built from June 1961 until October 1962 had the larger engine. Displacing 1,988 cubic centimeters, it developed 48 horsepower at 3,800 revolutions per minute. Compression ratio was raised to 21 to 1.

Again, these diesel models proved to be considerably better sellers than the gasoline-powered versions which shared the body style and exterior and interior appointments.

To graphically illustrate the dependability of this diesel model, several 180Ds were entered in the rugged Mille Miglia race in 1955. Usually the exclusive field for fast and exotic sports cars, the rather austere and totally uncomplicated diesel-engined passenger models presented a most unusual sight to the inhabitants of the localities where this 922-mile-long race was held. Three 180D models won the first three places in their special diesel classification, averaging a quite respectable speed of over 60 miles per hour.

When the 180D became available in the United States, it sold for $3,394.

Prices and Production

The 180D four-door sedan sold in 1954-1955 for .....DM 10,300
in 1956 ....DM 9,850
in 1956-1958 ....DM 9,480
in 1958-1961 ....DM 9,200
from August 1961 ....DM 9,450
from April 1962 ....DM 9,850

Production of the 180D model [120 I] (from October 1953/February 1954 until July 1959)

was in	1953	11 units
	1954	15,532 units
	1955	20,345 units
	1956	21,013 units
	1957	22,910 units
	1958	26,693 units
	1959	9,981 units
	total	116,485 units

Production of the 180Db [120 II] (from July 1959 until August 1961)

was in	1959	8,076 units
	1960	11,151 units
	1961	5,449 units
	total	24,676 units

Production of the 180Dc [120 III] (from June 1961 until October 1962)

was in	1961	4,822 units
	1962	7,000 units
	total	11,822 units

Specifications

	180D / 180Db	180Dc
Engine type	4 cyl diesel (OM 636)	4 cyl diesel (OM 621)
Bore and stroke	75 x 100mm (2.96 x 3.94 in)	87 x 83.6mm (3.43 x 3.29 in)
Displacement	1767 cc (107.7 cu in)	1988 cc (121 cu in)
Power output	40 hp (DIN) @ 3200 rpm 46 hp (SAE) @ 3500 rpm from Sept. '55: 43 hp @ 3500	48 hp (DIN) @ 3800 rpm
Compression ratio	19:1	21:1
Torque	10.3mgk @2000 rpm (75ft/lb)	11mkg @2200rpm (80ft/lb)
Fuel injection	Bosch injection pump (pre-combustion chamber)	
Engine speed at 100 km/hr	3330 rpm	3330 rpm
Gear ratios	I. 4.05:1 (15.0) II. 2.38:1 (8.81) III. 1.53:1 (5.66) IV. 1.00:1 (3.70)	I. 4.05:1 (15.0) II. 2.38:1 (8.81) III. 1.53:1 (5.66) IV. 1.00:1 (3.70)
Rear axle ratio	3.70 (37:10)	3.70 (37:10)
Chassis	unit frame and body	unit frame and body
Suspension	independent front, swing axle rear, with coil springs from Sept. '55: single swing axle	rear: single swing axle
Brakes and area	drum, 816 cm² (126.5 sq in)	drum, 1064 cm² (164.9 sq in)
Wheelbase	2650mm (104.3 in)	2650mm (104.3 in)
Track, front/rear	1430/1475mm (56.3/58.1 in)	1430/1475mm (56.3/58.1 in)
Length	4485mm (176.6 in)	4485mm (176.6 in)
Width	1740mm (68.5 in)	1740mm (68.5 in)
Height	1560mm (61.4 in)	1560mm (61.4 in)
Ground clearance	185mm (7.3 in)	185mm (7.3 in)
Tires	6.40 x 13	6.40 x 13
Turning circle	11.5 meters (38 ft)	11.5 meters (38 ft)
Steering type and ratio	recirculating ball, 18.5:1	recirculating ball, 18.5:1
Weight	1220 kg (2684 lbs)	1220 kg (2684 lbs)
Maximum speed	112 km/hr (70 mph) from Sept. '55: 115 km/hr	120 km/hr (75 mph)
Acceleration	39 sec 0-100 km from Sept. '55: 37 sec	36 sec 0-100 km
Fuel consumption	8 liters/100 km (29.3 mpg)	8 liters/100 km (29.3 mpg)
Fuel tank capacity	56 liters (14.8 gallons)	56 liters (14.8 gallons)

The frame-floor unit chassis of the 180, 1953

The OM 636 engine of the 180D, 1954

Model 300SL (1954-1963)

S = Sports, L (Leicht) = light

The 300SL sports car went into regular production in August 1954, but a more austere version had appeared on the international sports car racing scene in 1952. After an interval of many years, the company had decided to enter competition again and the 300SL was built. The designation SL (sport-light) described a new design in which the frame was replaced by a light but very stiff structure of a lattice pattern, made of thin welded steel tubing, and the outer cover was also very light since the lattice structure bears all stress.

The engine, developed from the 300S model, was mounted slanting 45 degrees for a lower hood line in order to allow the driver and passenger a better view ahead.

First tested in international competition in sports car races in Switzerland, at Le Mans, the Nürburgring, and the Panamericana in Mexico, the car earned its laurels. The magnificent victories, and the entire history of the 300SL, are related in another book by this author.

The production car incorporated many improvements gained from the racing experience. One of the striking features was the direct fuel injection which gave the 2,996 cubic centimeter six-cylinder engine 215 horsepower (240 SAE) at 5,800 revolutions per minute, and a maximum speed of 235 kilometers with the 3.64 rear axle and 260 kilometers (162 miles) per hour with the 3.25 axle fitted. The turbo brake drums were self-cooling and servo-assisted and were the same as on the 300S model. The speeds in the gears were 75 kilometers (47 miles) in first, 128 km (80 m) in second, 186 km (116 m) in third, and 240 kilometers (149 miles) in fourth at 6,000 revolutions per minute.

The 300SL roadster with conventional type doors was first shown at the Geneva Show in March 1957 and put into regular production in May. It was basically the same car as the gull-wing coupe, but the lower door line was closer to the ground and getting in and out was greatly facilitated. In many ways a superior sports car than the former, it never achieved the enthusiastic support of the

The 300SL coupe, 1956

original version, although actually more cars were produced during the seven years it was built.

The tubular frame was somewhat heavier because of the absence of the coupe body; the car weighed 1,330 kilograms to the 1,295 of the former, an increase of 77 pounds. The engine later had the competition camshaft installed with a higher compression ratio, 9.5 to 1, and was rated at 250 SAE horsepower at 6,200 revolutions per minute. The German specifications listed 215 horsepower at 5,800 revolutions per minute and the 8.55 compression ratio, as the earlier coupe model had. The U.S. cars also had the 3.89 rear axle ratio.

The various axle ratios gave the following maximum speeds: 3.25 at 155 miles per hour; 3.42 at 150, 3.64 at 146, 3.89 at 137, and 4.11 ratio at 129 miles per hour.

A hard top for the convertible roadster became available in September 1958 at extra cost, and in March 1961, four-wheel disc brakes were installed as a regular production item.

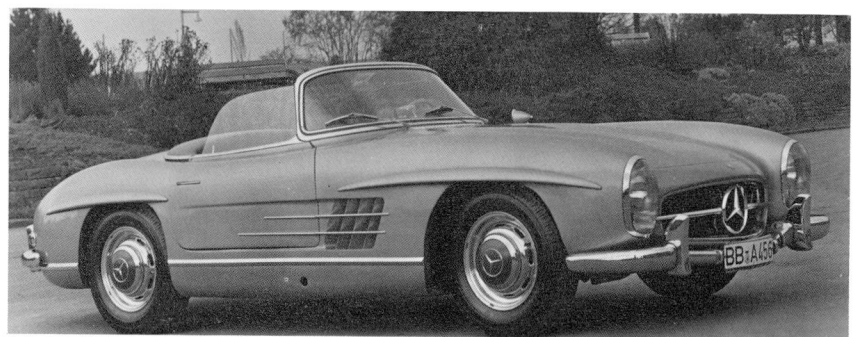

The 300SL roadster, 1957

Prices and Production

The 300SL coupe sold for . . . . .DM 29,000
Price in the United States was first . . . .$ 6,820
then rose to (finally) . . . .$ 8,902
The 300SL roadster sold for . . . . .DM 32,500
removable hardtop. . . . . .DM 1,500
Price in the United States was first . . . .$ 10,970
then . . . .$ 11,099
and. . . . .$ 11,573

Production of the 300 SL coupe [198 I] (from August 1954 until May 1957)

	was in 1954	146 units
	1955	867 units
	1956	311 units
	1957	76 units
	total	1,400 units

Production of the 300SL roadster [198 II] (from February/May 1957 until February 1963)

	was in 1957	554 units
	1958	324 units
	1959	211 units
	1960	249 units
	1961	250 units
	1962	244 units
	1963	26 units
	total	1,858 units

The 300SL coupe, 1956; just like this writer owned for two years

Specifications

	300SL (coupe)	300SL (roadster)	
Engine type	6 cyl overhead camshaft (45° slanted to the left) (M 198)		
Bore and stroke	85 x 88mm (3.35 x 3.46 in)	85 x 88mm (3.35 x 3.46 in)	
Displacement	2996 cc (182.7 cu in)	2996 cc (182.7 cu in)	
Power output	215 hp (DIN) @ 5800 rpm (240 hp SAE) (for U.S.: 250 hp @ 6200 rpm)		
Compression ratio	8.55:1	9.5:1	
Torque	28 mkg @ 4600 rpm (217 ft/lb @ 4800 rpm)	228 ft/lb	
Fuel injection	Bosch injection pump	Bosch injection pump	
Engine speed at 100 km/hr	3000 rpm	3000 rpm	
Gear ratios	I. 3.34:1 (12.15) II. 1.97:1 (7.18) III. 1.385:1 (5.03) IV. 1.00:1 (3.64)	I. 3.34:1 (12.15) II. 1.97:1 (7.18) III. 1.385:1 (5.03) IV. 1.00:1 (3.64)	for U.S. (13.0) (7.66) (5.40) (3.89)
Rear axle ratio	3.64; also 3.25; 3.42; 3.89; 4.11 upon request		
Chassis	tubular space frame with light alloy body		
Suspension	independent front, swing axle rear, with coil springs		
Brakes and area	drum, 1470 cm² (227.9 sq in) servo assisted; from Mar. '61 discs		
Wheelbase	2400mm (94.5 in)	2400mm (94.5 in)	
Track, front/rear	1385/1435mm (54.5/56.5 in)	1398/1448mm (55.0/57.0 in)	
Length	4520mm (178 in)	4570mm (180 in)	
Width	1790mm (70.5 in)	1790mm (70.5 in)	
Height	1300mm (51.2 in)	1300mm (51.2 in)	
Ground clearance	130mm (5.1 in)	130mm (5.1 in)	
Tires	6.50 x 15 super sport	6.70 x 15 super sport	
Turning circle	11.4 meters (37 ft)	11.4 meters (37 ft)	
Steering type and ratio	recirculating ball, 17.3:1 (3 turns)	recirculating ball, 17.3:1 (3 turns)	
Weight	1295 kg (2849 lbs)	1330 kg (2926 lbs)	
Maximum speed	3.64 axle: 235 km/hr (145 mph); 3.42-250 km/hr (155 mph); 3.25-260 km/hr (165 mph)		
Acceleration	8.7 sec 0-100 km/hr	8.1 sec 0-100 km/hr (for U.S. 7.2 sec)	
Fuel consumption	17 liters, super / 100 km (13.7 mpg)		
Fuel tank capacity	130 liters (34 U.S. gallons)	100 liters (26 U.S. gallons)	

The 190SL roadster, 1960

Model 190SL (1955-1963)

S = Sports, L (Leicht) = light

The 190SL model was announced early in 1954 as a smaller version of the 300SL, but initial production did not start until January 1955, when several important modifications had been made on the original design. This touring-sports car was based on the 180 model sedan and used the basic, but slightly altered, self-supporting frame-floor unit construction with the subframe assembly carrying the engine. The open roadster model needed greater support than the four-door sedan model.

The sporty body of the 190SL resembled that of the larger SL model but had regular fitted doors. A floor-located stick shift lever operated the four-speed synchro-meshed gear box. Speeds in gears were 46, 81, 128, and 190 kilometers (28, 50, 80, and 118 miles) per hour. Real leather bucket-type seats added greatly to the comfort and appearance of the silvery sports car.

The four-cylinder engine had a displacement of 1,897 cubic centimeters and a compression ratio of 8.5 to 1. The overhead camshaft engine, equipped with two Solex horizontal carburetors, developed 105 horsepower at 5,700 revolutions per minute (in the U.S. version 125 at 6,000). Maximum speed was given as 171 kilometers (106 miles) per hour. Torque was 101 ft/lbs.

The 190SL was advertised to sell in New York for $3,998 in 1955. The copy indicated a 125-horsepower engine and top speed of 118 miles per hour for this "blood brother" of the fabulous 300SL.

In September 1959 a new style hard top was designed with larger window area giving improved vision.

The 190SL was a popular selling car in this country, but owners hardly ever participated in competitive events, although the car proved fun to drive. It was not really an SL (sports, light) model. The car was too heavy for its particular class and was badly outperformed by the exotic sports cars available. However, in a 1958 Hong Kong rally, W. Sulke was the overall winner. Years later, the 190SL became a most desirable sports car and brought premium prices.

Prices and Production

The 190SL roadster, with cloth top, sold for ....DM 16,500
   with removable hard top.................DM 17,100
   with both types top.....................DM 17,650
In the U.S. the 190SL roadster sold in 1958
   East coast ....$ 5,020
   West coast ....$ 5,129

Production of the 190SL [121 II] (from January/May 1955 until February 1963)

was in	1955	1,727 units
	1956	4,032 units
	1957	3,332 units
	1958	2,722 units
	1959	3,949 units
	1960	3,977 units
	1961	3,792 units
	1962	2,246 units
	1963	104 units
total		25,881 units

EFFORTLESS STEERING is assured by the Mercedes-Benz ball-type steering mechanism with automatic return.

SINGLE-PIVOT SWING AXLE adds new safety and comfort to Mercedes-Benz' legendary road-holding qualities.

Specifications

	190SL
Engine type	4 cyl (M 121)
Bore and stroke	85 x 83.6mm (3.35 x 3.29 in)
Displacement	1897 cc (115.7 cu in)
Power output	105 hp (DIN) @ 5700 rpm (120 hp (SAE) @ 5700 rpm)
Compression ratio	8.5:1 from Sept. '59: 8.8:1
Torque	14.5 mkg @ 3200 rpm (105 ft/lb @ 3200 rpm)
Carburetion	2 dual downdraft carburetors Solex 44 PHH
Engine speed at 100 km/hr	3350 rpm
Gear ratios	I. 3.52:1 (13.7) II. 2.32:1 (9.02) III. 1.52:1 (5.92) IV. 1.00:1 (3.89)
Rear axle ratio	3.90 (39:10)
Chassis	unit frame and body
Suspension	independent front, single joint swing axle rear, with coil springs
Brakes and area	drum, 1064 cm² (164.9 sq in) servo optional
Wheelbase	2400mm (94.5 in)
Track, front/rear	1430/1475mm (56.2/58.1 in)
Length	4220mm (166.1 in)
Width	1740mm (68.5 in)
Height	1320mm (52 in)
Ground clearance	185mm (7.3 in)
Tires	6.40 x 13 sport
Turning circle	11 meters (36.1 ft)
Steering type and ratio	recirculating ball, 18.5:1
Weight	roadster: 1160 kg (2552 lbs) coupe: 1180 kg (2596 lbs)
Maximum speed	171 km/hr (106 mph)
Acceleration	14.5 sec 0-100 km
Fuel consumption	12.5 liters super/100 km (18.75 mpg)
Fuel tank capacity	65 liter (17 gallons)

The pre-production 190SL, 1954

The 190SL roadster with coupe top, 1955

The 190SL with the enlarged window, 1959

The 190 sedan, 1956

Model 190 (1956-1965)

The 190 sedan, introduced at the Frankfurt Auto Show in 1956, was one of three new models shown to the public at that time. The body style was the same as that of the 180 sedan, but the new single overhead camshaft four-cylinder engine of 1,897 cubic centimeters (actually a detuned version of the 190SL power unit) developed 75 horsepower at 4,600 revolutions per minute. It was mounted on four points on the U-frame, resulting in greater quietness of operation. Interior furnishings of the 190 sedan were somewhat superior to those of the 180 model but outwardly the only distinguishing feature was a decorative chrome line around the body.

The 190b model, built from June 1959 on, had a wider radiator shell and the bumper had no vertical bumper guard bar.

The 190c model, produced from April 1961 until August 1965, was quite different from the preceding models of the same designation. It was longer, larger, and lower, and had the body style of the 220 models of that period, with the slight tail fins. But it had a slightly shorter hood line, round lights, and simple bumpers.

From August 1963 on, the model was equipped with disc brakes and a twin circuit hydraulic system. An automatic transmission was also available from August 1962 on at extra cost.

Prices and Production

The 190 four-door sedan in 1956-1961 sold for	DM 9,450
Servo brakes available at additional	DM 300
The 190c four-door sedan sold in 1961 for	DM 9,950
from April 1962	DM 10,600
Servo brakes available at additional (until August 1963)	DM 300
Power steering (from May 1964)	DM 550
Automatic transmission (from August 1962)	DM 1,400

Production of the 190 model [121 I] (from March 1956 until August 1959)

was in	1956	16,001 units
	1957	22,578 units
	1958	15,791 units
	1959	6,975 units
	total	61,345 units

Production of the 190b model [121 III] (from June 1959 until August 1961)

was in	1959	6,613 units
	1960	12,986 units
	1961	8,864 units
	total	28,463 units

Production of the 190c model [110] (from April 1961 until August 1965)

was in	1961	9,249 units
	1962	31,275 units
	1963	35,457 units
	1964	33,776 units
	1965	20,797 units
	total	130,554 units

The 190 sedan, 1961

Specifications

	190	190b	190c
Engine type	4 cyl overhead camshaft (M 121)	4 cyl overhead camshaft (M 121)	4 cyl overhead camshaft (M 121)
Bore and stroke	85 x 83.6mm (3.35 x 3.29 in)	85 x 83.6mm (3.35 x 3.29 in)	85 x 83.6mm (3.34 x 3.29 in)
Displacement	1897 cc (115.7 cu in)	1897 cc (115.7 cu in)	1897 cc (115.7 cu in)
Power output	75 hp (DIN) @ 4600 rpm (84 SAE hp)	80 hp (DIN) @ 4800 rpm	80 hp (DIN) @ 5000 rpm (90 hp SAE @ 5200 rpm)
Compression ratio	7.5:1	8.5:1	8.7:1
Torque	13.9 mkg @ 2800 rpm (101 ft/lb)	14.2 mkg @ 2800 rpm (103 ft/lb)	14.5 mkg @ 2500 rpm (15.6 mkg @ 2700 rpm SAE 112.9 ft/lb)
Carburation	1 downdraft carburetor Solex 32 PAITA	1 downdraft carburetor Solex 32 PAITA	1 downdraft carburetor Solex 34 PJCB
Engine speed at 100 km/hr	3300 rpm	3300 rpm	3300 rpm
Gear ratios	I. 4.05:1 II. 2.38:1 III. 1.53:1 IV. 1.00:1	I. 4.05:1 II. 2.38:1 III. 1.53:1 IV. 1.00:1	I. 4.05:1　　automatic 3.98:1 II. 2.28:1　　　　　　　2.52:1 III. 1.53:1　　　　　　　1.58:1 IV. 1.00:1　　　　　　　1.00:1
Rear axle ratio	4.10	4.10	4.08
Chassis	unit frame and body	unit frame and body	unit frame and body
Suspension	independent front, single joint swing axle rear, with coil springs (from 1963; air suspension, optional)		
Brakes and area	drum, 1064 cm² (164.9 sq in) servo optional		drum, 1064 cm² (164.9 sq in) servo assisted from Aug. '63; disc, front
Wheelbase	2650mm (104.3 in)	2650mm (104.3 in)	2700mm (106.3 in)
Track, front/rear	1430/1475mm (56.2/58.1 in)	1430/1475mm (56.2/58.1 in)	1468/1485mm (58/58.5in) from Aug.'63 1482/1465mm
Length	4485mm (176.6 in)	4500mm (177.2 in)	4730mm (186.5 in)
Width	1740mm (68.5 in)	1740mm (68.5 in)	1795mm (70.7 in)
Height	1560mm (61.4 in)	1560mm (61.4 in)	1495,mm (58.8 in)
Ground clearance	185mm (7.3 in)	185,mm (7.3 in)	185mm (7.3 in)
Tires	6.40 x 13	6.40 x 13	7.00 x 13
Turning circle	11.5 meters (38 ft)	11.5 meters (38 ft)	11.8-11.6 meters (38 ft)
Steering type and ratio	recirculating ball, 18.5:1 (3.75 turns)	recirculating ball, 18.5:1 (3.75 turns)	recirculating ball, 21.4:1 (3.75 turns) from May '64: servo assist 17.3:1 (3.2 turns)
Weight	1240 kg (2728 lbs)	1240 kg (2728 lbs)	1280 kg (2816 lbs)
Maximum speed	139 km/hr (86 mph)	144 km/hr (89 mph)	150 km/hr (93 mph) automatic: 145 km/hr (90 mph)
Acceleration	20.5 sec 0-100 km	19 sec 0-100 km	18 sec 0-100 km/hr automatic: 22 sec 0-100 km/hr
Fuel consumption	11.5 liters, super/100 km (20.4 mpg)		11.5 liters, super/100 km (20.4 mpg) automatic: 12.5 liters (18.75 mpg)
Fuel tank capacity	56 liters (14.8 gallons)	56 liters (14.8 gallons)	52 liters (13.5 gallons)

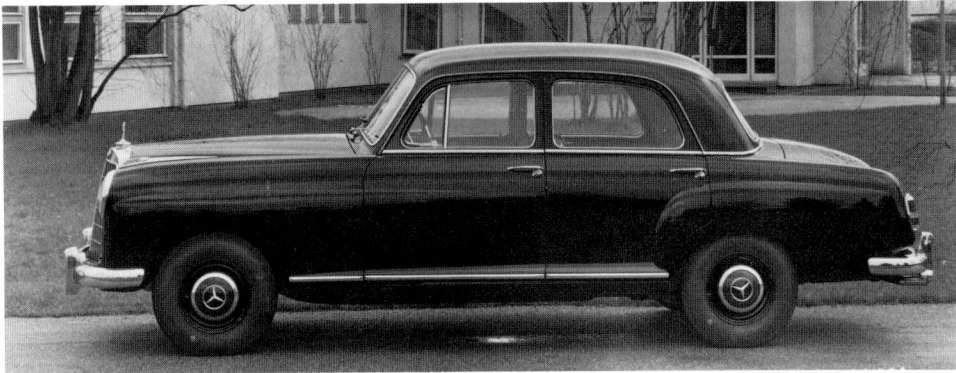

The 219 sedan, 1956

Prices and Production

The 219 four-door sedan sold for	DM 10,500
Servo brakes available at an additional	DM 300
Hydrak transmission	DM 450
Price in the U.S. was in 1956	$ 3,889

Production of the 219 model [105] (from March 1956 until July 1959)

was in	1956	5,474 units
	1957	8,505 units
	1958	9,296 units
	1959	4,570 units
	total	27,845 units

Model 219 (1956-1959)

The 219 sedan was the second model introduced at the Frankfurt Auto Show in 1956. The body style was identical to that of the 190 sedan, but the wheelbase was slightly larger, 2,750 millimeters to 2,650 millimeters for the 190 (3.937 inches longer). The six-cylinder engine was the same as that of the former 220 sedan, the proven 2,195 cubic centimeter unit developing 85 horsepower (92 SAE) at 4,800 revolutions per minute. Power output was increased in August 1957 to 90 horsepower (100 SAE), and the compression ratio from 7.6 to 8.7 to 1. With the increase in power, a slight increase in fuel consumption was also experienced, naturally, but only by one liter for 100 kilometers.

The 219 model was considered the middle range of the three newly developed sedans and the lowest priced six-cylinder one. The maximum speed, and cruising speed, was given as 148 kilometers (92 miles) per hour, with the 190 model doing 139 kilometers (86 miles) per hour and the 220S having a maximum speed of 99.4 miles, or 160 kilometers, per hour.

The 219 model was an economical car, yet quite powerful with the six-cylinder engine. It was available, as the other two similar models, with a sliding roof and in front a bench-type seat instead of the bucket seats.

As an optional extra, a hydraulic transmission was available. In this Hydrak system made by Fichtel and Sachs, a hydraulic coupling was used in connection with a conventional clutch automatically controlled. When the driver moved the gear lever, the clutch action was initiated. The system made for easier driving and provided engine braking at all times. It ensured smoothness of operation and saved the engine.

This Hydrak transmission, however, did not find too many enthusiastic supporters and, over the years, it seemed the one great handicap of these particular models whenever such a car became for sale as a used one. The operation was perhaps too tricky for the average driver — who usually held onto the lever — and a burned-out clutch seemed a regular occurrence. In retrospect, the Hydrak was an unfortunate choice.

Specifications

	219
Engine type	6 cyl overhead camshaft (M 180)
Bore and stroke	80 x 72.8mm (3.15 x 2.87 in)
Displacement	2195 cc (133.9 cu in)
Power output	85 hp (DIN) @ 4800 rpm (92 hp SAE) from Aug. '57: 90 hp (DIN) (100 hp SAE)
Compression ratio	7.6:1 from Aug. '57: 8.7:1
Torque	16 mkg @ 2400 rpm (116 ft/lb) from Aug. '57: 17 mkg (123 ft/lb)
Carburetion	1 dual downdraft carburetor Solex 32 PAATJ
Engine speed at 100 km/hr	3320 rpm
Gear ratios	I. 3.52:1 (14.4) II. 2.32:1 (9.51) III. 1.52:1 (6.23) IV. 1.00:1 (4.10)
Rear axle ratio	4.10 from Aug. '57: 3.90
Chassis	unit frame and body
Suspension	independent front, single joint swing axle rear, with coil springs
Brakes and area	drum, 1064 cm^2 (164.9 sq in)
Wheelbase	2750mm (108.3 in)
Track, front/rear	1430/1470mm (56.2/57.9 in)
Length	4680mm (184.3 in)
Width	1740mm (68.5 in)
Height	1560mm (61.4 in)
Ground clearance	185mm (7.3 in)
Tires	6.40 x 13
Turning circle	11.5 meters (38 ft)
Steering type and ratio	recirculating ball, 21.4:1 (4 turns)
Weight	1290 kg (2838 lbs)
Maximum speed	148 km/hr (92 mph)
Acceleration	17 sec 0-100 km
Fuel consumption	14.5 liters/100 km (16.2 mpg) from Aug. '57 13.5 liters
Fuel tank capacity	56 liters (14.8 gallons)

The Hydrak transmission, 1956

The 220S sedan, 1956

# Model 220S (1956-1959)
S = Super

The sedan was the third of the new models shown to the public at the Frankfurt Show in 1956. It was also the most powerful one of the trio and the most expensive one as well. The 2,195 cubic centimeter six-cylinder engine was of the same size as that of the 219, but it developed 100 horsepower (112 SAE) at 4,800 revolutions per minute. From August 1957 on, with the compression ratio increased from 7.6 to 8.7 to 1, it developed 106 horsepower at 5,200 revolutions per minute. In the United States the engine was rated at 120 SAE horsepower. The Hydrak automatic transmission was also available from August 1957 on at an additional cost of DM 450.

The 220S was considered the refined successor of the 220a model, but the body style had not undergone many changes. A convertible appeared in May 1956 and the hard top coupe in 1957.

Prices and Production

The 220S four-door sedan sold for . . . . .DM 12,500
The 220S two-door convertible coupe sold for . . . . . . .DM 21,500
The 220S two-door hard top coupe sold for . . . . .DM 21,500
    Hydrak transmission . . . . .DM   450
Price in the United States was in 1956. . . . .$ 4,283

Production of the 220S [180 II] (from March 1956 until August 1959)

was in 1956	10,525	units
1957	15,459	units
1958	20,181	units
1959	9,114	units
total	55,279	units

Production of the 220S convertible and coupe [180 II] (from July 1956 until October 1959)

was in 1956	297	units
1957	1,066	units
1958	1,280	units
1959	786	units
total	3,429	units

The 220S convertible A, 1956

Specifications

	220S
Engine type	6 cyl overhead camshaft (M 180)
Bore and stroke	80 x 72.8mm (3.15 x 2.87 in)
Displacement	2195 cc (133.9 cu in)
Power output	100 hp (DIN) @ 4800 rpm (112 hp SAE) from Aug. '57: 106 @ 5200 (124 hp SAE)
Compression ratio	7.6:1 from Aug. '57: 8.7:1
Torque	16.5 mkg @ 3500 rpm (119 ft/lb) from Aug. '57: 17.5 mkg (127 ft/lb)
Carburetion	2 downdraft carburetors Solex 32 PAJTA
Engine speed at 100 km/hr	3320 rpm
Gear ratio	I. 3.52:1 II. 2.32:1 III. 1.52:1 IV. 1.00:1
Rear axle ratio	4.10
Chassis	unit frame and body
Suspension	independent front, single joint swing axle rear, with coil springs
Brakes and area	drum, 1064 cm² (164.9 sq in) servo assisted
Wheelbase	2820mm (111 in); coupe and convertible: 2,700mm (106.3 in)
Track, front/rear	1430/1470mm (56.2/57.9 in)
Length	4750mm (187 in); coupe and convertible: 4670mm (183.9 in)
Width	1740mm (68.5 in); coupe and convertible: 1765mm (69.5 in)
Height	1560mm (61.4 in); coupe and convertible: 1530mm (60.2 in)
Ground clearance	185mm (7.3 in)
Tires	6.70 x 13 sport
Turning circle	11.7 meters (38 ft); coupe and convertible: 11.4 meters (37 ft)
Steering type and ratio	recirculating ball, 21.4:1 (4 turns)
Weight	1350 kg (2970 lbs); coupe: 1410 kg (3102 lbs); convertible: 1450 kg (3219 lbs)
Maximum speed	160 km/hr (99.5 mph)
Acceleration	17 sec 0-100 km
Fuel consumption	13.5 liters super/100 km (17.4 mpg) coupe and convertible: 14 liters super
Fuel tank capacity	64 liters (16.9 gallons)

The 220S convertible A, 1956

The 220S sedan, 1956

The joint swing axle of the 220SE, 1958

The 220SE sedan, 1958

Model 220SE (1958-1960)

S = Super, E (Einspritzung) = fuel injection

The 220SE was first introduced in September 1958. Early pre-production was actually begun in April of that year, but the regular production lines did not get underway until October. The sedan had the same body style and furnishing of the 220S and was only different in the fuel-injected engine. The regular carburetor engine was equipped with two Solex downdraft carburetors and developed 100 horsepower (112 SAE) for the 220S; while the injection engine, using a Bosch two-plunger injection pump, developed 120 horsepower (134 SAE). It was also considerably more flexible than the carburetor unit.

The manifold injection system cost about $400 more to produce than the regular carburetion system, but the engineers estimated that it resulted in 18 percent more power, 5 percent greater torque, and reduced fuel consumption by 8 percent.

The air collection chamber and six intake pipes fed the air to the individual ports and fuel was injected just ahead of the junction of the manifold and the cylinder head. A calibrated jet was used for each individual cylinder and the fuel was being fed from the two plunger pumps which operated at engine speed. Injection was also controlled by temperature and barometric pressure. It was not a direct injection, but a manifold injection system.

The 220SE two-door convertible and coupe models were also shown at the same time as the sedan model. When in August 1959 production of the sedan ceased, the convertible and coupe models remained in production until the end of 1960, but were equipped with the newer, 120-horsepower fuel injection engine of the 220SEb type.

Prices and Production

The 220SE four-door sedan sold for . . . . .DM 14,400
The 220SE two-door convertible sold for . . . . .DM 23,400
The 220SE two-door coupe sold for . . . . .DM 23,400
    Hydrak transmission . . . . .DM 450
The 220SE convertible or coupe sold
    after August 1959 for. . . . . .DM 23,200

Production of the 220SE [128] (from April/October 1958 until August 1959)

was in	1958	201 units
	1959	1,773 units
	total	1,974 units

Production of the 220SE convertible and coupe [128] (from July/October 1958 until November 1960)

was in	1958	114 units
	1959	628 units
	1960	1,200 units
	total	1,942 units

Specifications

	220SE
Engine type	6 cyl overhead camshaft (M 180)
Bore and stroke	80 x 72.8mm (3.15 x 2.87 in)
Displacement	2195 cc (133.9 cu in)
Power output	115 hp (DIN) @ 4800 rpm (134 hp SAE @ 5000 rpm)
Compression ratio	8.7:1
Torque	19 mkg @ 3800 rpm (152 ft/lb @ 4100)
Fuel injection	Bosch two-plunger pump (into manifold)
Engine speed at 100 km/hr	3320 rpm
Gear ratios	I. 3.52:1　　U.S. cars: I. 3.65:1 (14.9) II. 2.32:1　　　　　　　II. 2.36:1 (9.68) III. 1.52:1　　　　　　　III. 1.53:1 (6.27) IV. 1.00:1　　　　　　　IV. 1.00:1 (4.10)
Rear axle ratio	4.10
Chassis	unit frame and body
Suspension	independent front, single joint swing axle rear, with coil springs
Brakes and area	drum, 1064 cm² (164.9 sq in) servo assisted
Wheelbase	2820mm (111 in); coupe and convertible: 2700mm (106.3 in)
Track, front/rear	1430/1470mm (56.2/57.9 in)
Length	4750mm (187 in); coupe and convertible: 4670mm (183.9 in)
Width	1740mm (68.5 in); coupe and convertible: 1765mm (69.5 in)
Height	1560mm (61.4 in); coupe and convertible: 1530mm (60.2 in)
Ground clearance	185mm (7.3 in)
Tires	6.70 x 13 sport
Turning circle	11.7 meters (38 ft); coupe and convertible: 11.4 meters (37 ft)
Steering type and ratio	recirculating ball, 21.4:1 (4 turns)
Weight	1370 kg (3014 lbs); coupe: 1430 kg (3146 lbs); convertible: 1470 kg (3234 lbs)
Maximum speed	160 km/hr (99.5 mph)
Acceleration	15 sec 0-100 km
Fuel consumption	13 liters super/100 km (18 mpg); coupe and convertible: 13.5 liters (17.4 mpg)
Fuel tank capacity	62 liters (16.4 gallons)

The 220SE convertible, 1958

The 220SE coupe, 1958

The M 180 engine of the 220SE, 1958

The 190D sedan, 1958

Model 190D (1958-1965)

D = Diesel

The 190D model followed the gasoline-powered 190 model more than two years later. It was not put into production until August 1958. That year, the 180D was still being sold; in fact, over 26,000 units were produced and nearly 10,000 of them were sold the next year. Along with the new 190D model, the 180Db appeared in 1959 and the 180Dc in 1961. This smaller version (and older body style) was still a very popular car and in great demand. The 180D and 180Db had the 1,767 cubic centimeter displacement engine, while the 190D and 190Db had the larger 1,897 cubic centimeter diesel unit. The 180Dc had a 1,988 cubic centimeter engine and the 190Dc, as well as the 200D later, shared that same power plant.

The 190D model had the 1,897 cubic centimeter engine of 50 horsepower at 4,000 revolutions per minute. It was completely redesigned from the previous one, had a shorter stroke and single overhead camshaft instead of the older pushrod, long-stroke engine which was still being used in the 180D model. The maximum speed of the 190D was 126 kilometers (78 miles) per hour.

To dramatically introduce the new, larger, and more powerful diesel engine to the public, a car was entered to compete in the tortuous 8,727-mile African Rallye from Algiers to Capetown. Karl Kling drove the car to victory, averaging 55.5 miles per hour across the Dark Continent.

The 190Db, built from August 1959 to August 1961, shared the body with its gasoline engined counterpart, with the wider radiator grille and simpler bumper without guards.

The 190Dc, built until August 1965, was similar to the 190c. It had the same dimensions and shared that same newer body style with the tail fins, longer, larger, and lower than the previous one.

Prices and Production

The 190D four-door sedan sold in 1958-1961 for . . . . . DM 9,950
The 190Dc four-door sedan in 1961 sold for. . . . . DM 10,450
    from April 1962 for. . . . . DM 11,100
    Power steering (from May 1964) . . . . DM 550
    Automatic transmission (from September 1963) . . . . DM 1,400

Production of the 190D model [121 I] (from August 1958 until July 1959)

was in	1958	5,469 units
	1959	15,160 units
total		20,629 units

Production of the 190Db [121 II] (from June 1959 until September 1961)

was in	1959	13,709 units
	1960	29,116 units
	1961	18,484 units
total		61,309 units

Production of the 190Dc model [110] (from April/June 1961 until August 1965)

was in	1961	12,882 units
	1962	45,414 units
	1963	60,784 units
	1964	64,422 units
	1965	42,143 units
total		225,645 units

Specifications

	190D / 190Db	190Dc		
Engine type	4 cyl diesel, single overhead camshaft (OM 621)			
Bore and stroke	85 x 83.6mm (3.35 x 3.29 in)	87 x 83.6mm (3.43 x 3.29 in)		
Displacement	1897 cc (115.7 cu in)	1988 cc (121.27 cu in)		
Power output	50 hp (DIN) @ 4000 rpm (55 hp SAE)	55 hp (DIN) @ 4200 rpm (60 hp SAE)		
Compression ratio	21:1	21:1		
Torque	11mkg @2200 rpm (79.5 ft/lbs)	11.5 mkg 2400 rpm 12 mkg SAE 87 ft/lbs)		
Fuel injection	Bosch injection pump pre-combustion chamber	Bosch injection pump		
Engine speed at 100 km/hr	3300 rpm	3300 rpm		
Gear ratios	I. 4.05:1 II. 2.38:1 III. 1.53:1 IV. 1.00:1	I. 4.05:1 II. 2.28:1 III. 1.53:1 IV. 1.00:1	automatic	I. 3.98:1 II. 2.52:1 III. 1.58:1 IV. 1.00:1
Rear axle ratio	3.70	3.92		
Chassis	unit frame and body	unit frame and body		
Suspension	independent front, single joint swing axle rear, with coil springs from 1963: air suspension, optional			
Brakes and area	drum, 1064 cm² (164.9 sq in)	drum, 1064 cm² (164.9 sq in) servo assisted from Aug. '63: disc, front		
Wheelbase	2650mm (104.3 in)	2700mm (106.3 in)		
Track, front/rear	1430/1475mm (56.2/58.1 in)	1468/1485mm (58/58.5 in) from Aug.'63: 1482/1485mm (58.3/58.5 in)		
Length	4485mm (176.6 in) b: 4500mm (177.2 in)	4730mm (186.5 in)		
Width	1740mm (68.5 in)	1795mm (70.7 in)		
Height	1560mm (61.4 in)	1495mm (58.8 in)		
Ground clearance	185mm (7.3 in)	185mm (7.3 in)		
Tires	6.40 x 13	7.00 x 13		
Turning circle	11.5 meters (38 ft)	11.8-11.6 meters (38 ft)		
Steering type and ratio	recirculating ball, 18.5:1 (3.75 turns)	recirculating ball, 21.4:1; from May '64: servo assisted 17.3:1 (3.2 turns)		
Weight	1250 kg (2750 lbs)	1320 kg (2904 lbs)		
Maximum speed	126 km/hr (78 mph)	130 km/hr (81 mph); automatic 127 km/hr (79 mph)		
Acceleration	29 sec 0-100 km	29 sec 0-100 km/hr; automatic 30 sec 0-100 km/hr		
Fuel consumption	8.5 liters/100 km (27.75 mpg)	9 liters/100 km (26 mpg); automatic 10 liters/100 km (23.5 mpg)		
Fuel tank capacity	56 liters (14.8 gallons)	52 liters (13.5 gallons)		

The 190Db sedan, 1961

The 190D with sunroof and extra lights, 1963

Drawing of the upper cylinder of M 621 engine, 1958

The 220S sedan, 1963

Prices and Production

The 220b four-door sedan sold for	.DM 11,500
from April 1962 for	.DM 12,160
Power steering	.DM 550
Hydrak transmission (until 1961)	.DM 450
Automatic transmission (from August 1962)	.DM 1,400
Price in the United States was	.$ 4,370

Production of the 220b [111/1] (from May/August 1959 until August 1965)

was in	1959	3,375 units
	1960	13,127 units
	1961	14,842 units
	1962	11,618 units
	1963	10,492 units
	1964	11,327 units
	1965	4,910 units
	total	69,691 units

Prices and Production

The 220Sb four-door sedan sold for	.DM 13,250
from April 1962 for	.DM 13,750
Power steering	.DM 550
Hydrak transmission (until 1961)	.DM 450
Automatic transmission (from August 1962)	.DM 1,400
Price in the United States was	.$ 5,120

Production of the 220Sb [111/2] (from May/August 1959 until July 1965)

was in	1959	7,267 units
	1960	26,642 units
	1961	32,238 units
	1962	26,077 units
	1963	26,236 units
	1964	28,732 units
	1965	13,927 units
	total	161,119 units

Model 220 (1959-1965)

The 220b model sedan, shown to the public at the Frankfurt Auto Show in 1959, was one of four models which shared the new body style. The four-door sedans had a wider radiator shell, a longer body (4.875 millimeters, 191.9 inches, overall length) with slight rear fins, wrap-around windshield, and wide rear window, as well as dual vertically positioned headlights. Bumpers had a narrower one above the standard sized one.

The 220b model was the successor to the 219 sedan, which was then discontinued. The 2,195 cubic centimeter six-cylinder engine developed 95 horsepower (105 SAE) and had the higher compression ratio (8.7 to 1) of the later 219 production models. Maximum speed was also increased from 148 to 160 kilometers (99.4 miles) per hour.

The Hydrak transmission was available until 1961 and after August 1962 an automatic transmission became an optional extra item. A year later, in August 1963, the car was fitted with disc brakes on the front wheels and a hydraulic dual braking system. Power brakes were also available.

# Model 220S (1959-1965)
S = Super

The 220S, first shown publicly in late 1959, was the second model which also shared the new body style of the sedans. All outside dimensions were the same as that of the other three models.

The six-cylinder engine developed 110 horsepower (124 SAE) and maximum speed was given as 165 kilometers (102.5 miles) per hour. Disc brakes on the front wheels were fitted from April 1962, and from August 1963 a hydraulic dual braking system was installed.

The 220 sedan, 1959

Specifications

	220	220S
Engine type	6 cyl overhead camshaft (M 180)	6 cyl overhead camshaft (M 180)
Bore and stroke	80 x 72.8mm (3.16 x 2.87 in)	80 x 72.8mm (3.16 x 2.87 in)
Displacement	2195 cc (133.9 cu in)	2195 cc (133.9 cu in)
Power output	95 hp (DIN) @ 4800 rpm (105 hp SAE @ 5000 rpm)	110 hp (DIN) @ 5000 rpm (124 hp SAE @ 5200 rpm)
Compression ratio	8.7:1	8.7:1
Torque	17.2 mkg @ 3200 rpm (18.4 mkg 133.2 ft/lb @ 3300)	17.5 mkg @ 3500 rpm (19.2 mkg 139 ft/lb @ 3700 rpm)
Carburetion	2 downdraft carburetors Solex 34 PJCB	2 dual downdraft carburetors Solex 34 PAJTA from July '63: 35/40 INAT
Engine speed at 100 km/hr	3300 rpm	3300 rpm
Gear ratios	I. 3.64:1 automatic I. 3.98:1 II. 2.36:1 (later 2.28:1) II. 2.52:1 III. 1.53:1 III. 1.58:1 IV. 1.00:1 IV. 1.00:1	I. 3.64:1 automatic I. 3.98:1 II. 2.36:1 (later 2.28:1) II. 2.52:1 III. 1.53:1 III. 1.58:1 IV. 1.00:1 IV. 1.00:1
Rear axle ratio	3.90 4.10	3.90 4.10
Chassis	unit frame and body	unit frame and body
Suspension	independent front, single joint swing axle rear, with coil springs	independent front, single joint swing axle rear, with coil springs
Brakes and area	drum, 1064 cm² (164.9 sq in), servo assisted, optional from Aug. '63 disc, front	drum, 1064 cm² (164.9 sq in), servo assisted, optional from Apr. '62 disc, front
Wheelbase	2750mm (108.3 in)	2750mm (108.3 in)
Track, front/rear	1470/1485mm (57.9/58.5 in) from Aug. '63: 1482/1485mm (58.3/58.5 in)	1470/1485mm (57.9/58.5 in) from Apr. '62: 1482/1485mm (58.3/58.5 in)
Length	4875mm (191.9 in)	4875mm (191.9 in)
Width	1795mm (70.7 in)	1795mm (70.7 in)
Height	1500mm (59.1 in)	1500mm (59.1 in)
Ground clearance	165mm (6.5 in)	165mm (6.5 in)
Tires	6.70 x 13; from 1960: 7.25 x 13	6.70 x 13 sport; from 1960: 7.25 x 13 sport
Turning circle	12.1-11.9 meters (39 ft)	12.1-11.9 meters (39 ft)
Steering type and ratio	recirculating ball, 21.4:1 (3.75 turns)	recirculating ball, 21.4:1 (3.75 turns)
Weight	1320 kg (2904 lbs)	1345 kg (2959 lbs)
Maximum speed	160 km/hr (99.5 mph)	165 km/hr (103 mph)
Acceleration	16 sec 0-100 km/hr	15 sec 0-100 km/hr
Fuel consumption	14 liters, super/100 km (16.75 mpg); automatic: 15 liters, super (15.6 mpg)	14 liters, super/100 km (16.75 mpg) automatic: 15 liters, super 100km/hr (15.6 mpg)
Fuel tank capacity	65 liters (17.2 gallons)	65 liters (17.2 gallons)

The 220SE convertible, 1961

# Model 220SE (1959-1965)
S = Super, E (Einspritzung) = fuel injection

The 220SEb, first shown also in late 1959, was the third of the models to share the identical body style with the others, but was more luxuriously outfitted in its interior.

The fuel-injection engine was essentially the same as that of the previous 220SE model, but now developed 120 horsepower (134 SAE) instead of 115. The maximum speed was 172 kilometers (107 miles) per hour. As in the carbureter engined model, this one had disc brakes on the front wheels fitted from April 1962 and the hydraulic dual braking system available from August 1963 on.

Production of the sedans got under way in August 1959, and in September 1960 a newly styled coupe became available, but it was not produced in quantity until February 1961. The convertible appeared in September 1961. All specifications were the same for the three body styles, except for the weights of the different models. Disc brakes were fitted for the two latter ones from the beginning, and at the same time the dual braking system was available in all three.

The body styles of the convertible and coupe were more modern — the rear fins were eliminated and the edge slightly rounded — and the cars were much more luxuriously equipped. Real leather upholstery was standard and a four-speed automatic transmission with floor-mounted shift lever, as well as a tachometer, were standard equipment of these truly elegant automobiles.

Prices and Production

The 220SEb four-door sedan sold for ....DM 14,950
   from April 1962 ....DM 15,400
   Power steering ....DM 550
   Hydrak transmission (until 1961) ....DM 450
   Automatic transmission (from August 1961) .....DM 1,400
The 220SEb two-door coupe sold for ....DM 23,500
The 220SEb two-door convertible sold for ....DM 25,500
The price in the United States for the sedan was ......$ 5,187
The price in the United States for the coupe was .....$ 8,895

Production of the 220SEb sedan [111/3] (from August 1959 until August 1965)

was in	1959	1,579 units
	1960	9,247 units
	1961	10,761 units
	1962	10,786 units
	1963	12,848 units
	1964	14,336 units
	1965	6,529 units
	total	66,086 units

Production of the 220SEb [111/3] coupe and convertible (from September 1960/February 1961 until October 1965)

was in	1960	2 units
	1961	2,537 units
	1962	4,287 units
	1963	3,755 units
	1964	3,528 units
	1965	2,793 units
	total	16,902 units

The 200SE coupe, 1961

Specifications

	220SEb	220SEb (coupe and convertible)		
Engine type	6 cyl overhead camshaft (M 127)	6 cyl overhead camshaft (M 127)		
Bore and stroke	80 x 72.8mm (3.16 x 2.87 in)	80 x 72.8mm (3.16 x 2.87 in)		
Displacement	2195 cc (133.9 cu in)	2195 cc (133.9 in)		
Power output	120 hp (DIN) @ 4800 rpm (134 hp SAE @ 5000 rpm)	120 hp (DIN) @ 4800 rpm (134 hp SAE @ 5000 rpm)		
Compression ratio	8.7:1	8.7:1		
Torque	19.3 mkg @ 3900 rpm; (21.0 mkg @ 4100 rpm SAE 151.9 ft/lb)			
Fuel injection	Bosch two plunger pump	Bosch two plunger pump		
Engine speed at 100 km/hr	3470 rpm	3470 rpm		
Gear ratios	I. 3.64:1 II. 2.36:1 (later 2.28:1) III. 1.53:1 IV. 1.00:1	I. 3.64:1 II. 2.36:1 (later 2.28:1) III. 1.53:1 IV. 1.00:1	automatic	I. 3.98:1 II. 2.52:1 III. 1.58:1 IV. 1.00:1
Rear axle ratio	4.10	4.10		
Chassis	unit frame and body	unit frame and body		
Suspension	independent front, single joint swing axle rear, with coil springs			
Brakes and area	drum, 1064 cm² (164.9 sq in) servo assisted, optional; from Aug. '63: two circuit hydraulic	disc, front; drum, rear		
Wheelbase	2750mm (108.3 in)	2750mm (108.3 in)		
Track, front/rear	1470/1485mm (57.9/58.5 in)	1482/1485mm (58.3/58.4 in)		
Length	4875mm (191.9 in)	4880mm (192.1 in)		
Width	1795mm (70.7 in)	1845mm (72.7 in)		
Height	1500mm (59.1 in)	1440mm (57 in)		
Ground clearance	185mm (7.3 in)	185mm (7.3 in)		
Tires	6.70 x 13 sport from 1960: 7.25 x 13 sport	coupe: 7.25 x 13; conv: 750 x 13		
Turning circle	12.1-11.9 meters (39 ft)	12.1-11.9 meters (39 ft)		
Steering type and ratio	recirculating ball, 21.4:1 (3.75 turns) (with servo assistance: 17.3:1; 3.2 turns)	22.7:1 (4.1 turns)		
Weight	1380 kg (3036 lb)	coupe: 1410 kg (3102 lbs); conv: 1510 kg (3322 lbs)		
Maximum speed	172 km/hr (107 mph)	172 km/hr (107 mph)		
Acceleration	14 sec 0-100 km/hr	14 sec 0-100 km/hr		
Fuel consumption	14 liters, super/100 km (16.75 mpg); automatic: 15 liters (15.6 mpg) 14.5 liters/15.5 liters			
Fuel tank capacity	65 liters (17.2 gallons)	65 liter (17.2 gallons)		

The 220SE coupe, 1963

The instrument panel of the 220SE coupe, 1961

The 300SE sedan, 1961

Model 300SE (1961-1967)

S = Super, E (Einspritzung) = fuel injection

The 300SE was the fourth model to share the new basic body style first shown at the Frankfurt Auto Show in 1959. In appointments it was similar to the 220SE, but it had several important refinements, visible and hidden. The white-wall tires and wider use of chrome trim on the body made it look longer and more elegant than its lesser counterparts, but from afar it seemed the same. An air suspension system and disc brakes on all four wheels were standard. The hydraulic dual braking system was available from August 1963 on.

The 2,996 cubic centimeter light alloy engine with manifold fuel injection developed 160 horsepower at 5,000 revolutions per minute and from January 1964 on, 170 horsepower at 5,400 revolutions per minute. This was achieved by raising the compression ratio from 8.7 to 8.8 to 1; and instead of the two-plunger injection pump, a six-plunger Bosch pump was used. Maximum speeds varied according to rear axle ratios; the 160 horsepower engine with automatic transmission and 3.92 axle produced 175 kilometers per hour, while the 170 horsepower version with manual transmission and 3.75 axle gave the sedan a maximum speed of 200 kilometers (124 miles) per hour.

The 300SE coupe and convertible were added to the line in March 1962, and a longer (2,850 millimeter or 112.2 inch) wheelbase model sedan came out in March 1963.

Production

Production of the 300SE sedan [112/3] (from April 1961 until July 1965)

was in	1961	13 units
	1962	2,768 units
	1963	995 units
	1964	936 units
	1965	490 units
total		5,202 units

Production of the 300SE convertible and coupe [112/3] (from February 1962 until December 1967)

was in	1962	331 units
	1963	630 units
	1964	706 units
	1965	710 units
	1966	497 units
	1967	253 units
total		3,127 units

Production of the 300SE long sedan [112/3] (from December 1962/March 1963 until August 1965)

was in	1962	1 unit
	1963	387 units
	1964	751 units
	1965	407 units
total		1,546 units

Prices

The 330SE four-door sedan sold for	DM 23,100
The 300SE long four-door sedan sold for	DM 26,400
The 300SE two-door coupe sold for	DM 31,350
The 300SE two-door convertible sold for	DM 33,350
Automatic transmission	DM 1,400
The price in the United States	
for the sedan in January 1966 was	$ 7,980
for the coupe in January 1966 was	$ 11,511
for the convertible in January 1966 was	$ 12,295

Specifications

The 300SE coupe, 1962

	300SE / 300SE (long) / 300SE (coupe and convertible)
Engine type	6 cyl overhead camshaft (M 189)
Bore and stroke	85 x 88mm (3.34 x 3.47 in)
Displacement	2996 cc (182.8 cu in)
Power output	160 hp (DIN) @ 5000 rpm; from Jan. '64: 170 hp (DIN) @ 5400 rpm (185 hp SAE @ 5200 rpm) (195 hp SAE @ 5500 rpm)
Compression ratio	8.7:1 from Jan. '64: 8.8:1
Torque	25.6 mkg @ 3800 rpm 25.4 mkg @ 4000 rpm (28.3 mkg @ 4000 rpm SAE 204.5 ft/lb)
Fuel injection	Bosch two plunger pump; from Jan. '64: six plunger pump
Engine speed at 100 km/hr	3310 rpm
Gear ratios	I. 4.05:1 automatic I. 3.98:1 (16.3) II. 2.28:1 II. 2.52:1 (10.3) III. 1.53:1 III. 1.58:1 (6.47) IV. 1.00:1 IV. 1.00:1 (4.10)
Rear axle ratio	3.92 or 3.75 4.10 from 1963: 3.92 or 3.75
Chassis	unit frame and body
Suspension	independent front and rear, with coil springs, single joint swing axle, air suspension
Brakes and area	disc, 253/255mm (99.6/100.4), servo assisted, two circuit hydraulic
Wheelbase	2750mm (108.3 in); SE long: 2850mm (112.2 in)
Track, front/rear	1482/1490mm (58.3/58.6)
Length	4875mm (191.9 in); long: 5875mm (231.2 in); coupe & convertible: 4880mm (192.1 in)
Width	1795mm (70.7 in) coupe & convertible: 1845mm (72.6 in)
Height	1455mm (58 in) coupe: 1395mm; conv: 1400mm (55.1 in)
Ground clearance	185mm (7.3 in)
Tires	7.50 x 13
Turning circle	12.1-11.9 meters (39 ft); long: 12.4-12.2 meters (40 ft)
Steering type and ratio	recirculating ball, 17.3:1 (3.2 turns), servo assisted
Weight	1580 kg (3476 lbs); long: 1630 kg (3586 lbs); coupe: 1600 kg (3520 lbs); conv: 1700 kg (3740 lbs)
Maximum speed	160 hp manual, 3.92 axle 180 km/hr (112 mph); autom. 175 km/hr 170 hp manual, 3.92 axle 190 km/hr (118 mph); autom. 185 km/hr 170 hp manual, 3.75 axle 200 km/hr (124 pmh); autom. 195 km/hr
Acceleration	160 hp: 13 sec 0-100 km/hr; 170 hp: 12 sec 0-100 km/hr
Fuel consumption	17 liters, super/100 km (13.7 mpg); automatic: 19 liters (12.3 mpg)
Fuel tank capacity	65 liters (17.2 gallons); from Jan. '63: 82 liters (21.6 gallons)

The interior of the 300SE sedan, 1961

The 230SL coupe, 1963

Model 230SL (1963-1967)

S = Sports, L (Leicht) = light

The 230SL sports car was first introduced at the Geneva Auto Show in March 1963. It was the successor to the 190SL which was phased out in February of that year. The engine for the 230SL was an enlarged version of the 220SE power unit, displacing 2,306 cubic centimeters and developing 150 horsepower (170 SAE) at 5,500 (5,600) revolutions per minute. Compression ratio was 9.3 to 1. The fuel was injected into the intake duct in the cylinder head instead of into the intake suction pipe as in the other models.

The four-speed transmission lever was placed on the floor and an automatic transmission was available. The rear axle ratio was 3.75 to 1. Maximum speeds were for the manual transmission 200 kilometers (124.2 miles) per hour and using the automatic transmission, 195 kilometers (121.2 miles) per hour.

A two-circuit servo brake system was installed as well as a vacuum operated brake booster. Disc brakes were fitted in front and drum brakes on the rear wheels. The coupe version had a slightly converse top, giving it the appearance of a pagoda top. The large glass area afforded an excellent view for the driver in all directions.

To start the introduction of the new model off with an impressive event, Eugen Böhringer won the tortuous Spa-Sofia-Liége Rally, driving the new 230SL. It was a spectacular performance for driver and car to win this initial test against strong international competition.

This victory proved, without a doubt, that this SL model was truly a light sports car and deserved that designation. In the United States the car was well received, but for many owners, performance was not its strongest asset. Perhaps compared with the really brutal power of the 300SL, this 230SL was a rather sedate, but quite adequately performing sports car model.

Prices and Production

The 230SL roadster sold in 1963 for	DM 20,600
from April 1966 for	DM 21,100
The 230SL coupe sold in 1963 for	DM 20,950
from April 1966 for	DM 21,450
Hard top (for the roadster)	DM 1,100
Power steering	DM 550
Automatic transmission	DM 1,400
Prices in the United States were, in April 1966,	
for the 230SL roadster (East coast)	$ 6,185
(West coast)	$ 6,262
for the 230SL coupe (East coast)	$ 6,343
(West coast)	$ 6,420
for the 230SL coupe/roadster (East coast)	$ 6,587
(West coast)	$ 6,665
Power steering (April 1966)	$ 171
Automatic transmission	$ 342
Prices previously were for the roadster	$ 6,144
for the coupe	$ 6,301
for the coupe/roadster	$ 6,543

Production of the 230SL [113] (from March/July 1963 until January 1967)

was in	1963	1,465 units
	1964	6,911 units
	1965	6,325 units
	1966	4,945 units
	1967	185 units
	total	19,831 units

Specifications

	230SL
Engine type	6 cyl overhead camshaft (M 127)
Bore and stroke	82 x 72.8mm (3.23 x 2.87 in)
Displacement	2,306 cc (140.7 cu in)
Power output	150 hp (DIN) @ 5500 rpm (170 hp SAE @ 5600 rpm)
Compression ratio	9.3:1
Torque	20 mkg @ 4200 rpm (22 mkg @ 4500 rpm 159 ft/lbs)
Fuel injection	Bosch six plunger pump
Engine speed at 100 km/hr	3145 rpm
Gear ratios	until 1965 automatic: I. 4.42:1 (later 4.05) I. 3.98:1 (14.9) II. 2.28:1 (later 2.23) II. 2.52:1 (9.45) III. 1.53:1 (later 1.42) III. 1.58:1 (5.92) IV. 1.00:1 (later 1.00) IV. 1.00:1 (3.75)
Rear axle ratio	3.75; from Sept. '65: 3.69 or 3.92
Chassis	unit frame and body
Suspension	independent front, single joint swing axle rear, with coil springs
Brakes and area	disc, front; drum, rear, servo assist, two circuit hydraulic, 253/230mm (9.96/9.06 in)
Wheelbase	2400mm (94.5 in)
Track, front/rear	1486/1487mm (58.5/58.5 in)
Length	4285mm (168.8 in)
Width	1760mm (69.2 in)
Height	1305mm (51.4 in)
Ground clearance	139mm (5.5 in)
Tires	185 HR 14 radial
Turning circle	10.5 meters (34 ft)
Steering type and ratio	recirculating ball, 22.7:1 (4.1 turns); servo assisted 17.3:1 (3.2 turns)
Weight	roadster: 1300 kg (2860 lbs); coupe: 1380 kg (3036 lbs)
Maximum speed	200 km/hr (124 mph); automatic: 195 km/hr (121 mph)
Acceleration	11 sec 0-100 km/hr; automatic: 13 sec 0-100 km/hr
Fuel consumption	14 liter, super/100 km (16.75 mpg)
Fuel tank capacity	65 liters (17.2 gallons)

The 230SL roadster, 1963

The instrument panel of the 230SL, 1963

Model 250SL (1966-1968)

S = Sports, L (Leicht) = light

The 250SL model made its brief appearance toward the end of 1966. The first few cars (seventeen units) were built in late November and in December of that year. The body was the same as that of the former 230SL which it replaced. Minor improvements had been made in the interior furnishings and outfitting, such as a pressure-absorbing steering wheel, better seat belts, and modified lighting of some instruments, but basically it was the same.

With the larger engine of 2,496 cubic centimeter (152.3 cubic inch) displacement and 150 horsepower (DIN) and 170 SAE, and especially vastly increased torque from the former 159 ft/lbs. to 173.6 ft/lbs. (both at 4,500 revolutions per minute), this new model showed an appreciable improvement in performance. Fitted with the four- or five-speed transmission and a rear axle ratio of 3.69, the car reached 19.7 miles at 1,000 revolutions per minute in top gear — the same as that of the 230SL model, but it was much more responsive. The gear ratios of the later production of the former model were maintained. Along with the engine of the 250SE line, the sports car also got the disc brakes, front and rear, resulting in some improvement in stopping the car; power assist was standard.

While this newer SL model was superior to the one it replaced, its actual performance was only slightly better than that of its predecessor. The somewhat larger displacement engine produced the same horsepower, but had a 10 percent increase in torque. Yet, the acceleration figures and maximum speed remained the same as before.

The 250SL was actually a one-year production car. It was soon to be replaced by a yet larger engined model and was produced in any quantity only during the year 1967. Only two cars were built in 1968.

The next version, in fact the third of this body style, was to be a most satisfactory car in every respect. It sold better than the previous ones and became a much desired sports car practically everywhere. Here, it indeed commanded premium prices, and 15 years later double the original cost was the going rate.

The 250SL roadster, 1967

Prices and Production

The 250SL coupe sold in 1967 for	DM 22,800
Power steering	DM 550
Automatic transmission	DM 1,400
The 250SL roadster sold in the U.S. in September 1967	
(East coast) for	$ 6,485
(West coast) for	$ 6,568
The 250SL coupe sold (East coast) for	$ 6,647
The 250SL coupe/roadster sold (East coast) for	$ 6,897

Production of the 250SL [113 A] (from November/December 1966 until January 1968)

was in	1966	17 units
	1967	5,177 units
	1968	2 units
	total	5,196 units

Specifications

	250SL
Engine type	6 cyl overhead camshaft (M 129)
Bore and stroke	82 x 78.8mm (3.23 x 3.1 in)
Displacement	2496 cc (152.3 cu in)
Power output	150 hp (DIN) @ 5500 rpm (170 hp SAE @ 5600 rpm)
Compression ratio	9.3:1
Torque	22 mkg @ 4200 rpm (24 mkg SAE @ 4500 rpm 173.6 ft/lb)
Fuel injection	Bosch six plunger pump
Engine speed at 100 km/hr	3245 rpm
Gear ratios	I. 4.05:1 automatic I. 3.98:1 II. 2.23:1 II. 2.52:1 III. 1.42:1 III. 1.58:1 IV. 1.00:1 IV. 1.00:1
Rear axle ratio	3.69
Chassis	unit frame and body
Suspension	independent front and rear, with coil springs, single joint swing axle
Brakes and area	disc, servo assist, two circuit hydraulic, 273/279mm (10.75/10.99 in)
Wheelbase	2400mm (94.5 in)
Track, front/rear	1486/1487mm (58.5/58.5 in)
Length	4285mm (168.8 in)
Width	1760mm (69.2 in)
Height	1305mm (51.4 in)
Ground clearance	139mm (5.5 in)
Tires	185 H 14 radial
Turning circle	10.5 meters (34 ft)
Steering type and ratio	recirculating ball, 22.7:1 (4.1 turns); servo assisted, 17.3:1 (3.2 turns)
Weight	roadster: 1300 kg (2860 lbs); coupe: 1380 kg (3036 lbs)
Maximum speed	200 km/hr (124 mph); automatic: 195 km/hr (121 mph)
Acceleration	11 sec 0-100 km/hr; automatic: 13 sec 0-100 km/hr
Fuel consumption	14 liters, super/100 km (16.75 mpg)
Fuel tank capacity	82 liters (21.7 gallons)

The 250SL coupe, 1967

The 250SL on the test track, 1967

The 250SL on the rain track, 1967

The 280SL coupe, 1968

Prices

The 280SL sports coupe/roadster sold for ....DM	23,793
Power steering ....DM	550
Automatic Transmission.................DM	1,400

Prices were in March 1968 (East coast)
    for the 280SL roadster.....................$ 6,485
    coupe ....$ 6,647
    roadster/coupe ....$ 6,897

Prices were in March 1968 (West coast)
    for the 280SL roadster.....................$ 6,585
    coupe ....$ 6,731
    roadster/coupe ....$ 6,981

Prices were in September 1968 (East coast)
    for the 280SL roadster.....................$ 6,638
    coupe ....$ 6,800
    roadster/coupe ....$ 7,050

Prices were in October 1969 (East coast)
    for the 280SL roadster.....................$ 6,952
    coupe ....$ 7,118
    roadster/coupe ....$ 7,374

Prices were in October 1970 (East coast)
    for the 280SL roadster.....................$ 7,444
    coupe ....$ 7,617
    roadster/coupe ....$ 7,884

Prices were in March 1971 (East coast)
    for the 280SL roadster.....................$ 7,469
    coupe ....$ 7,642
    roadster/coupe ....$ 7,909
    Power steering (October 1970)..............$ 198
    Automatic transmission ....$ 392

Model 280SL (1967-1971)

S = Sports, L (Leicht) = light

The 280SL sports car was the next, and last, graduation in the development of the particular model line. Begun in March 1963 as the 230SL, it had succeeded the popular 190SL of which nearly 26,000 units were produced. Yet in the three variations (230SL, 250SL, and 280SL) this model sold almost twice as many cars. It was not a competitive, but luxurious, fast touring sports car.

The six-cylinder 2,778 cubic centimeter displacement engine for the 280SL was entirely new. It retained the same design characteristics as the 250 engine, with single overhead camshaft and a seven main bearing crankshaft. An air cooler for the lubricating oil, similar to that employed on racing cars, replaced the oil-water heat exchanger of the previous engine design. Developing 180 SAE horsepower (up from 170) and 193 ft/lbs. torque (up from 174), the performance of this newest model sports car was tremendously enhanced, despite the restricting stricter emission controls. (The horsepower per liter ratio was for the 230SL/74, 250SL/68, and 280SL/65.)

For the American market a rear axle ratio of 4.08 was furnished, but the other two ratios, 3.92 and 3.69, were available upon special request. As on the two previous models, the five-speed manual gearbox was also available, while the four-speed one was standard. Power steering was not yet a standard item on the car. The 280SL was offered as a coupe, roadster, or combination roadster-coupe model.

Production

Production of the 280SL [113 E28] (from November 1967/January 1968 until March 1971)

was in	1967	143 units
	1968	6,930 units
	1969	8,047 units
	1970	7,935 units
	1971	830 units
	total	23,885 units

Specifications

	280SL
Engine type	6 cyl overhead camshaft (M 130)
Bore and stroke	86.5 x 78.8mm (3.41 x 3.10 in)
Displacement	2778 cc (169.5 cu in)
Power output	170 hp (DIN) @ 5700 rpm (180 SAE hp @ 5700 rpm) or 180 hp (DIN) @ 5900 rpm, but not for U.S.
Compression ratio	9.5:1
Torque	24.5 mkg @ 4250 rpm (26.7 mkg SAE @ 4500 rpm 193 ft/lb)
Fuel injection	Bosch six plunger pump
Engine speed at 100 km/hr	3500 rpm
Gear ratios	I. 4.05:1 automatic I. 3.98:1 (16.21) II. 2.23:1 II. 2.52:1 (10.27) III. 1.42:1 III. 1.58:1 (6.44) IV. 1.00:1 IV. 1.00:1 (4.08)
Rear axle ratio	4.08 upon request: 3.92, 3.69
Chassis	unit frame and body
Suspension	independent front and rear, with coil springs, single joint swing axle
Brakes and area	disc, servo assist, two circuit hydraulic, 273/279mm (10.75/10.99 in)
Wheelbase	2400mm (94.5 in)
Track, front/rear	1486/1487mm (58.5/58.5 in)
Length	4285mm (168.8 in)
Width	1760mm (69.2 in)
Height	1305mm (51.4 in)
Ground clearance	139mm (5.5 in)
Tires	185 H 14 radial
Turning circle	10.5 meters (34 ft)
Steering type	recirculating ball, servo assisted 17.2:1 (3.2 turns)
Weight	roadster: 1340 kg (2948 lbs); coupe: 1420 kg (3124 lbs)
Maximum speed	195 km/hr (121 mph); automatic: 190 km/hr (118 pmh)
Acceleration	10 sec 0-100 km/hr; automatic: 11 sec 0-100 km/hr
Fuel consumption	14 liters, super/100 km (16.75 mpg)
Fuel tank capacity	82 liters (21.7 gallons)

The 280SL coupe, 1968, U.S. version

The 280SL roadster, 1968

The 280SL roadster, 1968

Model 600 (1963-1981)

The 600 model — the Grosser Mercedes — was introduced at the Frankfurt Auto Show in 1963. It restored the tradition of sumptuous luxury and ultimate prestige of Mercedes-Benz.

A new V-type eight-cylinder engine of 6.3 liters (6,329 cubic centimeters) developing 250 horsepower (300 SAE) powered this newest edition of the great Mercedes to a maximum speed of 205 kilometers (127 miles) per hour. The 600 model was available in two body styles: a 5/6-seat limousine or 7/8-passenger pullman with wheelbases of 3,200 millimeters (126 inches) and 3,900 millimeters (153.5 inches), respectively. Overall length was 218 and 246 inches. From 1965 on, a landaulet also became available.

This fine automobile incorporated all modern design elements: fuel injection, overhead camshaft engine, air suspension and shock absorbers adjustment, disc brakes on all four wheels, automatic four-speed transmission and power steering, central vacuum locking system for the doors and luggage compartment, adjustable steering wheel, and two separate heating and ventilating systems. It was truly a majestic car of the highest order and an honorable descendant of the distinctive Great Mercedes automobiles of former years.

That year, 1963, the company offered fourteen passenger car models for sale. However, not all of them were made available to the American public, and most of them were naturally not entirely new models.

Prices

The 600 four-door limousine sold for	DM 56,500
The 600 four-door pullman sold for	DM 63,500
In the United States, advertised in May 1964, prices were for the limousine (called 5-passenger sedan)	$ 19,500
and for the pullman (called 7-passenger sedan)	$ 24,000
The price list of October 1965 offered the limousine (East coast) for	$ 20,143
(West coast) for	$ 20,291
pullman (East coast) for	$ 23,098
(West coast) for	$ 23,245
The price list of October 1970 (registration 1971 vehicles) offered the limousine (East coast) for	$ 25,707
(West coast) for	$ 25,920
pullman (East coast) for	$ 29,385
(West coast) for	$ 29,617
The price list of December 1971 (registration 1972 vehicles) offered the limousine (East coast) for	$ 32,695
pullman (East coast) for	$ 37,928
Other prices were, in September 1966 (East coast) limousine	$ 22,299
pullman	$ 25,582
in September 1968 (East coast) limousine	$ 23,007
pullman	$ 26,290
in October 1969 (East coast) limousine	$ 23,580
pullman	$ 26,953

The M 100 V-8 engine of the 600, 1963

The 600 limousine, 1963

Production

Production of the 600 and 600 long model [100]
(from August 1963/September 1964 until June 1981)

		Limousine	Pullman
was in	1963	2 units	1 unit
	1964	99 units	8 units
	1965	345 units	63 units
	1966	293 units	30 units
	1967	138 units	21 units
	1968	184 units	39 units
	1969	279 units	57 units
	1970	198 units	38 units
	1971	186 units	51 units
	1972	172 units	38 units
	1973	64 units	18 units
	1974	24 units	28 units
	1975	25 units	17 units
	1976	33 units	14 units
	1977	36 units	19 units
	1978	28 units	12 units
	1979	36 units	17 units
	1980	33 units	11 units
	1981	15 units	5 units
total		2,190 units	487 units

The 600 pullman, 1964

The 600 landaulet, 1965

Specifications

	600	Pullman
Engine type	V-8 cyl overhead camshaft, one for each bank (M 100)	
Bore and stroke	103 x 95mm (4.06 x 3.74 in)	103 x 95mm (4.06 x 3.74 in)
Displacement	6332 cc (386.3 cu in)	6332 cc (386.3 cu in)
Power output	250 hp (DIN) @ 4000 rpm (300 hp SAE @ 4100 rpm)	
Compression ratio	9.0:1	9.0:1
Torque	51 mkg @ 2800 rpm (434 ft/lbs @ 3000 rpm)	
Fuel injection	Bosch eight plunger pump	Bosch eight plunger pump
Engine speed at 100 km/hr	2475 rpm	2475 rpm
Gear ratios	I. 3.98:1 (12.86) II. 2.52:1 (8.14) III. 1.58:1 (5.10) IV. 1.00:1 (3.23)	I. 3.98:1 (12.86) II. 2.52:1 (8.14) (later 2.46:1) III. 1.58:1 (5.10) IV. 1.00:1 (3.23)
Rear axle ratio	3.23	3.23
Chassis	unit frame and body	unit frame and body
Suspension	independent front, single joint swing axle rear, air suspension	
Brakes and area	discs, 291/294.5mm (114.6/115.9 in), servo assisted, two circuit hydraulic	
Wheelbase	3200mm (126 in)	3900mm (153.5 in)
Track, front/rear	1587/1581mm (62.5/62 in)	1587/1581mm (62.5/62 in)
Length	5540mm (218 in)	6240mm (246 in)
Width	1950mm (76.8 in)	1950mm (76.8 in)
Height	1500mm (59.5 in)	1510mm (59.5 in)
Ground clearance	200mm (7.9 in) (later: 152mm (6.0 in)	
Tires	9.00 x 15 super sport	9.00 x 15 super sport
Turning circle	12.4 meters (40.7 ft) (later: 12.7m)	14.6 meters (47.8 ft) (later: 15.0m)
Steering type and ratio	recirculating ball, servo assisted, 17.3:1 (3.3 turns)	
Weight	2470 kg (5434 lbs) (later: 2475 kg)	2640 kg (5808 lbs) (later: 2660 kg)
Maximum speed	205 km/hr (127 mph)	200 km/hr (124 mph)
Acceleration	10 sec 0-100 km/hr (later: 9.7 sec)	12 sec 0-100 km/hr
Fuel consumption	24 liters, super/100 km (10.2 mpg)	26 liters, super/100 km (9 mpg)
Fuel tank capacity	112 liters (30 gallons)	112 liters (30 gallons)

The 200 sedan, 1965

Prices and Production

The 200 four-door sedan sold for	DM 10,800
from April 1966 for	DM 11,000
Power steering	DM 500
Automatic transmission	DM 1,400
The price in the United States was in 1965	
(East coast)	$ 3,929
(West coast)	$ 4,039
in September 1966 (East coast)	$ 4,084
in September 1967 (East coast)	$ 4,179
Power steering (1965)	$ 171
Automatic transmission	$ 342

Production of the 200 model [110] (from July 1965 until February 1968)

was in	1965	16,864 units
	1966	26,842 units
	1967	26,169 units
	1968	332 units
	total	70,207 units

Model 200 (1965-1968)

The 200 model was first shown, together with four other new models, at the Frankfurt Auto Show in 1965. It used the same body as the former 190c sedan which it replaced. Outwardly the change was a relocation of the indicator lights from the cowl to the front, just below the headlights, a redesigned cluster of rear lights, and a narrow chrome strip at the rear window for the air ventilation exit.

The four-cylinder engine had been increased from 1.9 liters to 2 liters (1,988 cubic centimeters) and developed 95 horsepower (105 SAE) instead of the former 80 horsepower (90 SAE). A five-bearing crankshaft gave it smoother and quieter operation. With the same weight as previously, performance was improved by some 20 percent. Acceleration figures from 0 to 100 kilometers (62 miles) were 15 seconds and maximum speed was 161 kilometers (100 miles) per hour. The 200 sedan was the smallest of the seventeen different models of passenger cars the company offered that year.

The M 121 engine of the 200, 1965

Specifications

	200
Engine type	4 cyl overhead camshaft (M 121)
Bore and stroke	87 x 83.6mm (3.43 x 3.29 in)
Displacement	1988 cc (121.27 cu in)
Power output	95 hp (DIN) @ 5200 rpm (105 hp SAE @ 5400 rpm)
Compression ratio	9.0:1
Torque	15.7 mkg @ 3600 rpm (16.9 mkg @ 3800 rpm 122.3 ft/lb)
Carburetion	2 downdraft carburetors Solex 38 PDSJ
Engine speed at 100 km/hr	3310 rpm
Gear ratios	I. 4.09:1 automatic I. 3.98:1 II. 2.25:1 II. 2.52:1 III. 1.42:1 III. 1.58:1 IV. 1.00:1 IV. 1.00:1
Rear axle ratio	4.08
Chassis	unit frame and body
Suspension	independent front, single joint swing axle rear, with coil springs
Brakes and area	disc, front; drum, rear; servo assist, two circuit hydraulic, 253/230mm (9.96/9.06 in)
Wheelbase	2700mm (106.3 in)
Track, front/rear	1482/1485mm (58.3/58.5 in)
Length	4730mm (186.5 in)
Width	1795mm (70.7 in)
Height	1495mm (58.8 in)
Ground clearance	185mm (7.3 in)
Tires	7.00 x 13
Turning circle	11.8-11.6 meters (39 ft)
Steering type and ratio	recirculating ball, 22.7:1 (4.1 turns); servo assisted 17.3:1 (3.2 turns)
Weight	1275 kg (2805 lbs)
Maximum speed	161 km/hr (100 mph); automatic: 158 km/hr (98 mph)
Acceleration	15 sec 0-100 km/hr; automatic: 16 sec 0-100 km/hr
Fuel consumption	12.5 liters, super/100 km (18.75 mpg); automatic: 13.5 liters, super (17.4 mpg)
Fuel tank capacity	65 liters (17.2 gallons)

Front view of the 200 sedan, 1965

The 200D sedan, 1965

Model 200D (1965-1968)

D = Diesel

The 200D was another new car, introduced at the time of the Frankfurt Show in 1965. As always, this diesel-engined model shared all of the appointments with the gasoline-engined model in its category. The body was exactly the same, and it, too, replaced the former 190Dc. Unlike its companion car, the engine of the 200D was of the same displacement as the previous one which already had displaced 1,988 cubic centimeters.

A five-bearing crankshaft, along with other noise attenuating measures, were built into the engine for quieter and smoother operation and less fatigue to the driver. These design features released greater power and increased the maximum speed of the car to 130 kilometers (80.8 miles) per hour. Fuel consumption remained extremely moderate, averaging between 7 to 9 liters (31 to 40 gallons) at regular cruising speeds. The standard consumption, according to DIN, was 35 miles per gallon (8.1 liters per 100 kilometers) at 60 miles per hour.

Since 1936, some 500,000 diesel-engined Mercedes-Benz cars had been built, attesting to the popularity of these economic and robust automobiles.

Prices and Production

The 200D four-door sedan sold for	DM 11,300
from April 1966 for	DM 11,500
Power steering	DM 500
Automatic transmission	DM 1,400
The price in the United States was in 1965	
(East coast)	$ 4,142
(West coast)	$ 4,252
in September 1966 (East coast)	$ 4,305
in September 1967 (East coast)	$ 4,380
Power steering (1965)	$ 171
Automatic transmission	$ 342

Production of the 200D model [110] (from July 1965 until February 1968)

was in	1965	30,937 units
	1966	61,707 units
	1967	68,399 units
	1968	575 units
	total	161,618 units

The instrument panel of the 200D sedan,

Specifications

	200D
Engine type	4 cyl diesel, overhead camshaft (OM 621)
Bore and stroke	87 x 83.6mm (3.43 x 3.29 in)
Displacement	1988 cc (121.27 cu in)
Power output	55 hp (DIN) @ 4200 rpm (60 hp SAE)
Compression ratio	21:1
Torque	11.5 mkg @ 2400 rpm (12 mkg SAE 87 ft/lbs)
Fuel injection	Bosch injection pump
Engine speed at 100 km/hr	3300 rpm
Gear ratios	I. 4.09:1 automatic I. 3.98:1 II. 2.25:1 II. 2.52:1 III. 1.42:1 III. 1.58:1 IV. 1.00:1 IV. 1.00:1
Rear axle ratio	3.92
Chassis	unit frame and body
Suspension	independent front, single joint swing axle rear, with coil springs air suspension, optional
Brakes and area	disc front; drum, rear, servo assist, 253/230mm (9.96/9.06 in) two circuit hydraulic
Wheelbase	2700mm (106.3 in)
Track, front/rear	1482/1485mm (58.3/58.5 in)
Length	4730mm (186.5 in)
Width	1795mm (70.7 in)
Height	1495mm (58.8 in)
Ground clearance	185mm (7.3 in)
Tires	7.00 x 13
Turning circle	11.8-11.6 meters (39 ft)
Steering type and ratio	recirculating ball, 22.7:1 (4.1 turns); servo assisted 17.3:1 (3.2 turns)
Weight	1325 kg (2915 lbs)
Maximum speed	130 km/hr (81 mph)
Acceleration	29 sec 0-100 km/hr; automatic: 30 sec 0-100 km/hr
Fuel consumption	9 liters/100 km (26 mpg); automatic: 10 liter/100 km (23 mpg)
Fuel tank capacity	65 liters (17.2 gallons)

The 200D sedan, 1965

The 200D sedan, 1965

The 230 sedan, 1965

Prices and Production

The 230 four-door sedan sold for	DM 11,700
from April 1966 for	DM 11,950
Power steering	DM 500
Automatic transmission	DM 1,400
The price in the United States was in 1965	
(East coast)	$ 4,113
(West coast)	$ 4,223
in September 1966 (East coast)	$ 4,280
in September 1967 (East coast)	$ 4,405
Power steering (1956)	$ 171
Automatic transmission	$ 342

Production of the 230 model [110] (from July 1965 until February 1968)

was in	1965	8,548 units
	1966	14,951 units
	1967	16,441 units
	1968	318 units
	total	40,258 units

Model 230 (1965-1968)

The 230 model, also first shown at the Frankfurt Show in 1965, was the successer to the 220 model. The body style was the same as that of the 200 line introduced at the same time. However, with the six-cylinder engine this model combined the compact dimensions with the performance and efficiency of a modern six-cylinder car.

The new engine had a bore of 82 millimeters, instead of the 80 millimeters of the former 2,195 cubic centimeter engine, resulting in an increase to 2,281 cubic centimeters (139.2 cubic inches). With a compression ratio of 9 to 1 and the new camshaft, the engine developed 105 horsepower at 5,200 revolutions per minute or 118 SAE horsepower at 5,400 revolutions per minute. The weight of this six-cylinder engine, now with a seven main bearing crankshaft for greater smoothness, was but slightly more than that of the four-cylinder unit and resulted in greatly improved performance over that model. Maximum speed was increased to 168 kilometers (104 miles) per hour. Automatic transmission and power steering were optional items for this model, of course.

Special attention was placed on internal safety in these cars. The passenger compartment was of extremely sturdy construction while the front and rear ends were deformable and yielded on impact in crash tests. The instrument panel was made of shock-absorbing material and the operating knobs were recessed. In the event of a collision, the inside mirror would become detached, and the steering wheel had the well-known padded center plate.

The unitized body system with strong side and cross members combined the four-door body and frame into a jointly supported torsionally stiff, welded unit. And the dual circuit power brake system was another safety feature of this new line of the New Medium Class of cars.

Specifications

	230
Engine type	6 cyl overhead camshaft (M 180)
Bore and stroke	82 x 72.8mm (3.23 x 2.87 in)
Displacement	2281 cc (139.2 cu in)
Power output	105 hp (DIN) @ 5200 rpm (118 hp SAE @ 5400 rpm)
Compression ratio	9:1
Torque	17.7 mkg @ 3600 rpm (19 mkg SAE @ 3800 rpm 137.4 ft/lb)
Carburetion	2 downdraft carburetors Solex 38 PDSJ
Engine speed at 100 km/hr	3470 rpm
Gear ratios	I. 4.09:1 automatic I. 3.98:1 II. 2.25:1 II. 2.52:1 III. 1.42:1 III. 1.58:1 IV. 1.00:1 IV. 1.00:1
Rear axle ratio	4.08
Chassis	unit frame and body
Suspension	independent front, single joint swing axle rear, with coil springs air suspension, optional
Brakes and area	disc front; drum rear, servo assist, two circuit hydraulic, 253/230mm (9.96/9.06 in)
Wheelbase	2700mm (106.3 in)
Track, front/rear	1482/1485mm (58.3/58.5 in)
Length	4730mm (186.5 in)
Width	1795mm (70.7 in)
Height	1495mm (58.8 in)
Ground clearance	185mm (7.3 in)
Tires	7.00 S 13
Turning circle	11.8-11.6 meters (39 ft)
Steering type and ratio	recirculating ball, 22.7:1 (4.1 turns); servo assisted 17.3:1 (3.2 turns)
Weight	1305 kg (2871 lbs)
Maximum speed	168 km/hr (104 mph); automatic: 165 km/hr (103 mph)
Acceleration	14 sec 0-100 km/hr; automatic: 16 sec 0-100 km/hr
Fuel consumption	15 liters, super/100 km (15.6 mpg); automatic: 16 liters, super (14.7 mpg)
Fuel tank capacity	65 liters (17.2 gallons)

The 230 sedan, 1965

The 230 sedan, 1965

The 230S sedan, 1965

Model 230S (1965-1968)

S = Super

The 230S model differed only slightly from the 230 model with which it was first shown at the Frankfurt Show in 1965. The body was practically identical except in the arrangement of the headlights which were combined into one large covered unit. The car replaced the former 220S model and was now the top model of the new class series of passenger cars.

The six-cylinder engine with overhead camshaft had two two-phase downdraft carburetors with automatic starting device. The valve timing permitted a maxium engine speed of 6,250 revolutions per minute without any risk. The horsepower output of the 2,281 cubic centimeter displacement engine was 120 horsepower at 5,400 revolutions per minute (or 135 SAE at 5,600), the same as that of the former 220S model. Compression ratio was 9 to 1. Maximum speed was given at 176 kilometers (110 miles) per hour, and in third gear a top speed of 125 kilometers (78 miles) per hour could be achieved.

Here, again as before, the S-model was indeed the Super version of the regular 230 model. The dual carburetors gave the engine more power, increased the torque, and improved the all-around performance.

Prices and Production

The 230S four-door sedan sold for	.DM 13,750
from April 1966 for	.DM 14,000
Power steering	.DM 500
Automatic transmission	.DM 1,400
The price in the United States was in 1965	
(East coast)	$ 4,754
(West coast)	$ 4,869
in September 1966 (East coast)	$ 4,910
in September 1967 (East coast)	$ 5,035
Power steering (1965)	$ 171
Automatic transmission	$ 342

Production of the 230S model [111/1A] (from July 1965 until January 1968)

was in	1965	12,621 units
	1966	17,230 units
	1967	11,176 units
	1968	80 units
total		41,107 units

The interior of the 230S sedan, 1965

Specifications

	230S
Engine type	6 cyl overhead camshaft (M 180)
Bore and stroke	82 x 72.8mm (3.23 x 2.87 in)
Displacement	2281 cc (139.2 cu in)
Power output	120 hp (DIN) @ 5400 rpm (135 hp SAE @ 5600 rpm)
Compression ratio	9:1
Torque	18.2 mkg @ 4200 rpm (20 mkg SAE 144.7 ft/lb)
Carburetion	2 dual downdraft carburetors Zenith 35/40 INAT
Engine speed at 100 km/hr	3415 rpm
Gear ratios	I. 4.05:1 automatic I. 3.98:1 II. 2.23:1 II. 2.52:1 III. 1.42:1 III. 1.58:1 IV. 1.00:1 IV. 1.00:1
Rear axle ratio	4.08
Chassis	unit frame and body
Suspension	independent front, single joint swing axle rear, with coil springs, air suspension
Brakes and area	disc front; drum rear, servo assist, two circuit hydraulic, 253/230mm (9.96/9.06 in)
Wheelbase	2750mm (108.2 in)
Track, front/rear	1482/1485mm (58.3/58.5 in)
Length	4730mm (186.5 in)
Width	1795mm (70.7 in)
Height	1495mm (58.8 in)
Ground clearance	185mm (7.3 in)
Tires	7.25 x 13
Turning circle	12.0-11.8 meters (39 ft)
Steering type and ratio	recirculating ball, 22.7:1 (4.1 turns); servo assisted, 17.3:1 (3.2 turns)
Weight	1350 kg (2970 lbs)
Maximum speed	176 km/hr (109 mph); automatic: 174 km/hr (108 mph)
Acceleration	13 sec 0-100 km/hr; automatic: 15 sec 0-100 km/hr
Fuel consumption	15 liters, super/100 km (15.6 mpg); automatic: 16 liters, super (14.7 mpg)
Fuel tank capacity	65 liters (17.2 gallons)

Impact-absorbing front and rear sections, 1967

Telescopically collapsing steering wheel column, 1967

Model 250S (1965-1969)

S = Super

The 250S model, also first shown at Frankfurt in 1965, had a brand new body style. The tail fins had been entirely eliminated and the overall appearance was similar to that of the coupe models. The body waist line was lowered and window area increased, with the windshield being 17 percent larger than that of the 220S model. The flat roof made it look wider, but width had increased by only 15 millimeters (0.59 inches). Height was reduced by 60 millimeters (2.36 inches).

The 2,496 cubic centimeter (152.3 cubic inch) engine was developed from the 2.2-liter power unit, but it had a larger bore and stroke and a seven-bearing crankshaft. A higher compression ratio and larger valves and induction passages were other changes. A double exhaust pipe was standard. The engine developed 130 horsepower at 5,400 revolutions per minute or 146 SAE horsepower at 5,600 revolutions.

Maximum speed of the 250S sedan was given as 180 kilometers (112 miles) per hour, and maximum allowable engine speed was 6,300 revolutions per minute.

The 250S sedan, 1965

Prices and Production

The 250S four-door sedan sold for	DM 15,300
from April 1966 for	DM 15,800
Power steering	DM 550
Automatic transmission	DM 1,400
The price in the United States was in 1965	
(East coast)	$ 5,696
(West coast)	$ 5,806
in September 1966 (East coast)	$ 5,747
in September 1967 (East coast)	$ 5,897
Power steering (1965)	$ 171
Automatic transmission	$ 342

Production of the 250S model [108 II] (from July/September 1965 until March 1969)

was in	1965	2,844 units
	1966	31,564 units
	1967	37,866 units
	1968	2,014 units
	1969	389 units
total		74,677 units

Front view of the 250S sedan, 1965

Specifications

	250S
Engine type	6 cyl overhead camshaft (M 108)
Bore and stroke	82 x 78.8mm (3.23 x 3.1 in)
Displacement	2496 cc (152.3 cu in)
Power output	130 hp (DIN) @ 5400 rpm (146 hp SAE @ 5600 rpm)
Compression ratio	9:1
Torque	19.8 mkg @ 4000 rpm (21.75 mkg SAE @ 4200 rpm 157.3 ft/lb)
Carburetion	2 dual downdraft carburetors Zenith 35/40 INAT
Engine speed at 100 km/hr	3245 rpm
Gear ratios	I. 4.05:1 automatic I. 3.98:1 (15.6) II. 2.23:1 II. 2.52:1 (9.88) III. 1.42:1 III. 1.58:1 (6.19) IV. 1.00:1 IV. 1.00:1 (3.92)
Rear axle ratio	3.92
Chassis	unit frame and body
Suspension	independent front, single joint swing axle rear, with coil springs, air suspension standard
Brakes and area	disc, servo assist, two circuit hydraulic, 273/279mm (10.75/10.99 in)
Wheelbase	2750mm (108.3 in)
Track, front/rear	1482/1485mm (58.3/58.5 in)
Length	4900mm (192.9 in)
Width	1810mm (71.3 in)
Height	1440mm (56.7 in)
Ground clearance	145mm (5.7 in)
Tires	7.35 H 14 or 185 H 14
Turning circle	12.1-11.9 meters (39 ft)
Steering type and ratio	recirculating ball, 22.7:1 (4.1 turns); servo assisted 17.3:1 (3.2 turns)
Weight	1440 kg (3168 lbs)
Maximum speed	182 km/hr (113 mph); automatic: 177 km/hr (110 mph)
Acceleration	13 sec 0-100 km/hr; automatic: 14 sec 0-100 km/hr
Fuel consumption	16 liters, super/100 km (14.7 mpg); automatic: 17 liters, super (13.7 mpg)
Fuel tank capacity	82 liters (21.7 gallons)

The M 108 engine of the 250S, 1965

The M 129 engine of the 250SE, 1965

The 250SE sedan, 1965

The 250SE coupe, 1965

Prices

The 250SE four-door sedan sold for	DM 16,850
from April 1966 for	DM 17,350
The two-door coupe sold for	DM 24,350
from April 1966 for	DM 24,950
The two-door convertible sold for	DM 26,350
from April 1966 for	DM 26,950
Power steering	DM 550
Automatic transmission	DM 1,400
In the United States the sedan sold for in 1965	
(East coast)	$ 6,331
(West coast)	$ 6,445
in September 1966 (East coast)	$ 6,385
in September 1967 (East coast)	$ 6,222
The 250SE coupe sold for in 1965 (East coast)	$ 8,890
in September 1966 (East coast)	$ 9,099
in September 1967 (East coast)	$ 9,099
The 250SE convertible sold for in 1965 (East coast)	$ 9,673
in September 1966 (East coast)	$ 9,892
in September 1967 (East coast)	$ 9,892
Power steering (1965)	$ 171
Automatic transmission	$ 342

# Model 250SE (1965-1968)
S = Super, E (Einspritzung) = fuel injection

The 250SE model, introduced first at the Frankfurt Auto Show, was the fuel injected version of the 250S model. Both cars appeared identical. They shared the same body and running gear. The suspension system had been improved and the reinforced rear axle was equipped with the new hydro-pneumatic compensating spring. Larger wheels (14") and disc brakes all around were fitted.

The engine had a six-plunger fuel injection pump, with the fuel being injected intermittently into the suction pipe. Power output was rated at 150 horsepower at 5,500 revolutions per minute or 170 horsepower (SAE) at 5,600 revolutions per minute. As in the carburetor engine, maximum engine speed allowed was 6,300 revolutions per minute and the top speed of the 250SE sedan was 193 kilometers (120 miles) per hour.

In addition to the sedan, the elegant coupe and convertible were also available with the fuel-injection engine. The 220SE coupe and convertible — with identical bodies — were still being manufactured, but the more powerful version of the 250SE had, of course, better acceleration and higher maximum and cruising speed.

Production

Production of the 250SE model [108 III] (from August/September 1965 until January 1968)

was in	1965	1,334 units
	1966	26,555 units
	1967	27,242 units
	1968	50 units
total		55,181 units

Production of the 250SE coupe and convertible model [111 III] (from August/September 1965 until December 1967)

was in	1965	1,205 units
	1966	3,601 units
	1967	1,407 units
total		6,213 units

Specifications

	250SE / 250SE (coupe and convertible)		
Engine type	6 cyl overhead camshaft (M 129)		
Bore and stroke	82 x 78.8mm (3.23 x 3.1 in)		
Displacement	2496 cc (152.3 cu in)		
Power output	150 hp (DIN) @ 5500 rpm (170 hp SAE @ 5600 rpm)		
Compression ratio	9.3:1		
Torque	22 mkg @ 4200 rpm (24 mkg SAE @ 4500 rpm 173.6 ft/lb)		
Fuel injection	Bosch six plunger pump		
Engine speed at 100 km/hr	3245 rpm		
Gear ratios	I. 4.05:1 automatic I. 3.98:1 (15.6) II. 2.23:1 II. 2.52:1 (9.88) III. 1.42:1 III. 1.58:1 (6.19) IV. 1.00:1 IV. 1.00:1 (3.92)		
Rear axle ratio	3.92		
Chassis	unit frame and body		
Suspension	independent front and rear, with coil springs, single joint swing axle		
Brakes and area	disc, servo assist, two circuit hydraulic, 273/279mm (10.75/10.99 in)		
Wheelbase	2750mm (108.3 in)		
Track, front/rear	1482/1485mm (58.3/58.5 in)		
Length	4900mm (192.9 in)	coupe: 4880mm (192.1 in)	conv: 4880mm (192.1 in)
Width	1810mm (71.3 in)	coupe: 1845mm (72.6 in)	conv: 1845mm (72.6 in)
Height	1440mm (56.7 in)	coupe: 1420mm (55.9 in)	conv: 1435mm (56.5 in)
Ground clearance	152mm (5.9 in)		
Tires	7.35 H 14 or 185 H 14	7.75 H 14 or 195 H 14	
Turning circle	12.1-11.9 meters (39 ft)		
Steering type and ratio	recirculating ball, 22.7:1 (4.1 turns); servo assisted 17.3:1 (3.2 turns)		
Weight	1510 kg (3322 lbs)	coupe: 1490 kg (3278 lbs)	conv: 1575 kg (3465 lbs)
Maximum speed	193 km/hr (120 mph); automatic: 188 km/hr (117 mph)		
Acceleration	12 sec 0-100 km/hr; automatic 13 sec 0-100 km/hr		
Fuel consumption	16 liters, super/100 km (14.7 mpg); automatic: 17 liters, super (13.7 mpg)		
Fuel tank capacity	82 liters (21.7 gallons)		

The instrument panel of the 250SE, 1965

The 300SE sedan, 1965

Model 300SE/SEL (1965-1967)

S = Super, E (Einspritzung) = fuel injection

SE L (Lang) = long wheelbase chassis

The new 300SE, as well as the 300SEL, were also introduced to the public at the Frankfurt Auto Show in 1965. Both had the newly styled body. The longer car had a wheelbase of 2,850 millimeters (112.2 inches) just 100 millimeters (3.9 inches) longer than the regular sedan.

The six-cylinder light alloy fuel injection engine was equipped with the six-plunger pump which adjusted automatically to accelerator pedal pressure, engine speed, atmospheric pressure, and cooling water temperature, thus giving the best possible mixture for all driving conditions. Maximum power output was 170 horsepower at 5,400 revolutions per minute, or 190 horsepower (SAE) at 5,500 revolutions. With the regular 3.92 rear axle ratio and automatic transmission the car was capable of a maximum speed of 185 kilometers (115 miles) per hour. The faster ratio of 3.69 to 1 gave it 200 kilometer (124 miles) top speed (with manual transmission).

The elegant coupe and convertible models were also fitted with the 300SE engine and power train. These models had, however, the air suspension system, as did the 300SEL now.

Prices

The 300SE four-door sedan sold for	DM 21,500
from April 1966 for	DM 22,100
The 300SEL four-door sedan sold for	DM 28,000
from April 1966 for	DM 28,600
The 300SE two-door coupe sold for	DM 31,350
from April 1966 for	DM 31,950
The 300SE two-door convertible sold for	DM 33,350
from April 1966 for	DM 35,350
Automatic transmission	DM 1,400
In the U.S. the price of the 300SE sedan was in 1965	
(East coast)	$ 7,980
(West coast)	$ 9,980
in September 1966 (East coast)	$ 8,283
The price for the 300SEL sedan was in 1965	
(East coast)	$ 9,863
(West coast)	$ 9,980
in September 1966 (East coast)	$ 10,144
The price for the 300SE coupe was in 1965	
(East coast)	$ 11,511
(West coast)	$ 11,657
in September 1966 (East coast)	$ 11,807
The price for the 300SE convertible was in 1965	
(East coast)	$ 12,295
(West coast)	$ 12,440
in September 1966 (East coast)	$ 12,591
Power steering (1965)	$ 171
Automatic transmission (but standard equipment on the coupe and convertible models sold in the U.S.)	$ 342

Production

Production of the 300SE sedan [108 IV] (from August 1965 until December 1967)

was in	1965	214 units
	1966	1,989 units
	1967	534 units
	total	2,737 units

Production of the 300SEL sedan [109 III] (from September 1965/March 1966 until December 1967)

was in	1965	1 unit
	1966	1,404 units
	1967	964 units
	total	2,369 units

Specifications

300SE / 300SEL / 300SE (coupe and convertible)

Engine type	6 cyl overhead camshaft (M 189)
Bore and stroke	85 x 88mm (3.34 x 3.47 in)
Displacement	2996 cc (182.8 cu in)
Power output	170 hp (DIN) @ 5400 rpm (195 hp SAE @ 5500 rpm)
Compression ratio	8.8:1
Torque	25.4 mkg @ 4000 rpm (28.1 mkg @ 4100 rpm 203.3 ft/lb)
Fuel injection	Bosch six plunger pump
Engine speed at 100 km/hr	3245 rpm
Gear ratios	I. 4.05:1 automatic I. 3.98:1 (16.3) II. 2.23:1 II. 2.52:1 (10.3) III. 1.42:1 III. 1.58:1 (6.47) IV. 1.00:1 IV. 1.00:1 (4.10)
Rear axle ratio	3.92 or 3.69
Chassis	unit frame and body
Suspension	independent front and rear, with coil springs, single joint swing axle
Brakes and area	disc, servo assist, two circuit hydraulic, 273/279mm (10.75/10.99 in)
Wheelbase	2750mm (108.3 in) SEL: 2850mm (112.2 in)
Track, front/rear	1482/1485mm (58.3/58.6 in) SEL: rear 1490mm (58.7 in)
Length	4900mm (192.9 in) SEL: 5000mm (196.9 in) coupe & conv: 4880mm (192in)
Width	1810mm (71.3 in) coupe & conv: 1845mm (72.6 in)
Height	1440mm (56.7 in) SEL: 1415mm (55.7 in) coupe: 1395mm (54.9 in) conv: 1400mm (55.1 in)
Ground clearance	152mm (5.9 in)
Tires	7.35 H 14 or 185 H 14 conv: 7.75 H 14 or 195 H 14
Turning circle	12.1-11.9 meters (39 ft) SEL: 12.4-12.2 meters (40 ft) coupe & conv: 12.1-11.9 meters (39 ft)
Steering type and ratio	recirculating ball, 17.3:1 (3.2 turns) servo assisted
Weight	1575 kg (3465 lbs) SEL: 1655 kg (3641 lbs) coupe: 1650 kg (3630 lbs) conv: 1715 kg (3773 lbs)
Maximum speed	manual, 3.92 axle 190 km/hr (118 mph) automatic, 3.92 axle 185 km/hr (115 mph) manual, 3.69 axle 200 km/hr (124 mph) automatic, 369 axle 195 km/hr (121 mph)
Acceleration	12 sec 0-100 km/hr
Fuel consumption	17-19 liters, super/100 km (13.7 to 12.3 mpg)
Fuel tank capacity	82 liters (21.7 gallons)

The 300SE convertible, 1966

Model 300SEL 6.3 (1968-1972)

SE L (Lang) = long wheelbase chassis

The 300SEL 6.3 model was introduced in the United States in June 1968, quite appropriately at the Laguna Seca race course, with Rudolf Uhlenhaut in attendance. He pointed out that the car had better road-holding ability, braking potential, suspension stability, and maneuverability than any comparable automobile in the world. It had first been shown in Europe in March 1968.

With the 6,332 cubic centimeter fuel-injected 300-horsepower (SAE) V-8 engine installed in the slightly modified but outwardly regular sedan body of the New Generation type, the car weighed 3,835 pounds and had a power-to-weight ratio of 12.8 pounds per horsepower. Performance was truly fantastic, especially when Uhlenhaut demonstrated to us the car's abilities. Zero to 60 miles acceleration took 6.5 seconds and the maximum speed of the 6.3 was 137 miles (220 kilometers) per hour.

The sedan had the air suspension system of the 600 series and many extra features were included as standard items, such as air conditioning, radio, leather upholstery, power steering, and power windows. Except for the numbers 6.3 on the trunk lid, the car was not distinguishable from the regular 300SEL model.

After exhaustively testing the car, *Road & Track* magazine called it "the greatest sedan in the world" and summarized the test, stating that the 6.3 was "truly the executive road racer . . . does more different things well than any other single car." This author concurred. The 300SEL 6.3 was certainly an outstanding automobile in every way.

The 300SEL 6.3 sedan, 1968

Prices and Production

The 300SEL 6.3 four-door sedan sold in 1968 for . . . . .DM 39,160
    in 1969 . . . . .DM 39,500
    in 1970 . . . . .DM 43,180
    in 1971 . . . . .DM 45,400
The 300SEL 6.3 sedan sold in the U.S.
(when introduced) for . . . .$ 13,998
The price was in September 1968 (East coast). . . . . . .$ 14,065
    in October 1969 (East coast) . . . .$ 14,530
    in October 1970 (East coast) . . . .$ 15,875
    in March 1971 (East coast) . . . .$ 16,275

Production of the 300SEL 6.3 sedan [109 E63] (from December 1967 until September 1972)

was in	1967	1 unit
	1968	1,094 units
	1969	2,578 units
	1970	1,797 units
	1971	670 units
	1972	386 units
	total	6,526 units

Sales of the 300SEL 6.3 sedan in this country were

in 1968	98 cars
1969	601 cars
1970	642 cars
1971	487 cars
1972	9 cars
1973	2 cars
	1,839 cars

Specifications

	300SEL 6.3
Engine type	V-8 cyl overhead camshaft for each cylinder bank (M 100)
Bore and stroke	103 x 95mm (4.06 x 3.74 in)
Displacement	6332 cc (386.3 cu in)
Power output	250 hp (DIN) @ 4000 rpm (300 hp SAE @ 4100 rpm)
Compression ratio	9.0:1
Torque	51 mkg @ 2800 rpm 369 ft/lb (60 mkg SAE @ 3000 rpm 434 ft/lb)
Fuel injection	Bosch eight plunger pump
Engine speed at 100 km/hr	2510 rpm
Gear ratios	I. 3.98:1 (11.34) II. 2.46:1 (7.00) III. 1.58:1 (4.50) IV. 1.00:1 (2.85)
Rear axle ratio	2.85
Chassis	unit frame and body
Suspension	independent front and rear, air springs, self leveling and air suspension, single joint swing axle
Brakes and area	disc, ventilated, servo assist, two circuit hydraulic, 273/279mm (107.5/109.9 in)
Wheelbase	2865 mm (112.8 in)
Track, front/rear	1482/1490mm (58.3/58.7 in)
Length	5000mm (196.9 in)
Width	1810mm (71.3 in)
Height	1410mm (55.5 in)
Ground clearance	160mm (6.3 in)
Tires	FR 70 VR 14 (Dunlop) or 7.75/195 H14 (Conti)
Turning circle	12.2 meters (40.4 ft)
Steering type and ratio	recirculating ball, 15.7:1 (3.0 turns)
Weight	1740 kg (3828 lbs)
Maximum speed	220 km/hr (137 mph)
Acceleration	6.5 sec 0-100 km/hr
Fuel consumption	15.5 liters, super/100 km (15.2 mpg)
Fuel tank capacity	105 liters (27.7 gallons)

	300SEL-6.3 No. 1	300SEL-6.3 No. 2
ENGINE CAPACITY	6.3	6.3
FINAL DRIVE RATIO	2.85	2.85
CURB WEIGHT LBS	4070	4070
TIME FOR 1/4 MILE SEC	14.4	14.25
TERMINAL SPEED AFTER 1/4 MILE MPH	93.8	97
TIME 0-60 MILES SEC	5.8	5.7
TIME 0-100 MILES SEC	15.9	15.0
TOP SPEED MPH	141 OBSERVED	144 OBSERVED
ENGINE SPEED AT TOP CAR SPEED RPM	5410	5530

Performance chart of the 300SEL 6.3, 1968

The M 100 V-8 engine of the 6.3, 1968

The 200 sedan, 1967

Model 200 (1967-1976)

The new 200 sedan was the least expensive car of the fifteen models of the New Generation class, introduced to the public in January 1968. All of the four- and smaller six-cylinder models shared the same body and basic construction. At the Frankfurt Auto Show in 1967 the main emphasis was placed on safety rather than on speed. Such safety features as collapsible steering column, padded instrument panel with softer knobs and soft ignition key, breakaway rear mirror, and seatback locks activated by the doors were standard equipment. The body was designed for maximum crash resistance and the front and rear ends for easier crushing in collisions to protect the passengers in the vehicle. A new rear axle was designed for improved roadability. Fourteen-inch wheels were again used on these new models and they had a slightly longer (50 mm = 2 inch) wheelbase and a narrower track. The entire instrument panel was also redesigned for improved legibility.

These new body styles of the Lower Range of models were quite similar to those of the Intermediate Line of cars earlier, as the 250S of 1965. In fact, there was practically only the arrangement of the headlights to quickly differentiate these cars from each other. Despite the smaller overall size, the interior space was nearly the same as previously.

The engine for the 200 model was of the proven type and only minor improvements were made in it. The 1,988 cubic centimeter four-cylinder powerplant developed 95 DIN horsepower and 122.2 ft/lbs. torque, as it had in the former model. All performance figures were identical.

In 1972 all of the smaller models were equipped with the new, safer four-spoke steering wheel. In 1973, because of the fuel crisis, the compression of the engine was lowered to 8 to 1, so that normal octane gasoline could be used. That engine developed 85 DIN horsepower instead of the former 95.

Prices and Production

The 200 four-door sedan sold in 1968 for	DM 11,500
in 1970 for	DM 12,745
in 1972 for	DM 13,390
in 1974 for	DM 15,140
in 1975 for	DM 16,710
Power steering	DM 515
Automatic transmission	DM 1,440
The 200 sedan sold in the U.S. first for (East coast)	$ 4,360
in September 1968 (East coast) for	$ 4,450
in October 1969 (East coast) for	$ 4,680
in October 1970 (East coast) for	$ 5,217
Power steering (1970)	$ 198
Automatic transmission	$ 392

Production of the 200 model [115 V20] (from October 1967/January 1968 until December 1976)

was in		
1967	67	units
1968	20,954	units
1969	26,138	units
1970	29,733	units
1971	35,122	units
1972	40,562	units
1973	37,337	units
1974	37,640	units
1975	48,214	units
1976	13,018	units
total	288,785	units

Specifications

	200
Engine type	4 cyl overhead camshaft (M 115)
Bore and stroke	87 x 83.6mm (3.43 x 3.29 in)
Displacement	1988 cc (121.27 cu in)
Power output	95 hp (DIN) @ 5200 rpm (105 hp SAE @ 5400 rpm)
Compression ratio	9.0:1
Torque	15.7 mkg @ 3600 rpm (16.9 mkg @ 3800 rpm 122.2 ft/lb)
Carburetion	2 downdraft carburetors Solex 38 PCSJ
Engine speed at 100 km/hr	3310 rpm
Gear ratios	I. 4.09:1 3.90:1 automatic I. 3.98:1 II. 2.25:1 2.30:1 II. 2.52:1 III. 1.42:1 1.41:1 III. 1.58:1 IV. 1.00:1 1.00:1 IV. 1.00:1
Rear axle ratio	3.92 (4.08 for U.S.)
Chassis	unit frame and body
Suspension	independent front and rear, with coil springs, diagonal-pivot swing axle, anti-sway bars
Brakes and area	disc, power assisted standard, 273/279mm (10.75/10.99 in)
Wheelbase	2750mm (108.3 in)
Track, front/rear	1440/1434mm (56.7/56.5 in)
Length	4680mm (184.3 in)
Width	1770mm (69.7 in)
Height	1440mm (56.7 in)
Ground clearance	175mm (6.9 in)
Tires	6.95 x 14 or 175 x 14
Turning circle	11.7 meters (38.4 ft)
Steering type and ratio	recirculating ball (4.6 turns); servo assisted (4.0 turns)
Weight	1275 kg (2805 lbs)
Maximum speed	161 km/hr (100 mph); automatic: 158 km/hr (98 mph)
Acceleration	15 sec 0-100 km/hr; automatic: 16 sec 0-100 km/hr
Fuel consumption	12.5 liters, super/100 km (18.75 mpg); automatic: 13.5 liters, super (17.4 mpg)
Fuel tank capacity	65 liters (17.2 gallons)

The 200 sedan, 1973

Front view of the 200 sedan, 1968, U.S. version

Model 200D (1967-1976)

D = Diesel

The 200D model was, as previously, the same as the gasoline-engined sedan of that size. One of the fifteen New Generation models, it shared the body style along with all of the new safety features and construction changes made for the 1968 model year. The body was nearly the same as that of the 250S line of 1966, which had a lower silhouette, lower center of gravity, and wider radiator design in the traditional manner, of course.

The engine of the 200D was the same as that of the earlier model. Displacing 1,988 cubic centimeters and developing 55 DIN (60 SAE) horsepower and 87 ft/lb. torque, it gave this economical diesel-engined model a most satisfactory performance. Power steering and power brakes were optional items, as was automatic transmission.

As before, the diesel version of the smaller model marketed by Daimler-Benz was again a best-seller and more of these 200D sedans were sold than those of the gasoline-powered version. The diesel cars offered actually the same comforts as the others and had in addition the tremendous cost advantages inherent only not in the simpler maintenance of the diesel engine, but also the economy of fuel, both in lower initial cost and in increased mileage achieved.

The 200D sedan, 1968

Prices and Production

The 200D four-door sedan sold in 1968 for	DM 12,000
in 1970 for	DM 13,265
in 1972 for	DM 14,430
in 1974 for	DM 15,585
in 1975 for	DM 17,185
Power steering	DM 515
Automatic transmission	DM 1,440
The 200D sedan sold in the U.S. first for (East coast)	$ 4,494
in September 1968 (East coast) for	$ 4,580
in October 1969 (East coast) for	$ 4,782
in Ocotber 1970 (East coast) for	$ 5,324
Power steering (1970)	$ 198
Automatic transmission	$ 392

Production of the 200D model [115 D20] (from October 1967/ January 1968 until December 1976)

was in	1967	106 units
	1968	23,293 units
	1969	27,663 units
	1970	32,841 units
	1971	35,000 units
	1972	41,065 units
	1973	45,287 units
	1974	50,613 units
	1975	62,978 units
	1976	21,081 units
total		339,927 units

The instrument panel of the 200D, 1973

Specifications

	200D
Engine type	4 cyl diesel, overhead camshaft (OM 615)
Bore and stroke	87 x 83.6mm (3.43 x 3.29 in)
Displacement	1988 cc (121.27 cu in)
Power output	55 hp (DIN) @ 4200 rpm (61 hp SAE @ 4200 rpm)
Compression ratio	21:1
Torque	11.5 mkg @ 2400 rpm (83.2 ft/lb)
Fuel injection	Bosch four plunger pump
Engine speed at 100 km/hr	3375 rpm
Gear ratios	I. 3.90:1 II. 2.30:1 III. 1.41:1 IV. 1.00:1
Rear axle ratio	3.92 (for U.S. 4.08)
Chassis	unit frame and body
Suspension	independent front and rear, with coil springs, diagonal-pivot swing axle, anti-sway bars
Brakes and area	disc, power assisted standard, 273/279mm (10.75/10.99 in)
Wheelbase	2750mm (108.3 in)
Track, front/rear	1440/1434mm (56.7/56.5 in)
Length	4680mm (184.3 in)
Width	1770mm (69.7 in)
Height	1440mm (56.7 in)
Ground clearance	175mm (6.9 in)
Tires	6.95 x 14 or 175 x 14
Turning circle	11.7 meters (38.4 ft)
Steering type and ratio	recirculating ball, (4.6 turns), servo assisted (4.0 turns)
Weight	1350 kg (2970 lbs)
Maximum speed	130 km/hr (81 mph)
Acceleration	30 sec 0-100 km/hr
Fuel consumption	8.1 liters/100 km (29 mpg)
Fuel tank capacity	65 liters (17.2 gallons)

Longitudinal section of the OM 615 engine, 1967

Cross section of the OM 615 engine for the 200D, 1967

The 220 sedan, 1968

Model 220 (1967-1973)

The 220 model was basically the same car as the smaller-engined one. It was the third of the New Generation models to share the same body style, including all of the new safety features. It was meant to replace the 200 sedan in the United States market.

Over the previous model, this new style featured the lower silhouette, an increased wheelbase and narrower track, offered increased visibility, a new headlight treatment with the lower half of the unit having amber color, and protective strips with rubber inserts all around the body. The single front and rear bumpers also had a rubber insert for added scratch protection. New larger rear light clusters had been designed for brighter, improved visibility.

The engine had two single throat Solex carburetors and developed 116 SAE horsepower at 5,200 revolutions per minute and torque of 142 ft/lbs. at 3,000 revolutions. Maximum speed was 100 miles per hour.

Optional equipment was the power assisted steering, air conditioning, sliding sun roof, leather upholstery, power windows, and other features. The base price of the 220 sedan was $4,360 on the East coast in 1968.

Prices and Production

The 220 four-door sedan sold in 1968 for	DM 12,000
in 1970 for	DM 13,165
in 1972 for	DM 14,375
in 1973 for	DM 14,985
Power steering	DM 515
Automatic transmission	DM 1,440
The 220 sedan sold in the United States in January 1968 for	
(East coast)	$ 4,360
(West coast)	$ 4,446
in September 1971, including automatic transmission	
(East coast)	$ 6,206
in September 1972, including automatic transmission	
(East coast)	$ 6,560
in March 1973, including automatic transmission	
(East coast)	$ 6,889
Power steering (1970)	$ 198
Power steering (1973)	$ 251
Automatic transmission (1970)	$ 392

Production of the 220 model [115 V22] (from October 1967/ February 1968 until August 1973)

was in	1967	131 units
	1968	23,486 units
	1969	22,493 units
	1970	22,652 units
	1971	24,140 units
	1972	23,691 units
	1973	12,146 units
	total	128,739 units

Cross section of M115 engine, 1968

Specifications

	220
Engine type	4 cyl overhead camshaft (M 115)
Bore and stroke	87.0 x 92.4mm (3.43 x 3.64 in)
Displacement	2197 cc (134 cu in)
Power output	105 hp (DIN) (116 hp SAE) @ 5200 rpm
Compression ratio	9:1
Torque	17.5 mkg @ 3600 rpm (19.7 mkg @ 3000 rpm 142.5 ft/lb)
Carburetion	2 dual downdraft carburetors Solex 36/40 PDSI (U.S.: 2 Stromberg carburetors 175 CDT)
Engine speed at 100 km/hr	3300 rpm
Gear ratios	I. 3.90:1 II. 2.30:1 III. 1.41:1 IV. 1.00:1
Rear axle ratio	3.92 (4.08 for U.S.)
Chassis	unit frame and body
Suspension	independent front and rear, with coil springs, diagonal pivot swing axle, anti-sway bars
Brakes and area	disc, power assist standard, 273/279mm (10.75/10.99 in)
Wheelbase	2750mm (108.3 in)
Track, front/rear	1440/1434mm (56.7/56.5 in)
Length	4680mm (184.3 in)
Width	1770mm (69.7 in)
Height	1440mm (56.7 in)
Ground clearance	175mm (6.9 in)
Tires	6.95 x 14 or 175 x 14
Turning circle	11.7 meters (38.4 ft)
Steering type and ratio	recirculating ball (4.6 turns); servo assisted (4.0 turns)
Weight	1314 kg (2890 lbs)
Maximum speed	161 km/hr (100 mph)
Acceleration	14 sec 0-100 km/hr
Fuel consumption	12 liters, super/100 km (19.5 mpg)
Fuel tank capacity	65 liters (17.2 gallons)

Individual front wheel suspension, 1967

Diagonal swing axle, 1967

The 220D sedan, 1968, U.S. version

Model 220D (1967-1976)

D = Diesel

The 220D was the fourth of the New Generation cars to share the same body style with the 200-220-200D models. It, too, was introduced to replace the smaller sedan in the United States market.

All of the outward specifications were identical with the gasoline version of this model. It was the luxury edition of the economical and reliable diesel-powerd automobile which actually went back to 1936 when a diesel passenger car was first built by Mercedes-Benz.

The four-speed manual transmission was standard, either column or floor mounted. Automatic transmission was an optional extra, as were power brakes and power steering.

The 2.2-liter diesel engine had Bosch four-plunger fuel injection and a five main bearing crankshaft. With the usual 21:1 compression ratio and maximum torque of 96 ft/lbs. at 2,400 revolutions per minute, the engine developed 65 SAE horsepower at 4,200 revolutions per minute and gave the car a maximum and cruising speed of over 80 miles per hour. (This diesel engine met the U.S. government standards for emission of hydrocarbons, carbon monoxide, and oxide of nitrogens through 1974, and the CO limit for 1975.)

Symbolic of the popularity of the diesel automobile, on May 9, 1968, the two millionth passenger car to come off the assembly lines at the Sindelfingen plant since 1946 was a 220D model — cream-colored and flower-covered.

A long wheelbase model sedan became available in December 1968. It had seats for eight persons and was similar to the 230 long limousine. The wheelbase was 3,400 mm (133.86 in) weight was 1,540 kg (3,388 lbs). Maximum speed was 130 km/hr (81 mph) and fuel consumption 11 liters per 100 km. With the optional automatic transmission, these figures were 125 km/hr and 12 liters/100 km (18 miles per gallon).

Prices and Production

The 220D four-door sedan sold in 1968 for	DM 12,500
in 1970 for	DM 13,690
in 1972 for	DM 14,930
in 1973 for	DM 15,485
Power steering	DM 515
Automatic transmission	DM 1,440
The 220D long limousine sold in 1969 for	DM 18,315
the price rose yearly until 1975 it was	DM 26,075
The 220D sedan sold in the U.S. in January 1968 for	
(East coast)	$ 4,494
(West coast)	$ 4,580
in September 1971 (East coast)	$ 5,900
in September 1972 (East coast)	$ 6,345
in March 1973 (East coast)	$ 6,662
with automatic transmission	$ 7,100
Power steering (1970)	$ 198
Power steering (1973)	$ 251
Automatic transmission (1970)	$ 392

Production of the 220D model [115 D22] (from July 1967/ January 1968 until December 1976)

was in	
1967	364 units
1968	50,630 units
1969	59,628 units
1970	63,314 units
1971	64,297 units
1972	73,729 units
1973	54,321 units
1974	27,510 units
1975	21,226 units
1976	5,254 units
total	420,273 units

Specifications

220D	
Engine type	4 cyl diesel, overhead camshaft (OM 615)
Bore and stroke	87.0 x 92.4mm (3.43 x 3.64 in)
Displacement	2197 cc (134 cu in)
Power output	60 hp (DIN) (65 hp SAE) @ 4200 rpm
Compression ratio	21:1
Torque	12.8 mkg @ 2400 rpm (92.6 ft/lb)
Fuel injection	Bosch four plunger pump
Engine speed at 100 km/hr	3375 rpm
Gear ratios	I. 3.90:1 (15.37) II. 2.30:1 (9.01) III. 1.41:1 (5.52) IV. 1.00:1 (3.92)
Rear axle ratio	3.92 (for U.S. 4.08)
Chassis	unit frame and body
Suspension	independent front and rear, with coil springs, diagonal-pivot swing axle, anti-sway bars
Brakes and area	disc, power assist standard, 273/279mm (10.75/10.99 in)
Wheelbase	2750mm (108.3 in)
Track, front/rear	1440/1434mm (56.7/56.5 in)
Length	4680mm (184.3 in)
Width	1770mm (69.7 in)
Height	1440mm (56.7 in)
Ground clearance	175mm (6.9 in)
Tires	6.95 x 14 or 175 x 14
Turning circle	11.7 meters (38.4 ft)
Steering type and ratio	recirculating ball, (4.6 turns); servo assisted 22.7:1 (4.0 turns)
Weight	1363 kg (2997 lbs)
Maximum speed	135 km/hr (84 mph)
Acceleration	28.1 sec 0-100 km/hr
Fuel consumption	8.5 liters/100 km (27.75 mpg)
Fuel tank capacity	65 liters (17.2 gallons)

Front view of the 220D sedan, 1968

The OM 615 engine of the 220D, 1973

The 230 sedan, 1967

Model 230/6 (1973-1976)

The 230/6 model made its appearance in late 1973 when the fuel crisis became a matter of serious concern to motorists and manufacturers in Europe. Utilizing the same body style as that of the other ten cars in the medium price range, the small six-cylinder engine was placed into it to create a lower priced as well as lower fuel consumption car than the regular 2.8-liter models.

A five-speed transmission was available on request in this model as on the 250, 280, and the three coupe styles. A fifth gear was designed as a high speed gear or overdrive. It lowered the engine speed and reduced fuel consumption, engine noise, and wear. The automatic torque converter four-speed transmission, as used on the 2.8-liter models, could also be fitted.

The 230.6 model was superior in performance to the four-cylinder model which it closely resembled. The car offered the flexibility of a six-cylinder engine and even greater fuel economy than the four-cylinder model at a considerably lower price than the regular sixes.

Production figures included in the previously described 230 sedan [114 V23] until November 1976

Model 230 (1967-1976)

The 230 model, in the center of the medium price range of the New Generation cars, had the same body style as that of the 200, 220, and the 250 sedans. It replaced the former 230 model, first built in 1965.

The interior dimensions were the same as those of the other models which shared the body style, the rear center arm rest, larger door pockets, increased visibility (11 percent more glass area), arm rests on all doors, and roof-mounted assist handles, but it had the grip handles attached to the arm rest of the right front door, while the 250 model had them on all three doors (except the driver's).

The engine of the 230 model was the same as before, except for redesigned cams which improved the torque at lower engine speeds and molybdenum coated piston rings (1, 2 and 3) for longer wear and reduced oil consumption. The new gear box and newly designed clutch, now with new diaphragm spring clutch having fewer moving parts (that is, one diaphram spring instead of nine pressure springs), were fitted to all of the models which had the same chassis and body as the 230 sedan. The new hydro-pneumatic leveling device, automatic transmission, and power steering were optional items.

A long-wheelbase sedan to seat eight passengers became available in October 1968. It was also made with the 220D engine two months later. The wheelbase was 3,400 mm (133.86 in) and the total weight was 1,515 kg (3,344 lbs). The maximum speed was 170 km/hr (106 mph) and fuel consumption 16 liters per 100 kilometers. With automatic transmission these figures were 165 km/hr and 17 liters/100 km.

Prices

The 230/6 four-door sedan sold in 1973 for	DM 16,765
in 1974 for	DM 17,485
in 1975 for	DM 19,270
The 230/6 long four-door sedan sold in 1973 for	DM 23,145
in 1974 for	DM 24,200
in 1975 for	DM 26,685
Power steering	DM 515
Automatic transmission	DM 1,440

Specifications

	230	230/6
Engine type	6 cyl overhead camshaft (M 180)	
Bore and stroke	81.7 x 72.8mm (3.23 x 2.87 in)	
Displacement	2292 cc (139.9 cu in)	
Power output	120 hp (DIN) @ 5400 rpm (135 hp SAE @ 5600 rpm)	
Compression ratio	9:1	
Torque	18.2 mkg @ 3600 rpm; 20 mkg @ 3800 rpm (144.7 ft/lb)	
Carburetion	2 dual downdraft carburetors Zenith 35/40 INAT	
Engine speed at 100 km/hr	3180 rpm	
Gear ratios	I. 3.90:1 II. 2.30:1 III. 1.41:1 IV. 1.00:1	
Rear axle ratio	3.92 (4.08 for U.S.)	
Chassis	unit frame and body	
Suspension	independent front and rear, with coil springs, diagonal-pivot swing axle, anti-sway bars	
Brakes and area	disc, power assist standard, 273/279mm (10.95/10.99 in)	
Wheelbase	2750mm (108.3 in)	2750mm (108.3 in)
Track, front/rear	1444/1440mm (56.9/56.7 in)	1448/1440mm (57.0/56.7 in)
Length	4680mm (184.3 in)	4680mm (184.3 in)
Width	1770mm (69.7 in)	1770mm (69.7 in)
Height	1440mm (56.7 in)	1440mm (56.7 in)
Ground clearance	175mm (6.9 in)	175mm (6.9 in)
Tires	6.95 x 14 or 175 x 14	175 SR 14
Turning circle	11.7 meters (38.4 ft)	11 meters (36.1 ft)
Steering type and ratio	recirculating ball (4.6 turns); servo assisted (4.0 turns)	recirculating ball (3.0 turns), servo assisted
Weight	1323 kg (2911 lbs)	1365 kg (3003 lbs)
Maximum speed	165 km/hr (102 mph)	175 km/hr (109 mph)
Acceleration	14 sec 0-100 km/hr	13.5 sec 0-100 km/hr
Fuel consumption	11.2 liters, super/100 km (21 mpg)	11.2 liters/100 km (21.5 mpg)
Fuel tank capacity	65 liters (17.2 gallons)	65 liters (17.2 gallons)

Prices and Production

The 230 four-door sedan sold in 1968 for .... DM 13,150
   in 1970 for. .... DM 14,620
   in 1972 for. .... DM 16,100
   in 1973 for. .... DM 16,765
   Power steering .... DM 515
   Automatic transmission .... DM 1,440
The 230 long limousine sold in 1968 for .... DM 18,980
   the price rose gradually every year and in 1975 was.. DM 26,685
The 230 four-door sedan sold in the United States
   in January 1968 for (East coast)................ $ 4,544
     (West coast)............................... $ 4,631
   in December 1968 (East coast)................. $ 4,764
   Power steering (1970) .... $ 198
   Automatic transmission .... $ 392

Production of the 230 model [114 V 23] (from September 1967/January 1968 until November 1976)

	was in	1967	252 units
		1968	22,064 units
		1969	23,835 units
		1970	25,252 units
		1971	30,520 units
		1972	35,270 units
		1973	31,378 units
		1974	25,314 units
		1975	22,992 units
		1976	4,906 units
	total		221,783 units

The 250 sedan, 1967

Prices and Production

The 250 four-door sedan sold in 1967 for	DM 14,630
in 1970 for	DM 16,185
in 1972 for	DM 17,875
Power steering	DM 515
Automatic transmission	DM 1,440
The 250 four-door sedan sold in the United States	
in January 1968 for (East coast)	$ 5,060
(West coast)	$ 5,150
in October 1969 (East coast)	$ 5,208
in October 1970 (including automatic transmission) (East coast)	$ 6,208
in September 1971 (including automatic transmission) (East coast)	$ 7,205
Power steering (1970)	$ 198

Production of the 250 model [114 V25] (from July/December 1967 until May 1972)

was in	1967	2,215 units
	1968	20,475 units
	1969	18,692 units
	1970	17,329 units
	1971	15,180 units
	1972	4,412 units
total		78,303 units

Model 250 (1967-1972)

The 250 model represented the top of the medium price range in the passenger car production line of the New Generation cars. It was distinguished by several styling refinements over the others which shared the body with this model. As the 230 model, it was fitted with a wider-spaced grill design — the box type instead of the pierced type which the 200 and 220 models had. The 250 also had a double bumper on the front and a chrome door strip.

As the best of the Medium Range, the interior was fancier than the poorer relations, the 200 and 230 models. The left side stalk on the steering column activated the headlight dimming, the windshield wipers, and the directional signals. The center console had the shift lever for the new four-speed automatic transmission, a much improved unit over the earlier one. It started always in first gear, giving an easy gliding-like move when starting off. In fact, the entire operation was considerably smoother than before and seemed a definite technological advancement.

The six-cylinder engine for the 250 was newly developed. It produced 146 SAE horsepower at 5,600 revolutions per minute. Suspension was the same as the other, less expensive models, which shared the same body style. The optional hydro-pneumatic leveler controlled the rear suspension unit, leveling the car when loaded. It had the advantage of constant leveling because the system was operative when the engine was running and maintained a constant bumper height.

The conclusion reached by the testing editors of a prestigious automotive magazine was that the car was Substantial, Safe, Spacious, and 'Spensive.

Specifications

	250
Engine type	6 cyl overhead camshaft (M 114)
Bore and stroke	81.7 x 78.8mm (3.23 x 3.1 in)
Displacement	2496 cc (152.4 cu in)
Power output	130 hp (DIN) @ 5000 rpm (146 hp SAE @ 5600 rpm)
Compression ratio	9:1
Torque	20 mkg @ 3600 rpm (22.2 mkg @ 3800 rpm 161 ft/lb)
Carburetion	2 dual downdraft carburetors Zenith 35/40 INAT
Engine speed at 100 km/hr	3180 rpm
Gear ratios	I. 3.90:1 II. 2.30:1 III. 1.41:1 IV. 1.00:1
Rear axle ratio	3.92 (4.08 for U.S.)
Chassis	unit frame and body
Suspension	independent front and rear, with coil springs, diagonal-pivot swing axle, anti-sway bars
Brakes and area	disc, power assist standard, 273/279mm (10.8/11.0 in)
Wheelbase	2750mm (108.3 in)
Track, front/rear	1444/1440mm (56.9/56.7 in)
Length	4680mm (184.3 in)
Width	1770mm (69.7 in)
Height	1440mm (56.7 in)
Ground clearance	175mm (6.9 in)
Tires	6.95 H 14 or 175 x 14
Turning circle	11.7 meters (38.4 ft)
Steering type and ratio	recirculating ball (4.6 turns); servo assisted (4.0 turns)
Weight	1370 kg (3014 lbs)
Maximum speed	180 km/hr (112 mph)
Acceleration	13 sec 0-100 km/hr
Fuel consumption	12.5 liters, super/100 km (18.75 mpg)
Fuel tank capacity	65 liters (17.2 gallons)

The 250 sedan, 1968, U.S. version

The automatic transmission, 1967

Model 280S (1967-1972)

S = Super

The 280S sedan, 1968

The 280S model was the lowest priced car in the higher priced range of the New Generation automobiles. The body style was that of the new 280SE and the 300SE models, as well as that of the older 250S first introduced in 1965, which remained in production.

The body was longer than that of the smaller-engined 250 model cars, but the wheelbase remained at 108.3 inches. Track was slightly larger and these sedans were somewhat wider, allowing more inside room for the passengers. A distinctive difference was the arrangement of the headlights. Two vertical lights made up the cluster which in the other models consisted of one headlight and amber indicator and parking lights.

The interior was more luxuriously appointed in these types than in the less expensive models. There was a definite feel of staid elegance in the dashboard layout, greater comfort in seats, and all-around conception in this model.

The engine had the dual downdraft carburetor, air oil cooler, and a new cylinder arrangement for increased cooling, and developed 140 (DIN) horsepower at 5,200 (or 157 SAE at 5,400) revolutions per minute. The seven-bearing crankshaft made for quieter and more flexible operation of this newly designed powerplant.

With this more flexible and more powerful unit, the new M130 engine, the 1,460-kilogram sedan reached a respectable maximum speed of 115 miles per hour.

The 280S was a comfortable, fast touring car in the best Mercedes tradition and it found many willing purchasers, as sales indicated. The more expensive model, the SE with identical fuel consumption but slightly superior performance, sold nearly as well over the years. This would suggest that the fuel-injection car was becoming ever more popular over the carburetor version.

Prices and Production

The 280S four-door sedan sold in 1968 for ....DM	17,000
in 1970 for ....DM	18,815
in 1971 for ....DM	19,760
Power steering ....DM	515
Automatic transmission ....DM	1,440
The 280S four-door sedan sold in the United States	
in January 1968 for (East coast) ....$	5,897
(West coast) ....$	6,011
in October 1969 (East coast) ....$	6,273
in October 1970 (including automatic transmission) (East coast) ....$	7,019
in March 1971 (including automatic transmission) (East coast) ....$	7,370
Power steering (1970) ....$	198

Production of the 280S model [108 V28] (from November 1967/ January 1968 until September 1972)

was in	1967	762 units
	1968	20,110 units
	1969	25,249 units
	1970	24,882 units
	1971	16,234 units
	1972	6,429 units
total		93,666 units

Specifications

	280S
Engine type	6 cyl overhead camshaft (M 130)
Bore and stroke	86.5 x 78.8mm (3.41 x 3.10 in)
Displacement	2778 cc (169.5 cu in)
Power output	140 hp (DIN) @ 5200 rpm (157 hp SAE @ 5400 rpm)
Compression ratio	9:1
Torque	23 mkg @ 3600 rpm (25.1 mkg @ 3800 rpm 181.6 ft/lb)
Carburetion	2 dual downdraft carburetors Zenith 35/40 INAT
Engine speed at 100 km/hr	3140 rpm
Gear ratios	I. 3.90:1 II. 2.30:1 III. 1.41:1 IV. 1.00:1
Rear axle ratio	3.92 (4.08 for U.S.)
Chassis	unit frame and body
Suspension	independent front and rear, with coil springs, single joint swing axle, anti-sway bars
Brakes and area	disc, power assist standard, 273/279mm (10.8/11.0 in)
Wheelbase	2750mm (108.3 in)
Track, front/rear	1444/1440mm (56.9/56.7 in)
Length	4900mm (192.9 in)
Width	1810mm (71.3 in)
Height	1440mm (56.7 in)
Ground clearance	175mm (6.9 in)
Tires	7.35 H 14
Turning circle	12.5 meters (41 ft)
Steering type and ratio	recirculating ball (4.0 turns); servo assisted (3.0 turns)
Weight	1460 kg (3212 lbs)
Maximum speed	185 km/hr (115 mph); automatic: 180 km/hr (112 mph)
Acceleration	12.5 sec 0-100 km/hr
Fuel consumption	12.5 liters/100 km (18.75 mpg)
Fuel tank capacity	82 liters (21.7 gallons)

The 280S sedan, 1968, U.S. version

The 280S sedan, 1969

The 280SE sedan, 1968

Model 280SE/SEL (1967-1972)

S = Super, E (Einspritzung) = fuel injection

The 280SE model was available as a sedan and the more luxurious coupe and convertible. The sedan body was the same as that of the 280S New Generation model, but the coupe and convertible had the same body style as the earlier 250SE which they replaced, and which were discontinued. There were no distinguishing marks between the 280S and SE sedans, except, of course, for the engine. The interior was no more elegant than that of the carburetor-engined car but the overall weight of the SE was 50 pounds more.

The fuel injected six-cylinder engine had a six-plunger pump for increased engine performance with improved economy and was not affected by altitude or by temperature. It also provided an efficient smog control system. Otherwise the 2.8-liter engines were alike. The seven main bearing crankshaft made for less vibration and longer bearing life and the greater separation between cylinders ensured better cooling. The new viscose cooling fan was also more efficient and the redesigned cams and molybdenum covered rings were all appreciable improvements. The 280SE engine developed 160 (DIN) horsepower at 5,500 (or 180 SAE at 5,750) revolutions per minute.

The 280SEL sedan went into production in January 1968. It had a longer wheelbase, by 3.9 inches, than the regular sedan, but otherwise was the same car in practically every respect.

Production

Production of the 280SE model [108 E28] (from November 1967/January 1968 until September 1972)

was in	units
1967	365 units
1968	18,685 units
1969	25,081 units
1970	25,627 units
1971	14,871 units
1972	6,422 units
total	91,051 units

Production of the 280SEL model [108 E28] (from January 1968 until April 1971)

was in	units
1968	1,688 units
1969	2,610 units
1970	3,674 units
1971	278 units
total	8,250 units

Production of the 280SE coupe and convertible model [111 E28] (from November 1967/February 1968 until May 1971)

was in	units
1968	55 units
1969	1,950 units
1970	2,501 units
1971	613 units
1972	68 units
total	5,187 units

The 280SE coupe, 1968

Prices

The 280SE four-door sedan sold in 1968 for. . . . . . . .DM	18,600
in 1970 for. . . . . .DM	20,535
in 1971 for. . . . . .DM	21,590
The 280SEL four-door sedan sold in 1968 for. . . . . . .DM	25,100
The 280SE coupe sold in 1968 for . . . . .DM	26,510
in 1970 for. . . . . .DM	29,140
in 1971 for. . . . . .DM	30,680
The 280SE convertible sold in 1968 for. . . . . .DM	28,510
in 1970 for. . . . . .DM	31,140
in 1971 for. . . . . .DM	32,680
Power steering . . . . .DM	515
Automatic transmission . . . . .DM	1,440
The 280SE four-door sedan sold in the United States	
in January 1968 for (East coast). . . . .$	6,222
(West coast) . . . .$	6,336
in October 1969 (East coast) . . . .$	6,561
in September 1968 (East coast) . . . .$	6,310
in October 1970 (including automatic transmission)	
(East coast) . . . .$	7,297
in September 1971 (including automatic transmission)	
(East coast) . . . .$	9,546
The 280SEL sedan sold in January 1968 for	
(East coast) . . . .$	6,622
(West coast) . . . .$	6,712
in September 1968 (East coast) . . . .$	6,722
in October 1969 (East coast) . . . .$	6,992
in October 1970 (including automatic transmission)	
(East coast) . . . .$	8,088
in September 1971 (including automatic transmission)	
(East coast) . . . .$	10,925
The 280SE coupe sold in January 1968 for (East coast) . .$	9,174
(West coast) . . . .$	9,262
in September 1968 (East coast) . . . .$	9,424
in October 1969 (East coast) . . . .$	11,112
in January 1970 (East coast) . . . .$	11,612
The 280SE convertible sold in January 1968 for	
(East coast) . . . .$	9,967
(West coast) . . . .$	10,054
in September 1968 (East coast) . . . .$	10,217
in October 1969 (East coast) . . . .$	11,924
in January 1970 (East coast) . . . .$	12,444
Power steering (1970) (standard on SEL model). . . .$	198
Automatic transmission . . . .$	392

Specifications

	280SE /280SEL / 280SE (coupe and convertible)
Engine type	6 cyl overhead camshaft (M 130)
Bore and stroke	86.5 x 78.8mm (3.41 x 3.10 in)
Displacement	2778 cc (169.5 cu in)
Power output	160 hp (DIN) @ 5500 rpm (180 hp SAE @ 5750 rpm)
Compression ratio	9.5:1
Torque	24.5 mkg @ 4250 rpm (26.7 mkg @ 4500 rpm 193.2 ft/lb)
Fuel injection	Bosch six plunger pump
Engine speed at 100 km/hr	3140 rpm
Gear ratios	I. 3.98:1 II. 2.39:1 III. 1.46:1 IV. 1.00:1
Rear axle ratio	3.92 (4.08 for U.S.)
Chassis	unit frame and body
Suspension	independent front and rear, with coil springs, single joint swing axle, anti-sway bars
Brakes and area	disc, power assisted, standard, 273/279mm (10.8/11.0 in)
Wheelbase	2750mm (108.3 in) SEL: 2850mm (112.2 in)
Track, front/rear	1482/1490mm (58.4/58.7 in)
Length	4900mm (192.9 in) SEL: 5000mm (196.9 in)
Width	1810mm (71.3 in) coupe and conv: 72.6 in
Height	1440mm (56.7 in) coupe: 55.9 in; conv: 56.5 in
Ground clearance	175mm (6.9 in)
Tires	7.35 H 14 or 185 H 14
Turning circle	12.5 meters (41 ft) SEL: (42 ft)
Steering type and ratio	recirculating ball (4.0 turns); servo assisted (3.0 turns)
Weight	1486 kg (3270 lbs) SEL: 3305 lbs coupe: 3330 lbs conv: 3495 lbs
Maximum speed	190 km/hr (118 mph); automatic: 185 km/hr (115 mph)
Acceleration	10.5 sec 0-100 km/hr
Fuel consumption	12.5 liters, super/100 km (18.75 mpg)
Fuel tank capacity	82 liters (21.7 gallons)

The 300SEL sedan, 1967

Model 300SEL (1967-1970)

SE L (Lang) = long wheelbase chassis

The 300SEL sedan was the top of the line of New Generation cars for 1968. It retained the body of the former 300SE, first built in 1965, but now came equipped with the fuel injection engine of 2,778 cubic centimeter displacement and 180 SAE horsepower. The only outward difference between this and the 280 line was a more generous use of chrome around the window areas. Inwardly, the furnishings were of the finest as befitting this most elegant limousine of the New Generation class. Only the great 600 automobiles were more luxuriously built.

Such optional extras as automatic transmission, power steering, and air suspension system were standard on the 300SEL sedan. The body dimensions and chassis specifications were practically the same as those for the 300SEL 6.3 model, and the price of the car surely indicated that it was a superb automobile.

But the production life of this model was a rather short one. Sales for the first two years were quite respectable, but the superb 6.3 model, costing nearly $4,000 more, actually outsold this one by more than twice in 1969, thus accelerating its demise.

And the new V-8 engines were ready to take over from the six-cylinder units, in the top range of models.

Prices and Production

The 300SEL four-door sedan sold in 1968 for........DM 29,760
The 300SEL sedan sold in the United States
   in January 1968 for (East coast)...............$ 9,400
                    (West coast).............................$ 9,489
   in September 1968 (East coast)...............$ 9,525
   in October 1969 (East coast).................$ 10,823
   in January 1970 (East coast).................$ 11,327

Production of the 300SEL model [109 E28] (from December 1967/February 1968 until January 1970)

was in	1967	37 units
	1968	1,325 units
	1969	1,137 units
	1970	20 units
	total	2,519 units

The 300SEL sedan, 1967

Specifications

	300SEL
Engine type	6 cyl overhead camshaft (M 189)
Bore and stroke	86.5 x 78.8mm (3.41 x 3.10 in)
Displacement	2778 cc (169.5 cu in)
Power output	160 hp (DIN) @ 5500 rpm (180 hp SAE @ 5750 rpm)
Compression ratio	9.5:1
Torque	24.5 mkg @ 4250 rpm (26.7 mkg @ 4500 rpm 193.2 ft/lb)
Fuel injection	Bosch six plunger pump
Engine speed at 100 km/hr	3140 rpm
Gear ratios	I. 3.98:1 II. 2.46:1 III. 1.58:1 IV. 1.00:1
Rear axle ratio	4.08
Chassis	unit frame and body
Suspension	independent front and rear, air springs, self-leveling and air suspension, single joint swing axle
Brakes and area	disc, servo assisted, 273/279mm (10.8/11.0 in)
Wheelbase	2850mm (112.2 in)
Track, front/rear	1482/1490mm (58.4/58.7 in)
Length	5000mm (196.9 in)
Width	1810mm (71.3 in)
Height	1415mm (55.7 in)
Ground clearance	175mm (6.9 in)
Tires	7.35 H 14 or 185 H 14
Turning circle	12.2 meters (40 ft)
Steering type and ratio	recirculating ball, servo assisted (3.0 turns)
Weight	1620 kg (3564 lbs)
Maximum speed	190 km/hr (118 mph)
Acceleration	11.5 sec 0-100 km/hr
Fuel consumption	12.2 liters/100 km (19 mpg)
Fuel tank capacity	82 liters (21.7 gallons)

The 300SEL sedan, 1968

The interior of the 300SEL sedan, 1967

The 250C coupe, 1970; just like this writer owned for eleven years

Model 250C/CE (1968-1976)

C = Coupe, E (Einspritzung) = fuel injection

The 250C and 250CE coupe models were introduced toward the end of 1968 as the last of the New Generation cars. The chassis, wheelbase and track, were the same as those of the 250 sedan, but the roof was nearly two inches lower and the passenger compartment was shorter. There were no pillars between the front and rear side windows and the chrome strips on the roof made the car look considerable more sportier than the staid model.

Powered either by the carburetor engine of 130 DIN (146 SAE) horsepower or the electronically controlled fuel injection engine of 150 DIN (170 SAE) horsepower, for the United States the 280 engine was fitted. This developed 157 SAE horsepower and the car had the final drive of 3.92:1 instead of the 4.08 for the former cars. The four-speed manual transmission was optional. Caliper-type disc brakes ensured safe stopping and radial tires provided superb road-holding. The base price of the 250C sporty coupe model, however, at first did not include such extras as air conditioning, automatic transmission, and power steering. (Other countries, as Great Britain, also got the 280 engine.)

Production

Production of the 250C coupe model [114 V25] (from October 1968 until May 1972)

was in	1968	3 units
	1969	2,949 units
	1970	2,627 units
	1971	2,348 units
	1972	897 units
total		8,824 units

Production of the 250CE model [114 E25] (from October 1968 until May 1972)

was in	1968	3 units
	1969	5,840 units
	1970	8,002 units
	1971	5,898 units
	1972	2,044 units
total		21,787 units

Production of the 250C model (2,778 cc engine) [114 V28] (from July 1969 until June 1976)

was in	1969	1,213 units
	1970	2,425 units
	1971	3,621 units
	1972	2,839 units
	1973	649 units
	1974	490 units
	1975	442 units
	1976	89 units
total		11,768 units

Prices

The 250C coupe sold in 1969 for	DM 16,820
in 1970 for	DM 18,430
in 1971 for	DM 19,370
The 250CE coupe sold in 1969 for	DM 17,710
in 1970 for	DM 19,370
in 1971	DM 20,370
Power steering	DM 515
Automatic transmission	DM 1,440
The 250C (2.8-liter engine) sold in the United States in January 1970 for (East coast)	$ 6,625
(West coast)	$ 6,761
in October 1970 (including automatic transmission) (East coast)	$ 7,348
in September 1971 (including automatic transmission) (East coast)	$ 8,059
Power steering (1970)	$ 198

Specifications

	250C / 250CE (coupe)
Engine type	6 cyl overhead camshaft (M 114) (for U.S. M 130)
Bore and stroke	81.7 x 78.8mm (3.23 x 3.10 in) for U.S.: 86.5 x 78.8mm (3.41 x 3.10 in)
Displacement	2496 cc (152.4 cu in) for U.S.: 2778 cc (169.5 cu in)
Power output	C: 130 hp (DIN) @ 5400 rpm (146 hp SAE @ 5600 rpm) CE: 150 hp (DIN) @ 5500 rpm (170 hp SAE @ 5500 rpm) for U.S.: 157 hp SAE @ 5400
Compression ratio	9:1 (later: 8.7:1)
Torque	C: 20.3 mkg @ 3600 rpm (22.3 mkg @ 3800 rpm 161.3 ft/lb) CE: 21.5 mkg @ 4500 rpm (23.5 mkg @ 4650 rpm 170 ft/lb) for U.S.: 25.1 mkg @ 3800 rpm 181.6 ft/lb
Carburetion or Fuel injection	2 dual downdraft carburetors Zenith 35/40 INAT CE: Bosch electronic
Engine speed at 100 km/hr	3180 rpm
Gear ratios	I. 3.90:1 (optional) I. 3.96:1 II. 2.30:1 II. 2.34:1 III. 1.41:1 III. 1.43:1 IV. 1.00:1 IV. 1.00:1 V. 0.87:1
Rear axle ratio	3.92 (later: 3.69; for 5-speed 3.92)
Chassis	unit frame and body
Suspension	independent front and rear, with coil springs, diagonal-pivot swing axle, anti-sway bars
Brakes and area	disc, power assisted, 273/279mm (10.8/11.0 in)
Wheelbase	2750mm (108.3 in)
Track, front/rear	1444/1440mm (56.9/56.7 in)
Length	4680mm (184.3 in)
Width	1770mm (69.7 in)
Height	1395mm (54.9 in)
Ground clearance	175mm (6.9 in)
Tires	6.95 H 14 or 175 H 14
Turning circle	11.7 meters (38.4 ft)
Steering type and ratio	recirculating ball, (4.0 turns), servo assisted
Weight	1395 kg (3069 lbs)
Maximum speed	180 km/hr (112 mph)
Acceleration	13 sec 0-100 km/hr
Fuel consumption	12.5 liters/100 km (18.75 mpg)
Fuel tank capacity	65 liters (17.2 gallons)

The 250CE coupe, 1972

The 250C coupe, 1975

The 280SE convertible, 1969

Model 280SE 3.5 (1969-1971)

S = Super, E (Einspritzung) = fuel injection

The 280SE 3.5 luxury coupe and convertible were introduced at the Frankfurt Auto Show in 1969. The basic body style actually dated back to the 1961 220SE model, and it was only slightly altered. The radiator was 70 millimeters lower and 100 millimeters wider and the bumpers had rubber inserts. The engine, however, was the most advanced one produced, with transistorized ignition, three-phase generator, and Bosch electronic fuel injection. Such accessories as stereo radio, air conditioning, automatic transmission, and electric windows were standard. Upholstery was of real leather and the elegant wood trim was especially selected.

The new V-8 engine, displacing 3,499 cubic centimeters (213.5 cubic inches), and developing 200 horsepower (230 SAE) was brand-new and did not share any components with the earlier and larger 6.3-liter unit. With the cast-iron block and aluminum head, it weighed only 55 pounds more (505 pounds) than the six-cylinder powerplant and gave the cars an acceleration rate of 9.5 seconds to 100 kilometers per hour and maximum speed of 125 miles per hour.

These luxurious models were the last of the long line of convertibles and coupes which were to become so very desirable and brought premium prices many years later.

Prices and Production

The 280SE 3.5 coupe sold in 1970 for	DM 32,025
in 1971 for	DM 33,690
The 280SE 3.5 convertible sold for an additional about	DM 2,000
The 280SE 3.5 coupe sold in the United States	
in January 1970 for (East coast)	$ 13,430
(West coast)	$ 13,574
in March 1971 (East coast)	$ 13,766
The 280SE 3.5 convertible sold in the United States	
in January 1970 for (East coast)	$ 14,155
(West coast)	$ 14,297
in March 1971 (East coast)	$ 14,509

Production of the 280SE 3.5 [111 E35/1] (from August/November 1969 until July 1971)

was in	1969	176 units
	1970	3,300 units
	1971	1,026 units
	total	4,502 units

The 280SE coupe, 1969

Specifications

	280SE 3.5 (coupe and convertible)
Engine type	V-8 cyl overhead camshafts, one for each bank (M 116)
Bore and stroke	92 x 65.8mm (3.62 x 2.59 in)
Displacement	3499 cc (213.5 cu in)
Power output	200 hp (DIN) @ 5800 rpm (230 hp SAE @ 6050 rpm)
Compression ratio	9.5:1
Torque	29.2 mkg @ 4000 rpm (32 mkg @ 4200 rpm 231.5 ft/lb)
Fuel injection	Bosch electronic
Engine speed at 100 km/hr	2945 rpm
Gear ratios	I. 3.98:1 (14.69) II. 2.39:1 (8.82) III. 1.46:1 (5.38) IV. 1.00:1 (3.69)
Rear axle ratio	3.69
Chassis	unit frame and body
Suspension	independent front and rear, with coil springs, single joint swing axle
Brakes and area	disc, servo assist, two circuit hydraulic, 273/279mm (10.8/11.0 in)
Wheelbase	2750mm (108.3 in)
Track, front/rear	1482/1485mm (58.4/58.6 in)
Length	4880mm (192 in)
Width	1845mm (72.6 in)
Height	1395mm (54.9 in)
Ground clearance	152mm (6 in)
Tires	7.35 H 14 or 185 H 14
Turning circle	12 meters (39.4 ft)
Steering type and ratio	recirculating ball (3.2 turns), servo assisted
Weight	convertible: 1574 kg (3463 lbs); coupe: 1655 kg (3641 lbs)
Maximum speed	205 km/hr (127 mph)
Acceleration	9.5 sec 0-100 km/hr
Fuel consumption	13 liters, super/100 km (18 mpg)
Fuel tank capacity	82 liters (21.7 gallons)

The timeless convertible, the 280SE 3.5 of 1971

The first of a long line, the 220SE of 1961

The 300SEL 3.5 sedan, 1969

Model 300SEL 3.5 (1969-1972)

SE L (Lang) = long wheelbase chassis

The 300SEL 3.5 sedan was the other car introduced at the 1969 Frankfurt Auto Show to have the new V-8 engine of 3.5-liter displacement installed. The body style was identical to the earlier 300SEL sedan which had the 6-cylinder-in-line engine of 2.8 liters and 180 SAE (160 DIN) horsepower. This, in turn, had replaced the first 300SEL sedan which actually had a 300 engine, the 2,996 cubic centimeter power unit of 160, and later 170 (DIN) horsepower.

The new 3.5-liter oversquare V-8 engine had the new Bosch electronic fuel injection system, a more accurate and less expensive method than the previously used mechanical injection. It developed a considerable 200 DIN (230 SAE) horsepower and with a torque of 231.5 ft/lb gave the 300SEL sedan a maximum speed of 205 kilometers (127 miles) per hour. It was designed for the future and would appear within only two years in enlarged form.

The new 300SEL 3.5 was again the top of the line, a most luxuriously appointed automobile, more advanced than the coming 280SE 3.5 sedan in chassis design, and, with the longer wheelbase, a somewhat better riding automobile. It had the air suspension system of the 6.3 model sedan and shared some other technological improvements of that model.

(This 300SEL 3.5 was the only one of the 3.5 models — the 280 SE 3.5 and the 280SEL 3.5 were the other two — which was sold in the U.S. Over the years 1,039 such units were sold here.)

Prices and Production

The 300SEL 3.5 four-door sedan sold in 1970 for . . . . .DM 31,025
    in 1971 for. . . . . .DM 32,635
The 300SEL 3.5 four-door sedan sold in the United States
    in January 1970 for (East coast). . . . .$ 12,572
    (West coast) . . . .$ 12,718
    in March 1971 (East coast) . . . .$ 12,886
    in September 1971 (East coast) . . . .$ 14,121
    in December 1971 (East coast). . . . .$ 13,768

Production of the 300SEL 3.5 model [109 E35/1] (from August/November 1969 until September 1972)

was in	1969	158 units
	1970	4,903 units
	1971	3,225 units
	1972	1,297 units
total		9,483 units

The 300SEL 3.5 sedan, 1969

Specifications

	300SEL 3.5
Engine type	V-8 cyl overhead camshafts, one for each bank (M 116)
Bore and stroke	92 x 65.8mm (3.62 x 2.59 in)
Displacement	3499 cc (213.5 cu in)
Power output	200 hp (DIN) @ 5800 rpm (230 hp SAE @ 6050 rpm)
Compression ratio	9.5:1
Torque	29.2 mkg @ 4000 rpm (32 mkg @ 4200 rpm 231.5 ft/lb)
Fuel injection	Bosch electronic
Engine speed at 100 km/hr	2945 rpm
Gear ratios	I. 3.98:1 (14.69) II. 2.39:1 (8.82) III. 1.46:1 (5.38) IV. 1.00:1 (3.69)
Rear axle ratio	3.69
Chassis	unit frame and body
Suspension	independent front and rear, air springs, self leveling and air suspension, single joint swing axle
Brakes and area	front vented disc, rear solid, servo assisted, 273/279mm (10.8/11.0 in)
Wheelbase	2850mm (112.2 in)
Track, front/rear	1482/1490mm (58.4/58.7 in)
Length	5000mm (196.9 in)
Width	1810mm (71.3 in)
Height	1415mm (55.7 in)
Ground clearance	175mm (6.9 in)
Tires	7.35 H 14 or 185 H 14
Turning circle	12.2 meters (40 ft)
Steering type and ratio	recirculating ball (3.0 turns), servo assisted
Weight	1673 kg (3680 lbs)
Maximum speed	205 km/hr (127 mph)
Acceleration	9.5 sec 0-100 km/hr
Fuel consumption	13 liters, super/100 km (18 mpg)
Fuel tank capacity	82 liters (21.7 gallons)

Longitudinal section of the M 116 engine, 1969

Cross section of the M 116 engine, 1969

The 250 sedan, 1970

Model 250 (1970-1976)

The 250 sedan, first produced March and placed into regular production in July 1970, was another model where the designation no longer indicated the displacement of the engine, for it had the 2,778 cubic centimeter engine. The true 250 was still being made (begun in July and put into production in December 1967, it was phased out in May 1972). After the appearance of the 2.8-liter 250 coupe the previous year, the 2.8-liter sedan was probably a natural 250 model to follow.

Sharing the body style of the larger 280SEL sedan, the 250 was shorter, had a smaller fuel tank, smaller sized tires, weighed 178 pounds less, but had the same specifications in other respects. In actual performance it was slightly superior to the larger sedan.

This 250 model, equipped with a 2.8-liter engine, proved that the once rigidly adhered-to model designations were now definitely discarded. A year before the 250C was — for the United States market — furnished with the 280 engine, and at the time (1970) the 280SE 3.5 and the 300 SEL 3.5 were introduced, it was believed that it was merely an exception. But now, when this new V-8 engine of 3.5 liter displacement seemed unquestionably designed for enlargement to at least 4.5 liters, it appeared certain that style designations could not be relied upon to indicate the engine's displacement in the car. Of course, the 600 limousine had actually a 6.3-liter engine, but a 630 would probably have not sounded as well. (A 600 sedan was built in 1924-1929, which had a 6.24-liter engine!) And then, earlier (in 1976), the 300SEL had a 2.8-liter engine, but it was not a 300SEL 2.8.

Prices and Production

The 250 four-door sedan sold in 1970 for	DM 16,185
in 1972 for	DM 17,875
in 1973 for	DM 18,760
The 250 four-door sedan sold in the United States	
in January 1970 for (East coast)	$ 5,539
(West coast)	$ 5,674
in October 1970 (including automatic transmission) (East coast)	$ 6,208
in September 1971 (including automatic transmission) (East coast)	$ 7,205
Power steering (1970)	$ 198

Production of the 250 model [114 V28] (from March/July 1970 until July 1976)

was in	1970	3,248 units
	1971	7,382 units
	1972	8,266 units
	1973	6,570 units
	1974	4,516 units
	1975	3,580 units
	1976	499 units
	total	34,061 units

Specifications

	250
Engine type	6 cyl overhead camshaft (M130)
Bore and stroke	86.5 x 78.8mm (3.41 x 3.10 in)
Displacement	2778 cc (169.5 cu in)
Power output	140 hp (DIN) @ 5200 rpm (157 hp SAE @ 5400 rpm)
Compression ratio	9:1
Torque	23 mkg @ 3600 rpm (25.1 mkg @ 3800 rpm 181.6 ft/lb)
Carburetion	2 dual downdraft carburetors Zenith 35/40 INAT
Engine speed at 100 km/hr	3140 rpm
Gear ratio	I. 3.90:1 II. 2.30:1 III. 1.41:1 IV. 1.00:1
Rear axle ratio	3.92
Chassis	unit frame and body
Suspension	independent front and rear, with coil springs, diagonal-pivot swing axle, anti-sway bars
Brakes and area	disc, power assist, two circuit hydraulic, 273/279mm (10.8/11.0 in)
Wheelbase	2750mm (108.3 in)
Track, front/rear	1444/1440mm (56.9/56.7 in)
Length	4680mm (184.3 in)
Width	1770mm (69.7 in)
Height	1440mm (56.7 in)
Ground clearance	175mm (6.9 in)
Tires	6.95 H 14
Turning circle	11.7 meters (38.4 ft)
Steering type and ratio	recirculating ball (4.0 turns), servo assisted
Weight	1445 kg (3179 lbs)
Maximum speed	190 km/hr (118 mph)
Acceleration	12 sec 0-100 km/hr
Fuel consumption	12.5 liters, super/100 km (18.75 mpg)
Fuel tank capacity	65 liters (17.2 gallons)

The 250 sedan, 1971, U.S. version

The suspension system of the 250 sedan, 1970

Model 280SEL 3.5 (1970-1972)

SE L (Lang) = long wheelbase chassis

The 280SEL 3.5 sedan introduced at the Auto Show in Amsterdam, was produced for only three years. First pre-production was begun in June 1970 with only three units being built that year. Regular production did not get underway until the following March. After placing that 3.5-liter V-8 engine into the luxury coupe and convertible of the 280SE line, it seemed only natural to equip the sedan in the same manner. However, the 300SEL sedan, a more elegant model, was already in production and selling in fair numbers, even when the less expensive 280SEL was available. (The 300SEL 3.5 sold nearly 9,500 units in four years, while the 280SEL 3.5 sold less than 1,000 units in two years.)

The 280SEL 3.5 sedan, 1971

Prices and Production

The 280SEL 3.5 four-door sedan sold in 1971 for . . . . . DM 31,420

Production of the 280SEL 3.5 model [108 E35] (from June 1970/ March 1971 until August 1972)

	was in 1970	3 units
	1971	565 units
	1972	383 units
	total	951 units

Prices and Production

The 280SE 3.5 four-door sedan sold in 1971 for . . . . . . DM 24,920

Production of the 280SE 3.5 model [108 E35] (from July 1970/ March 1971 until September 1972)

	was in 1970	3 units
	1971	7,450 units
	1972	3,856 units
	total	11,309 units

Model 280SE 3.5 (1970-1972)

S = Super, E (Einspritzung) = fuel injection

The 280SE 3.5 sedan, first produced in July 1970, but really not in regular series production until March of the following year, was a more powerful edition of the prevailing sedan model. The new V-type eight-cylinder engine had been first installed into the higher priced luxury coupe and convertible models and the longer wheelbase sedans of the 280SEL and 300SEL designation. It seemed natural to make that better performance car also available in the regular sedan style.

Still, the 280SE 3.5 sedan had a relatively short production run with slightly over 11,000 units in two years. It was then replaced by the more correctly named model and with the newer styled body and other notable improvements gained over the years.

Specifications

	280SEL 3.5	280SE 3.5
Engine type	V-8 cyl overhead camshafts, one for each bank (M 116)	V-8 cyl overhead camshafts (M 116)
Bore and stroke	92 x 65.8mm (3.62 x 2.59 in)	92 x 65.8mm (3.62 x 2.59 in)
Displacement	3499 cc (213.5 cu in)	3499 cc (213.5 cu in)
Power output	200 hp (DIN) @ 5800 rpm (230 hp SAE @ 6050 rpm)	200 hp (DIN) @ 5800 rpm (230 hp SAE @ 6050 rpm)
Compression ratio	9.5:1	9.5:1
Torque	29.2 mkg @ 4000 rpm (32 mkg @ 4200 rpm 231.5 ft/lb)	29.2 mkg @ 4000 rpm (32 mkg @ 4200 rpm 231.5 ft/lb)
Fuel injection	Bosch electronic	Bosch electronic
Engine speed at 100 km/hr	2945 rpm	2945 rpm
Gear ratios	I. 3.98:1 II. 2.39:1 III. 1.46:1 IV. 1.00:1	I. 3.98:1 II. 2.39:1 III. 1.46:1 IV. 1.00:1
Rear axle ratio	3.69	3.69
Chassis	unit frame and body	unit frame and body
Suspension	independent front and rear, with coil springs, single joint swing axle, anti-sway bars	independent front and rear, with coil springs, single joint swing axle, anti-sway bars
Brakes and area	front vented disc, rear solid, servo assisted, two circuit hydraulic, 273/279mm (10.8/11.0 in)	disc, front vented, rear solid, servo assisted, two circuit hydraulic, 273/279mm (10.8/11.0 in)
Wheelbase	2850mm (112.2 in)	2750mm (108.3 in)
Track, front/rear	1482/1490mm (58.4/58.7 in)	1482/1490mm (58.4/58.7 in)
Length	5000mm (196.9 in)	4900mm (192.9 in)
Width	1810mm (71.3 in)	1810mm (71.3 in)
Height	1440mm (56.7 in)	1440mm (56.7 in)
Ground clearance	175mm (6.9 in)	175mm (6.9 in)
Tires	7.35 H 14 or 185 H 14	7.35 H 14 or 185 H 14
Turning circle	12.2 meters (40 ft)	11.7 meters (38.4 ft)
Steering type and ratio	recirculating ball (4.0 turns), servo assisted	recirculating ball (4.0 turns), servo assisted
Weight	1762 kg (3876 lbs)	1737 kg (3821 lbs)
Maximum speed	200 km/hr (124 mph)	200 km/hr (124 mph)
Acceleration	10 sec 0-100 km/hr	10 sec 0-100 km/hr
Fuel consumption	13 liters, super/100 km (18 mpg)	13 liters, super/100 km (18 mpg)
Fuel tank capacity	82 liters, (21.7 gallons)	82 liters (21.7 gallons)

The 350SL roadster, 1971

Prices and Production

The 350SL model sold in 1971 for	DM 29,970
in 1972 for	DM 31,415
in 1973 for	DM 32,915
in 1974 for	DM 34,400
in 1975 for	DM 37,920
in 1977 for	DM 39,360
In the United States the 350SL sold	
in September 1971 (East coast) for	$11,059
in December 1971 (East coast)	$10,540

Production of the 350SL model [107 E35] (from November 1970/April 1971 until March 1980)

was in	1970	3 units
	1971	4,802 units
	1972	4,778 units
	1973	1,647 units
	1974	574 units
	1975	390 units
	1976	540 units
	1977	650 units
	1978	743 units
	1979	934 units
	1980	243 units
total		15,304 units

Model 350SL (1970-1980)

S = Sports, L (Leicht) = light

The 350SL model was introduced early in 1971, although the preproduction actually got started in November of the previous year. The impressive two-seater sports car was to replace the 280SL, which had actually started with the 230SL version in 1963. The body and chassis of this all-new car was considerably heavier (300 lbs.) and longer (3.3 in.) than that of the earlier sportscars, but still showed a slight resemblance to them. The front and rear axles were similar to those of the 200-250 models, with independent wheel suspension with double wishbones and anti-drive control at the front, diagonal swing axle at the rear. The steel coil springs had rubber helping springs, anti-roll bars, and double-acting hydraulic telescopic shock absorbers. Brakes were ventilated disc at front and solid on the rear, hydraulic dual circuit with vacuum boost. A fluid-coupling four-speed automatic transmission was available as an optional item. Some of the many new safety features of the 350SL were the four-spoke safety steering wheel, the fuel tank repositioned, collision-safe over the rear axle, the safety door handles, and a new type safety belt.

The engine was the 3.5-liter V-8 type with slight modifications from those of the other 3.5 models. The gear shift lever was placed on the floor and the regular four-speed transmission or automatic was available. Maximum speed was 210 km/hr and acceleration was 8.8 seconds to 100 kilometers per hour, with the standard transmission car.

The car came as an open roadster with removable hard top pagoda style roof.

The 350SL 4.5 was marketed in the U.S. It was the same car with few exceptions, but had the larger 4.5-liter engine installed. Rated at the same horsepower as the European version (3.5) the larger engine used 10 percent more fuel, but regular instead of super gasoline. Emission controls were met until 1974 with the 4.5 — the principal reason for the change to a larger displacement engine for the U.S.

Specifications

	350SL
Engine type	V-8 overhead camshafts (M 116)
Bore and stroke	92 x 65.8mm (3.62 x 2.59 in)
Displacement	3499 cc (213.5 cu in)
Power output	200 hp (DIN) @ 5800 rpm (230 hp SAE @ 6050 rpm); 1977: 195 hp (DIN) @ 5500 rpm
Compression ratio	9.5:1 1979: 9:1
Torque	29.2 mkg @ 4000 rpm (32 mkg @ 4200 rpm 231.5 ft/lb)
Fuel injection	Bosch electronic; 1979: mechanical, with air flow sensor
Engine speed at 100 km/hr	2945 rpm automatic: 3085 rpm
Gear ratios	I. 3.98:1 automatic I. 3.96:1 after July, 1972 I. 2.31:1 II. 2.39:1 II. 2.34:1 II. 1.46:1 III. 1.46:1 III. 1.43:1 III. 1.00:1 IV. 1.00:1 IV. 1.00:1
Rear axle ratio	3.46
Chassis	unit frame and body
Suspension	independent front and rear, double wishbones, diagonal-pivot swing axle
Brakes and area	disc, front vented, rear solid, 278/279mm (10.9/11.0 in)
Wheelbase	2460mm (96.9 in)
Track, front/rear	1452/1440mm (57.2/56.7 in)
Length	4380mm (172.4 in) 1979: 4390mm (172.8 in)
Width	1790mm (70.5 in)
Height	1300mm (51.2 in)
Ground clearance	140mm (5.5 in)
Tires	205/70 VR 14
Turning circle	10.34 meters (33.9 ft)
Steering type and ratio	recirculating ball (3.0 turns); servo assisted 15.6:1
Weight	1585 kg (3487 lbs) 1979: 1540 kg (3388 lbs)
Maximum speed	210 km/hr (130 mph); automatic: 205 km/hr (127 mph); 1977: 205 km/hr; automatic: 200 km/hr
Accleration	8.8 sec 0-100 km/hr; automatic: 9.0 sec 0-100 km/hr; 1979: 9.5 sec 0-100 km/hr; automatic: 10.1 sec
Fuel consumption	13 liters, super/100 km (18 mpg); 1979: at 120 km/hr, 13.8 liters; automatic: 14.5 liters
Fuel tank capacity	90 liters (23 gallons)

The 350SL hard top, 1972

The 350SLC coupe, 1971

# Model 350SLC (1971-1980)
S = Sports, L = Light, C = Coupe

The 350SLC model was first shown to the public at the Brussels Auto Show in 1971. It was a slightly longer edition of the SL model. The wheelbase as well as overall length was 360 millimeter (about 14 inches) longer and the car weighed 50 kilograms more. The coupe had, of course, rear passenger seats and larger trunk space than the 350SL model, but it looked just like it except for the short space of louvered rear side window area.

This newly designed luxury coupe took the place of the (111 factory designation) line of coupes and convertibles first produced as 220SE in September 1960 and followed by the steadily increased power of the 250SE and 280SE models.

It was over six inches shorter and three inches lower than the older body style car.

The 350SLC was an automobile with the sporty character of the SL model, giving superior performance, exclusive comfort, and elegant styling to the discriminating owner. Fitted with the four-speed manual or automatic transmission, the SLC had the same performance as the SL model.

For the United States, the 195 horsepower (DIN) 4.5-liter engine was installed and only the three-speed automatic transmission was available. Many items were standard equipment, such as air conditioning, automatic transmission, power brakes, power steering, central locking system, stereo radio, leather upholstery, and Michelin XVR tires, among others.

Prices and Production

The 350SLC model sold in 1971 for . . . . .DM 33,690
in 1972 for. . . . . .DM 35,635
in 1973 for. . . . . .DM 37,300
in 1974 for. . . . . .DM 38,980
in 1975 for. . . . . .DM 42,970
in 1977 for. . . . . .DM 44,910

Production of the 350SLC model [107 E35] (from June 1971/February 1972 until March 1980)

was in	1971	6 units
	1972	5,562 units
	1973	3,750 units
	1974	864 units
	1975	589 units
	1976	671 units
	1977	822 units
	1978	807 units
	1979	775 units
	1980	79 units
	total	13,925 units

The 350SLC coupe, 1972, U.S. version

Specifications

	350SLC
Engine type	V-8 cyl overhead camshafts (M 116)
Bore and stroke	92 x 65.8mm (3.62 x 2.59 in)
Displacement	3499 cc (213.5 cu in)
Power output	200 hp (DIN) @ 5800 rpm (230 hp SAE @ 6050 rpm); 1977: 195 hp (DIN) @ 5500 rpm
Compression ratio	9.5:1 1979: 9:1
Torque	29.2 mkg @ 4000 rpm (32 mkg @ 4200 rpm 231.5 ft/lb)
Fuel injection	Bosch electronic; 1979: mechanical with air flow sensor
Engine speed at 100 km/hr	2945 rpm automatic: 3085 rpm
Gear ratios	I. 3.98:1 automatic I. 3.96:1 after July, 1972 I. 2.31:1 II. 2.39:1 II. 2.34:1 II. 1.46:1 III. 1.46:1 III. 1.43:1 III. 1.00:1 IV. 1.00:1 IV. 1.00:1
Rear axle ratio	3.64
Chassis	unit frame and body
Suspension	independent front and rear, double wishbones, diagonal swing axle
Brakes and area	disc, front vented, rear solid, 278/279mm (10.9/11.0 in)
Wheelbase	2820mm (111.0 in)
Track, front/rear	1452/1440mm (57.2/56.7 in)
Length	4740mm (186.6 in) 1979: 4750mm (187 in)
Width	1790mm (70.5 in)
Height	1300mm (51.2 in)
Ground clearance	140mm (5.5 in)
Tires	205/70 VR
Turning circle	10.34 meters (33.9 ft)
Steering type and ratio	recirculating ball (3.0 turns); servo assisted 15.6:1
Weight	1635 kg (3597 lbs) 1979: 1590 kg (3498 lbs)
Maximum speed	210 km/hr (130 mph); automatic: 205 km/hr (127 mph); 1977: 205 km/hr; automatic: 200 km/hr (124 mph)
Acceleration	8.8 sec 0-100 km/hr; automatic: 9.0 sec 0-100 km/hr; 1979: 9.5 sec; automatic: 10.1 sec
Fuel consumption	13 liters, super/100 km (18 mpg); 1979: at 120 km/hr, 13.8 liters; automatic: 14.5 liters
Fuel tank capacity	90 liters (23 gallons)

The 350SLC on the test track, 1977

The 280 sedan, 1974, U.S. version

Model 280 (1971-1976)

The 280 sedan, fitted with the newly developed six-cylinder engine with two overhead camshafts, was introduced in early 1972. The design of an altered shape of combustion chamber and different positioning of valves and double camshafts made for more complete burning of fuel and less emission of noxious exhaust gases (15 percent less hydrocarbon and 10 percent less carbon monoxide) and was an answer to the ever-increasing stringent emission controls.

Although this newly designed twin-cam engine, particularly the detuned version for the United States market, was a considerably lower emission unit than the former six-cylinder engine it replaced. For the world market this new engine developed appreciably more power than the old one.

Equipped with the dual downdraft Solex carburetor, the M110 engine developed 160 DIN horsepower at 5,500 revolutions per minute and 23 mkg torque at 4,000. The new sedan came equipped with the all-synchromesh four-speed transmission with steering column or center floor gear shift, but had the manual five-speed transmission or the automatic unit as an optional item. It was a larger version of the 250 sedan.

Prices and Production

The 280 four-door sedan sold in 1972 for	DM 18,980
in 1973 for	DM 19,925
in 1974 for	DM 21,700
in 1975 for	DM 23,610
Power steering	DM 515
Automatic transmission	DM 1,440
In the United States the 280 sedan sold in 1972 for (including automatic transmission)	
(East coast)	$ 8,875
(West coast)	$ 8,978
in November 1973 (East coast)	$ 10,950
in September 1974 (East coast)	$ 12,325
in October 1975 (East coast)	$ 13,813

Production of the 280 model [114 V28] (from October 1971/May 1972 until September 1976)

was in	1971	2 units
	1972	9,828 units
	1973	13,718 units
	1974	11,755 units
	1975	6,535 units
	1976	2,699 units
	total	44,537 units

The 280 sedan, 1973

Specifications

	280
Engine type	6 cyl double overhead camshafts (M 110)
Bore and stroke	86 x 78.8mm (3.41 x 3.10 in)
Displacement	2746 cc (168 cu in)
Power output	160 hp (DIN) @ 5500 rpm (180 hp SAE) later, U.S.: 120 hp SAE @ 4800 rpm
Compression ratio	9:1　　　(U.S.: 8:1)
Torque	23 mkg @ 4000 rpm (166.4 ft/lb)
Carburetion	dual downdraft carburetor Solex 4 A 1
Engine speed at 100 km/hr	3140 rpm
Gear ratios	I.　3.90:1 II.　2.30:1 III.　1.41:1 IV.　1.00:1
Rear axle ratio	3.69
Chassis	unit frame and body
Suspension	independent front and rear, with coil springs, diagonal-pivot swing axle, anti-sway bars
Brakes and area	disc, power assisted, two circuit hydraulic, 273/279mm (10.8/11.0 in)
Wheelbase	2750mm (108.3 in)
Track, front/rear	1444/1440mm (56.9/56.7 in)
Length	4680mm (184.3 in)
Width	1770mm (69.7 in)
Height	1440mm (56.7 in)
Ground clearance	175mm (6.9 in)
Tires	185 HR 14
Turning circle	11.7 meters (38.4 ft)
Steering type and ratio	recirculating ball (4.0 turns), servo assisted
Weight	1455 kg (3200 lbs)
Maximum speed	190 km/hr (118 mph)
Acceleration	13 sec 0-100 km/hr (18.75 mpg)
Fuel consumption	12.5 liters, super/100 km (later, U.S.: no lead fuel)
Fuel tank capacity	65 liters (17.2 gallons)

Cross section of the M 110 engine, 1972

The 280 sedan, 1973

The 280E sedan, 1972

Model 280E (1971-1976)

E (Einspritzung) = fuel injection

The 280E sedan introduced in early 1971, but not produced in any quantity until the following year, had the new double overhead camshaft six-cylinder engine, but with electronic fuel enjection. This version of the M110 engine developed 185 DIN horsepower at 6,000 revolutions per minute and 24.3 mkg torque at 4,500 revolutions. Performance was slightly better than that of the carburetor model, with maximum speed of 200 kilometers (124 miles) against the 190 of the 280 sedan, but fuel consumption was rated equal.

Inside furnishing was exactly the same and so was the exterior body style except for the designation E on the trunk lid after the 280.

Prices and Production

The 280E four-door sedan sold in 1972 for	DM 20,535
in 1973 for	DM 21,535
in 1974 for	DM 22,500
in 1975 for	DM 25,465
Power steering	DM 515
Automatic transmission	DM 1,440

Production of the 280E model [114 E28] (from January 1971/April 1972 until September 1976)

was in	1971	18 units
	1972	8,371 units
	1973	8,214 units
	1974	3,612 units
	1975	2,277 units
	1976	344 units
	total	22,836 units

Model 280CE (1971-1976)

C = Coupe, E (Einspritzung) = fuel injection

The 280CE coupe was introduced at about the same time to the general public as the carburetor version of the car, but pre-production had actually begun in April of 1971. At that time, however, only two prototypes were made and production did not get underway until 1972 when over five thousand units of this double overhead camshaft engined model were built. The electronic fuel injected version developed 185 DIN horsepower at 6,000 revolutions per minute and a torque of 24.3 mkg at 4,500 revolutions per minute, giving the coupe a considerably livelier performance than the carburetor engined model.

Prices and Production

The 280CE sold in 1972 for	DM 22,980
in 1973 for	DM 24,090
in 1974 for	DM 26,240
in 1975 for	DM 28,405
Power steering	DM 515
Automatic transmission	DM 1,440

Production of the 280CE coupe [114 E28] (from April 1971/May 1972 until July 1976)

was in	1971	2 units
	1972	5,389 units
	1973	3,724 units
	1974	1,429 units
	1975	844 units
	1976	130 units
	total	11,518 units

The 280CE coupe, 1972

Specifications

	280E	280CE (coupe)		
Engine type	6 cyl double overhead camshafts (M 110)	6 cyl double overhead camshafts (M 110)		
Bore and stroke	86 x 78.8mm (3.41 x 3.10 in)	86 x 78.8mm (3.41 x 3.10 in)		
Displacement	2746 cc (168 cu in)	2746 cc (168 cu in)		
Power output	185 hp (DIN) @ 6000 rpm (205 hp SAE)	185 hp (DIN) @ 6000 rpm (205 hp SAE)		
Compression ratio	9:1	9:1		
Torque	24.3 mkg @ 4500 rpm (175.8 ft/lb)	24.3 mkg @ 4500 rpm (175.8 ft/lb)		
Fuel injection	Bosch electronic	Bosch electronic		
Engine speed at 100 km/hr	3140 rpm	3140 rpm		
Gear ratios	I. 3.90:1 II. 2.30:1 III. 1.41:1 IV. 1.00:1	I. 3.90:1 II. 2.30:1 III. 1.41:1 IV. 1.00:1	optional	I. 3.96:1 II. 2.34:1 III. 1.43:1 IV. 1.00:1 V. 0.87:1
Rear axle ratio	3.69	3.69 (for 5-speed 3.82)		
Chassis	unit frame and body	unit frame and body		
Suspension	independent front and rear, with coil springs, diagonal-pivot swing axle, anti-sway bars	independent front and rear, with coil springs, diagonal-pivot swing axle, anti-sway bars		
Brakes and area	disc, power assisted, 273/279mm (10.8/11.0 in)	disc, power assisted, 273/279mm (10.8/11.0 in)		
Wheelbase	2750mm (108.3 in)	2750mm (108.3 in)		
Track, front/rear	1444/1440mm (56.9/56.7 in)	1444/1440mm (56.9/56.7 in)		
Length	4680mm (184.3 in)	4680mm (184.5 in)		
Width	1770mm (69.7 in)	1770mm (69.7 in)		
Height	1440mm (56.7 in)	1395mm (54.9 in)		
Ground clearance	175mm (6.9 in)	175mm (6.9 in)		
Tires	185 HR 14	185 HR 14		
Turning circle	11.7 meters (38.4 ft)	11.7 meters (38.4 ft)		
Steering type and ratio	recirculating ball (4.0 turns), servo assisted	recirculating ball (4.0 turns), servo assisted		
Weight	1455 kg (3200 lbs)	1455 kg (3200 lbs)		
Maximum speed	200 km/hr (124 mph)	200 km/hr (124 mph)		
Acceleration	12 sec 0-100 km/hr	12 sec 0-100 km/hr		
Fuel consumption	12.5 liters, super/100 km (18.75 mpg)	12.5 liters, super/100km (18.75 mpg)		
Fuel tank capacity	65 liters (17.2 gallons)	65 liters (17.2 gallons)		

The 280C coupe, 1972

Prices and Production

The 280C coupe sold in 1972 for	DM 21,425
in 1973 for	DM 22,480
in 1974 for	DM 24,500
in 1975 for	DM 26,555
Power steering	DM 515
Automatic transmission	DM 1,440

In the United States the 280C coupe sold

in September 1972 for (East coast)	$ 9,518
(West coast)	$ 9,618
in November 1973 (East coast)	$ 11,630
in September 1974 (East coast)	$ 13,063
in October 1975 (East coast)	$ 14,639

Production of the 280C coupe [114 V28] (from December 1971/ June 1972 until August 1976)

was in	1971	1 unit
	1972	2,124 units
	1973	4,196 units
	1974	3,734 units
	1975	2,133 units
	1976	963 units
	total	13,151 units

Model 280C (1971-1976)

C = Coupe

The 280C coupe appeared on the scene in early 1972. It had been originated in the late period of the previous year, along with the sedan line, and one car was actually produced in December 1971. The new double overhead camshaft six-cylinder engine, equipped with the Solex dual compound downdraft carburetor, was fitted into the coupe body of the 250C model. Specifications, except for the new engine installation, were the same as those of the previous model, which remained in production, but minor alterations, such as simpler bumpers, and improved side mirror, were made.

The new regulation bumpers on the United States models were quite controversial, according to some designers. The huge, bulky rubber ends forming around the sides, front and back, were considered very ugly indeed by many experts, or design-conscious critics. It was urgently hoped that they were merely a temporary solution to the problem of compliance to stricter federal regulations, which were not always stated in precise terms and often changed quite rapidly. (Yet, on one of our visits to Germany, we found two owners of Mercedes cars who wanted to get them for their models.)

The 280C was a heavier coupe than the previous one and with the newer double overhead camshaft six-cylinder engine was a superior performing car than the older version, that is in the European trim. The U.S. version was not superior, for the engine was tuned down to develop only 120 horsepower instead of the 160 elsewhere. The same process was applied to the torque — higher in Europe, but lower in this country — which made the new coupe a rather less briskly performing, but still a pleasant car, to drive.

During the last three years of production the 280C outsold the 250C with the 2.8-liter engine by a wide margin (6,830 to 1,021), which only proved the decision a correct one.

Specifications

	280C (coupe)
Engine type	6 cyl double overhead camshafts (M 110)
Bore and stroke	86 x 78.8mm (3.41 x 3.10 in)
Displacement	2746 cc (168 cu in)
Power output	160 hp (DIN) @ 5500 rpm (180 hp SAE) later, U.S.: 120 hp SAE @ 4800 rpm; 1975 California: 123 hp SAE @ 5000 rpm
Compression ratio	9:1 (U.S.: 8:1)
Torque	23 mkg @ 4000 rom (166.4 ft/lb) later, U.S.: 15.5 mkg @ 2800 rpm (120 ft/lb); 1975: 143 ft/lb @ 2800 rpm California: 143 ft/lb @ 3600 rpm
Carburetion	dual downdraft carburetors Solex 4 A 1
Engine speed at 100 km/hr	3140 rpm
Gear ratios	I. 3.90:1 optional I. 3.96:1 II. 2.30:1 II. 2.34:1 III. 1.41:1 III. 1.43:1 IV. 1.00:1 IV. 1.00:1 V. 0.87:1
Rear axle ratio	3.69 (for 5-speed 3.92)
Chassis	unit frame and body
Suspension	independent front and rear, with coil springs, diagonal-pivot swing axle, anti-sway bars
Brakes and area	disc, power assisted, 273/279mm (10.8/11.0 in)
Wheelbase	2750mm (108.3 in)
Track, front/rear	1444/1440mm (56.9/56.7 in)
Length	4680mm (184.5 in)
Width	1770mm (69.7 in)
Height	1395mm (54.9 in)
Ground clearance	175mm (6.9 in)
Tires	185 HR 14
Turning circle	11.7 meters (38.4 ft)
Steering type and ratio	recirculating ball (4.0 turns), servo assisted
Weight	1455 kg (3200 lbs)
Maximum speed	190 km/hr (118 mph)
Acceleration	13 sec 0-100 km/hr
Fuel consumption	12.5 liters, super/100 km (18.75 mpg) (U.S.: no lead fuel)
Fuel tank capacity	65 liters (17.2 gallons)

The 280C coupe, 1972

The 280C coupe, 1974, U.S. version

The 280SE 4.5 sedan, 1971, U.S. version

Prices and Production

In the United Stated the 280SE 4.5 sedan sold
   in September 1972 for (East coast).............$ 10,283
   (West coast)..........................$ 10,393

Production of the 280SE 4.5 model [108 E45] (from April/May 1971 until November 1972)
          was in 1971   5,782 units
                 1972   7,745 units
              total   13,527 units

Prices and Production

In the United States the 280SEL 4.5 sedan sold
   in September 1972 for (East coast).............$ 10,875
   (West coast)..........................$ 10,985

Production of the 280SEL 4.5 model [108 E45] (from May 1971 until November 1972)
          was in 1971   1,871 units
                 1972   6,302 units
              total   8,173 units

Model 280SE 4.5 (1971-1972)

S = Super, E (Einspritzung) = fuel injection

The 280SE 4.5 sedan made its first appearance in early 1971, just a few months after the new 4.5-liter V-8 engine had made its debut. In fact, that model was available to the purchaser at about the same time the 3.5-liter engined sedan was produced, and gave the buyer another option in power for his car. It was, however, not the choice of as many buyers as was the 3.5-liter engined sedan the first year of production when nearly 6,000 units were sold, but the following year it outsold the smaller-engined version by a margin of two to one.

Inside and out, the two sedans were alike, with the more powerful one having, of course, better performance. Acceleration was slightly faster and the maximum speed was five miles better, but fuel consumption was 1.5 liters more for the 4.5- than for the 3.5-liter engined sedan.

The 280SE 4.5 sedan fitted into the policy of offering the customer the widest possible range in passenger automobiles. The U.S. customers were nearly the only ones who were offered this and the following two 4.5-liter engined cars, while others were able to buy and wisely preferred the 3.5-liter versions, not hampered by restrictive emission controls. (A total of 23,488 cars of the 280SE 4.5, the 280SEL 4.5, and the 300SEL 4.5 were sold in the U.S.)

Model 280SEL 4.5 (1971-1972)

SE L (Lang) = long wheelbase chassis

The 280SEL 4.5 sedan was produced at about the same time (in 1971) the regular length sedan was available. Again, this longer wheelbase car was identical to the other model, and the extra ten centimeters gave the rear-seat passengers additional space to stretch their legs. On longer journeys this was especially appreciated.

This 4.5-liter engined long sedan outsold the 3.5-liter version by about three to one during the first year of its availability and the following year this more powerful version was the choice of over 6,000 customers while only about 500 bought the less powerful car. Apparently the extra fuel consumption was of no serious concern to the buyers of the 4.5-liter long sedan.

Specifications

	280SE 4.5	280SEL 4.5
Engine type	V-8 cyl overhead camshafts (M 117)	V-8 cyl overhead camshafts (M 117)
Bore and stroke	92 x 85mm (3.62 x 3.35 in)	92 x 85mm (3.62 x 3.35 in)
Displacement	4520 cc (275.8 cu in)	4520 cc (275.8 cu in)
Power output	225 hp (DIN) @ 5000 rpm (250 hp SAE) U.S.: 230 hp SAE @ 5000 rpm	225 hp (DIN) @ 5000 rpm (250 hp SAE) U.S.: 230 hp SAE @ 5000 rpm
Compression ratio	8.8:1 U.S.: 8:1	8.8:1 U.S.: 8:1
Torque	38.5 mkg @ 3000 rpm (278.5 ft/lb)	38.5 mkg @ 3000 rpm (278.5 ft/lb)
Fuel injection	Bosch electronic	Bosch electronic
Engine speed at 100 km/hr	2865 rpm U.S.: 2740 rpm	2865 rpm U.S.: 2740 rpm
Gear ratios	I. 3.98:1 U.S. automatic I. 2.31:1 II. 2.39:1 II. 1.46:1 III. 1.46:1 III. 1.00:1 IV. 1.00:1	I. 3.98:1 U.S. automatic I. 2.31:1 II. 2.39:1 II. 1.46:1 III. 1.46:1 III. 1.00:1 IV. 1.00:1
Rear axle ratio	3.69 U.S.: 3.23	3.69 U.S.: 3.23
Chassis	unit frame and body	unit frame and body
Suspension	independent front and rear, with coil springs, single joint swing axle, anti-sway bars	independent front and rear, with coil springs, single joint swing axle, anti-sway bars
Brakes and area	disc, front and rear vented, servo assisted, two circuit hydraulic, 273/279mm (10.8/11.0 in)	disc, front and rear vented, servo assisted, two circuit hydraulic, 273/279mm (10.8/11.0 in)
Wheelbase	2750mm (108.3 in)	2850mm (112.2 in)
Track, front/rear	1482/1490mm (58.4/58.7 in)	1482/1490mm (58.4/58.7 in)
Length	4900mm (192.9 in)	5000mm (196.9 in)
Width	1810mm (71.3 in)	1810mm (71.3 in)
Height	1440mm (56.7 in)	1440mm (56.7 in)
Ground clearance	175mm (6.9 in)	175mm (6.9 in)
Tires	735 H 14 or 185 H 14	735 H 14 or 185 H 14
Turning circle	11.7 meters (38.4 ft)	12.2 meters (40 ft)
Steering type and ratio	recirculating ball (4.0 turns), servo assisted	recirculating ball (4.0 turns), servo assisted
Weight	1737 kg (3821 lbs)	1737 kg (3821 lbs)
Maximum speed	205 km/hr (127 mph) U.S.: 190 km/hr (118 mph)	205 km/hr (127 mph) U.S.: 190 km/hr (118 mph)
Acceleration	9.5 sec 0-100 km/hr U.S.: 12 sec 0-100 km/hr	9.5 sec 0-100 km/hr U.S.: 12 sec 0-100 km/hr
Fuel consumption	14.5 liters, super/100 km (16 mpg)	14.5 liters, super/100 km (16 mpg)
Fuel tank capacity	82 liters (21.7 gallons)	82 liters (21.7 gallons)

Model 300SEL 4.5 (1971-1972)

SE L (Lang) = long wheelbase chassis

The 300SEL 4.5 model sedan was produced at the same time the 280SE/SEL models, first in May 1971. It was natural that the larger and more powerful V-8 engine would be placed into the more luxurious of the longer wheelbase sedans, so as to allow this rather formal model to remain the very best of the top line. The sedan was greatly preferred as an official and generally chauffeur-driven automobile, whenever the prestigious 600 limousine was not desired.

This luxury sedan proved to be a superb fast touring car, offering the greatest comfort possible, and with its elegant interior appointment keeping up the best Mercedes tradition of superior automobiles. While the actual performance data compared with the 280SEL 4.5 model was identical, the owner of the 300SEL 4.5 sedan experienced the feeling of driving a car with truly unsurpassed roadability, the very best available model in every respect.

The 300SEL 4.5 sedan never achieved the popularity of the 280SEL 4.5 model, of course, but sales for the first year were over 600 units, while in 1972 nearly 2,000 such cars were sold. Total sales of the 300SEL 4.5 were 2,553 units and of the 280SEL 4.5 were 8,173 units during the two years of their production life.

The rather appreciative difference in price over the slightly lesser 280SEL 4.5 model contributed undoubtedly to the smaller sales of this car, yet enough buyers supported the stated Daimler-Benz policy of supplying the widest possible selection of car models to the broadest range of prospective purchasers.

The 300SEL 4.5 sedan, 1971, U.S. version

Prices and Production

In the United States the 300SEL 4.5 sedan sold
in September 1972 for (East coast)............$ 14,130
(West coast)..........................$ 14,240

Production of the 300SEL 4.5 model [109 E45] (from May 1971 until October 1972)

was in	1971	656 units
	1972	1,897 units
	total	2,553 units

The interior of the 300SEL 4.5, 1971

Specifications

	300SEL 4.5
Engine type	V-8 cyl overhead camshafts (M 117)
Bore and stroke	92 x 85mm (3.62 x 3.35 in)
Displacement	4520 cc (275.8 cu in)
Power output	225 hp (DIN) @ 5000 rpm (250 hp SAE) U.S.: 230 hp SAE @ 5000 rpm
Compression ratio	8.8:1 U.S.: 8:1
Torque	38.5 mkg @ 3000 rpm (278.5 ft/lb)
Fuel injection	Bosch electronic
Engine speed at 100 km/hr	2865 rpm U.S.: 2740 rpm
Gear ratios	I. 3.98:1 U.S. automatic I. 2.31:1 II. 2.39:1 II. 1.46:1 III. 1.46:1 III. 1.00:1 IV. 1.00:1
Rear axle ratio	3.69 U.S.: 3.23
Chassis	unit frame and body
Suspension	independent front and rear, with coil springs, single joint swing axle, anti-sway bars
Brakes and area	disc, front vented, rear solid, servo assisted, two circuit hydraulic, 273/279mm (10.8/11.0 in)
Wheelbase	2850mm (112.2 in)
Track, front/rear	1482/1490mm (58.4/58.7 in)
Length	5000mm (196.9 in)
Width	1800mm (71.3 in)
Height	1440mm (56.7 in)
Ground clearance	175mm (6.9 in)
Tires	735 H 14 or 185 H 14
Turning circle	12.2 meters (40 ft)
Steering type and ratio	recirculating ball (4.0 turns), servo assisted
Weight	1854 kg (4079 lbs)
Maximum speed	205 km/hr (127 mph) U.S.: 190 km/hr (118 mph)
Acceleration	9.5 sec 0-100 km/hr U.S.: 12 sec 0-100 km/hr
Fuel consumption	14.5 liters, super/100 km (16 mpg)
Fuel tank capacity	82 liters (21.7 gallons)

The instrument panel of the 300SEL 4.5, 1971

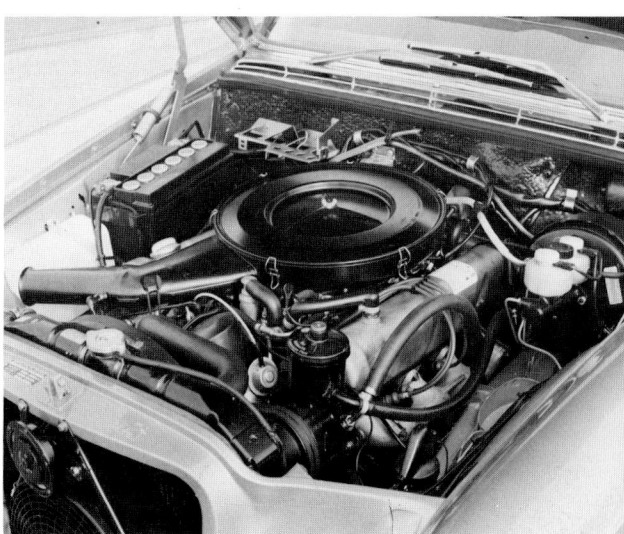

The M 117 engine for the 300SEL 4.5, 1971

Model 450SL (1971-1980)

S = Sports, L (Leicht) = light

The 450SL model was shown to the public at the Geneva Auto Show in 1973 but had been produced for the United States market earlier, in 1971. It was a more powerful car than the 3.5-liter version and retained all of the fine attributes of this new model sports car.

The U.S. version of the 450SL (outwardly identifiable by the different headlight arrangement only), had a lowered compression ratio to 8:1 and milder camshafts. The car was equipped with heavier bumpers and was fitted with the new three-speed automatic transmission only. Rear axle ratio was changed to 3.07 and the maximum speed was 124 miles per hour. The 4.5-liter engine actually developed less horsepower than the original 3.5-liter unit, but that was the price to pay for the more stringent emission controls prevailing here. The car weighed 148 pounds more than the European version and had, of course, not the performance of that more powerful and lighter car.

The difference in horsepower output by the same basic engine would become even more pronounced in the coming years, and there was certainly no similarity in the same models when driving a European version over there and then driving that model in this country.

The 450SL roadster, 1975, U.S. version

Prices and Production

The 450SL model sold in 1973 for	DM 36,630
in 1974 for	DM 38,300
in 1975 for	DM 42,215
in 1977 for	DM 43,856

In the United States the 450SL coupe/roadster sold

in September 1972 (East coast) for	$11,688
(West coast)	$11,800
in March 1973 (East coast)	$12,733
in November 1973 (East coast)	$15,450
in September 1974 (with automatic transmission) (East coast)	$17,056
in October 1975 (with automatic transmission) (East coast)	$19,357
in March 1977 (East coast)	$21,943
in February 1979 (East coast)	$30,729

Production of the 450SL model [107 E45] (from March/July 1971 until November 1980)

was in		
	1971	2,131 units
	1972	7,473 units
	1973	8,654 units
	1974	6,093 units
	1975	6,011 units
	1976	6,625 units
	1977	8,110 units
	1978	7,434 units
	1979	8,184 units
	1980	5,583 units
	total	66,298 units

The 450SL roadster, 1977, U.S. version

Specifications

	450SL
Engine type	V-8 cyl overhead camshaft (M 117)
Bore and stroke	92 x 85mm (3.62 x 3.35 in)
Displacement	4520 cc (275.8 cu in)
Power output	225 hp (DIN) @ 5000 rpm (250 hp SAE); U.S.: 230 hp SAE @ 5000 rpm (200 hp DIN); later, 190 hp SAE @ 4750 rpm; 1975 California: 180 hp SAE; 1977: 217 hp (DIN); 1979: 218 hp (DIN) U.S. 1977: 180 hp (SAE) @ 4750 rpm; 1980: 160 hp (SAE) @ 4200 rpm
Compression ratio	8.8:1 U.S.: 8:1
Torque	38.5 mkg @ 3000 rpm (278.5 ft/lb); U.S.: 33.0 mkg @ 3000 rpm (238.8 ft/lb); 1975 California: 232 ft/lb U.S. 1977: 32.25 mkg @ 3000 rpm (220 ft/lb); 1980: 31.9 mkg @ 2500 rpm (230 ft/lb)
Fuel injection	Bosch electronic
Engine speed at 100 km/hr	2865 rpm U.S.: 2700 rpm
Gear ratios	I. 3.98:1 U.S. automatic I. 2.31:1 II. 2.39:1 II. 1.46:1 III. 1.46:1 III. 1.00:1 IV. 1.00:1
Rear axle ratio	3.07 U.S. 1979: 3.06; 1980: 2.65
Chassis	unit frame and body
Suspension	independent front and rear, double wishbones, diagonal-pivot swing axle
Brakes and area	disc, front vented, rear solid, 278/279mm (10.9/11.0 in)
Wheelbase	2460mm (96.9 in) 1979: 2455mm (96.6 in)
Track, front/rear	1452/1440mm (57.2/56.7 in)
Length	4380mm (172.4 in) U.S.: 182.3 in (4630mm)
Width	1790mm (70.5 in)
Height	1300mm (51.2 in)
Ground clearance	140mm (5.5 in)
Tires	205/70 VR 14
Turning circle	10.2 meters (33.5 ft); later 10.34 meters (33.9 feet); U.S.: 10.48 meters (34.4 ft)
Steering type and ratio	recirculating ball (3.0 turns); servo assisted 15.9:1
Weight	1585 kg (3487 lbs); U.S.: 1718 kg (3780 lbs); 1977: 1730 kg (3815 lbs); 1979: 1695 kg (3740 lbs); 1980: 1700 kg (3750 lbs)
Maximum speed	215 km/hr (133.5 mph); 1977: 210 km/hr; U.S.: 200 km/hr (124 mph)
Acceleration	8.5 sec 0-100 km/hr; 1979: 9.3 sec 0-100 km/hr; U.S.: 11 sec 0-100 km/hr
Fuel consumption	14.5 liters, super/100 km (16 mpg) (U.S.: no lead fuel); 1979: at 120 km/hr, 15.8 liters (15 mpg)
Fuel tank capacity	90 liters (23.8 gallons)

The 450SL roadster, 1974

Model 450SLC (1972-1980)

S = Sports, L = Light, C = Coupe

The 450SLC model was also shown at the Geneva Show in 1973. Here again, the European version of that coupe was quite differently powered than that for sale in the United States. The restrictions placed on emission and safety added weight and lessened performance because of less horsepower developed. The 4.5-liter engine actually developed 225 DIN horsepower, while the U.S. version developed 230 SAE horsepower. Considering that the German (DIN) designation means the net horsepower available and the SAE (American) horsepower is the gross measurement, one can readily see that the heavier car with less power suffered greatly in comparison.

Outwardly there was no difference in the 350SLC or the 450SLC cars. Unlike the SL model, the coupe never was designated as the 350 4.5.

The 450SLC coupe, 1973

Prices and Production

The 450SLC model sold in 1973 for . . . . .DM 41,015
   in 1974 for . . . . .DM 42,860
   in 1975 for . . . . .DM 47,265
   In 1977 for . . . . .DM 49,406
In the United States the 450SLC coupe sold
   in September 1972 (East coast) for $15,094
     (West coast). $15,194
   in March 1973 (East coast). $16,498
   in November 1973 (East coast) $19,450
   in September 1974 (with automatic transmission)
     (East coast) $21,307
   in October 1975 (with automatic transmission)
     (East coast) $23,976
   in March 1977 (East coast). $27,090
   in February 1979 (East coast). $36,519

Production of the 450SLC coupe model [170 E45] (from February/July 1972 until October 1980)

was in	1972	700 units
	1973	5,594 units
	1974	2,961 units
	1975	2,993 units
	1976	3,802 units
	1977	4,569 units
	1978	4,382 units
	1979	4,510 units
	1980	2,228 units
	total	31,739 units

The 450SL and 450SLC on the test track, 1976

Specifications

	450SLC
Engine type	V-8 cyl overhead camshafts (M 117)
Bore and stroke	92 x 85mm (3.62 x 3.35 in)
Displacement	4520 cc (275.8 cu in)
Power output	225 hp (DIN) @ 5000 rpm (250 hp SAE); 1977: 217 hp (DIN); 1979: 218 hp (DIN) U.S.: 230 hp SAE @ 5000 rpm U.S. 1977: 180 hp SAE @ 4750 rpm; 1980: 160 hp SAE @ 4200 rpm later, 190 hp SAE @ 4750 rpm; 1975 California: 180 hp SAE
Compression ratio	8.8:1 U.S. 8:1
Torque	38.5 mkg @ 3000 rpm (278.5 ft/lb); U.S. 1977: 32.25 mkg @ 3000 rpm (220 ft/lb); 1980: 31.9 mkg @ 2500 rpm (230 ft/lb) U.S.: 33.0 mkg @ 3000 rpm (238.8 ft/lb); 1975 California: 232 ft/lb
Fuel injection	Bosch electronic
Engine speed at 100 km/hr	2865 rpm U.S.: 2700 rpm
Gear ratios	I. 3.98:1 U.S. automatic I. 2.31:1 II. 2.39:1 II. 1.46:1 III. 1.46:1 III. 1.00:1 IV. 1.00:1
Rear axle ratio	3.07 U.S. 1979: 3.06; 1980: 2.65
Chassis	unit frame and body
Suspension	independent front and rear, double wishbones, diagonal-pivot swing axle
Brakes and area	disc, front vented, rear solid, 278/279mm (10.9/11.0 in)
Wheelbase	2815mm (110.8 in)
Track, front/rear	1452/1440mm (57.2/56.7 in)
Length	4740mm (186.6 in); 1979: 4750mm (187 in) U.S.: 196.4 in (4990mm)
Width	1790mm (70.5 in)
Height	1330mm (51.2 in)
Ground clearance	140mm (5.5 in)
Tires	205/70 VR 14
Turning circle	11.2 meters (36.7 ft); later 11.55 meters (36.9 feet); U.S.: 11.68 meters (38.3 feet)
Steering type and ratio	recirculating ball (3.0 turns); servo assisted 15.9:1
Weight	1635 kg (3597 lbs) U.S.: 1735 kg (3817 lbs); 1977: 1750 kg (3860 lbs); 1979: 1720 kg (3795 lbs); 1980: 1700 kg (3750 lbs)
Maximum speed	215 km/hr (133.5 mph); 1979: 210 km/hr U.S.: 200 km/hr (124 mph)
Acceleration	8.5 sec 0-100 km/hr U.S.: 11 sec 0-100 km/hr
Fuel consumption	14.5 liters, super/100 km (16 mpg) (U.S. no lead fuel); 1979: at 120 km/hr, 15.8 liters (15 mpg)
Fuel tank capacity	90 liters (23.8 gallons)

The 450SLC coupe, 1977, U.S. version

The 280S sedan, 1972

Model 280S (1972-1980)

S = Super

The 280S model, one of the newly designed cars of the S-class, was first shown at the Paris Automobile Salon in 1972. It was the least expensive representative of the almost completely restyled new line of the large six- and eight-cylinder models which shared the same basic chassis and body.

The car appeared slightly wider, lower, and longer than the previous ones. The radiator shell was longer and wider and the front light section was integrated into a wide unit curving around to the side. The rear light cluster was also redesigned in the manner of the sports models, with the dirt-repelling feature. Many new safety features had been incorporated into the design.

The modified chassis had the new suspension system of the SL and SLC models which had proved superior to the former design.

The double overhead camshaft six-cylinder engine developed 160 DIN horsepower, but for the United States a detuned version of 120 SAE horsepower was supplied, with lowered compression ratio, for improved emission. It had a torque converter four-speed automatic transmission. That car also weighed 350 pounds more than the European model, and had consequently less performance. Still, the maximum speed was 170 kilometers (105 miles) per hour.

Prices and Production

The 280S four-door sedan sold in 1972 for	DM 23,810
in 1973 for	DM 25,030
in 1974 for	DM 26,165
in 1975 for	DM 28,050
in 1977 for	DM 30,158

In the United States the 280S sedan sold
in September 1974 (fully equipped) for
(East coast)................................$14,548
(West coast)...............................$14,698
in October 1975 (East coast)..................$16,545

Production of the 280S model [116 V28] from August/September 1972 until July 1980)

was in	1972	3,787 units
	1973	15,340 units
	1974	20,808 units
	1975	21,996 units
	1976	18,031 units
	1977	17,080 units
	1978	15,307 units
	1979	9,208 units
	1980	1,291 units
	total	122,848 units

The 280S sedan, 1974

Specifications

	280S
Engine type	6 cyl double overhead camshafts (M110)
Bore and stroke	86 x 78.8mm (3.41 x 3.10 in)
Displacement	2746 cc (168 cu in)
Power output	160 hp (DIN) @ 5500 rpm (180 hp SAE); 1977: 156 hp (DIN) U.S.: 120 hp SAE @ 4800 rpm; 1975 California: 123 hp SAE @ 5000 rpm
Compression ratio	9:1 U.S. 8:1
Torque	23 mkg @ 4000 rpm (166.4 ft/lb) U.S.: 15.5 mkg @ 2800 rpm (112.1 ft/lb) 1975: 143 ft/lb @ 2800 rpm; California: 143 @ 3600 rpm
Carburetion	dual downdraft carburetor Solex 4 A 1
Engine speed at 100 km/hr	3140 rpm by 1976: 3355 rpm
Gear ratios	I. 3.98:1 (14.69) 1976: I. 3.90:1 automatic (optional): I. 3.98:1 II. 2.39:1 (8.82) II. 2.30:1 II. 2.39:1 III. 1.46:1 (5.39) III. 1.41:1 III. 1.46:1 IV. 1.00:1 (3.69) IV. 1.00:1 IV. 1.00:1
Rear axle ratio	3.69
Chassis	unit frame and body
Suspension	independent front and rear, double wishbones, diagonal-pivot swing axle
Brakes and area	disc, front vented, rear solid, 278/279mm (10.9/11.0)
Wheelbase	2865mm (112.8 in)
Track, front/rear	1525/1505mm (60.0/59.3 in)
Length	4960mm (195.3 in)
Width	1865mm (73.4 in)
Height	1425mm (56.1 in)
Ground clearance	150mm (5.9 in)
Tires	185 HR 14
Turning circle	11.4 meters (37.4 ft)
Steering type and ratio	recirculating ball (2.7 turns); servo assisted 15.6:1
Weight	1610 kg (3542 lbs) U.S.: 3890 lbs
Maximum speed	190 km/hr (118 mph) U.S.: 170 km/hr (105.5 mph); 185 km/hr (115 mph)
Acceleration	13.5 sec 0-100 km/hr; (U.S.: no lead fuel)
Fuel consumption	12.5 liters/100 km (18.75 mpg) (U.S.: no lead fuel)
Fuel tank capacity	96 liters (25.4 gallons)

Front view of the 280S sedan, 1975, U.S. version

The 280SE sedan, 1972

Model 280SE (1972-1980)

S = Super, E (Einspritzung) = fuel injection

The 280SE model, also introduced at the Paris Salon in 1972, was the fuel-injected version of the six-cylinder sedan of the newly designed S-class of passenger cars. It had the same dimensions as the carburetor model and shared the body and chassis with the more powerful eight-cylinder cars.

The new model weighed 124 kilograms (273 pounds) more than the former 280SE model which it replaced, but with the double overhead camshaft engine of 185 DIN horsepower, against the 160 formerly, the performance was actually superior to the older model.

For the United States market in 1977 the car got a detuned engine of 142 SAE horsepower (137 in California) and consequently much lower torque. Horsepower and torque were also lowered in the European version. But the performance of this fine, fast six-cylinder touring sedan was still quite good, and in subsequent years the sedan was actually made lighter by 50 kilograms.

Prices and Production

The 280SE four-door sedan sold in 1972 for.........DM 25,530
  in 1973 for..............................DM 26,810
  in 1974 for..............................DM 28,020
  in 1975 for..............................DM 30,900
  in 1977 for..............................DM 32,289
In the United States the 280SE sedan sold
  in March 1977 (East coast) for.................$19,411
  in February 1979 (East coast)..................$26,177

Production of the 280SE model [116 E28] (from August/September 1972 until July 1980)

was in 1972	3,737	units
1973	18,266	units
1974	18,634	units
1975	17,376	units
1976	17,968	units
1977	26,903	units
1978	23,571	units
1979	22,568	units
1980	1,752	units
total	150,775	units

The 280SE sedan, 1974

Specifications

	280SE
Engine type	6 cyl double overhead camshafts (M 110)
Bore and stroke	86 x 78.8mm (3.41 x 3.10 in)
Displacement	2746 cc (168 cu in)
Power output	185 hp (DIN) @ 6000 rpm (205 hp SAE); 1977: 177 hp (DIN) U.S. 1977: 142 hp SAE @ 5750 rpm; 1980: 140 hp SAE @ 5500 rpm; California: 137 hp @ 5750 rpm
Compression ratio	9:1 U.S. 1977: 8:1
Torque	24.5 mkg @ 4500 rpm (175.8 ft/lb); U.S. 1977: 21.4 mkg @ 4600 rpm (149 ft/lb); California: 20.5 mkg @ 4600 rpm (142 ft/lb)
Fuel injection	Bosch electronic
Engine speed at 100 km/hr	3140 rpm; by 1976 (automatic optional): 3375 rpm
Gear ratios	I. 3.98:1 (14.69) 1976: I. 3.90:1 I. 3.98:1 automatic (optional) II. 2.39:1 (8.82) II. 2.30:1 II. 2.31:1 III. 1.46:1 (5.39) III. 1.41:1 III. 1.46:1 IV. 1.00:1 (3.69) IV. 1.00:1 IV. 1.00:1
Rear axle ratio	3.69 U.S. 1978: 3.58
Chassis	unit frame and body
Suspension	independent front and rear, double wishbones, diagonal-pivot swing axle
Brakes and area	disc, front vented, rear solid, 278/279mm (10.9/11.0 in)
Wheelbase	2865mm (112.8 in)
Track, front/rear	1525/1505mm (60.0/59.3 in) U.S. 1977 front: 1521mm (59.9 in)
Length	4960mm (195.3 in) U.S. 1977: 5220mm (205.5 in)
Width	1865mm (73.4 in) 1976: 1870mm (73.6 in)
Height	1425mm (56.1 in)
Ground clearance	150mm (5.9 in)
Tires	185 HR 14
Turning circle	11.4 meters (37.4 ft) U.S. 1979: 11.59 meters (38 ft)
Steering type and ratio	recirculating ball (2.7 turns); servo assisted 15.6:1 U.S. 1978: 3.2 turns
Weight	1610 kg (3542 lbs); U.S. 1977: 1770 kg (3905 lbs); 1978: 1615 kg (3560 lbs); 1979: 1730 kg (3820 lbs); 1980: 1720 kg (3795 lbs)
Maximum speed	200 km/hr (124 mph) automatic: 195 km/hr (121 mph)
Acceleration	12.5 sec 0-100 km/hr
Fuel consumption	12.5 liters/100 km (18.75 mpg)
Fuel tank capacity	96 liters (25.4 gallons)

The 280SE sedan, 1972, U.S. version

The 350SE sedan, 1972

Prices and Production

The 350SE four-door sedan sold in 1972 for . . . . .DM 28,860
   in 1973 for . . . . .DM 30,260
   in 1974 for . . . . .DM 31,615
   in 1975 for . . . . .DM 34,860
   in 1977 for . . . . .DM 36,430

Production of the 350SE model [116 E35] (from March/August 1972 until September 1980)

was in	1972	4,353 units
	1973	14,340 units
	1974	7,266 units
	1975	5,447 units
	1976	4,734 units
	1977	5,723 units
	1978	4,964 units
	1979	4,099 units
	1980	214 units
	total	51,140 units

The 350SEL four-door sedan sold in 1973 for . . . . .DM 34,865
   in 1974 for . . . . .DM 36,415
   in 1975 for . . . . .DM 40,160
   in 1977 for . . . . .DM 38,550

Production of the 350SEL model [116 E35] (from September/November 1973 until June 1980)

was in	1973	58 units
	1974	529 units
	1975	552 units
	1976	718 units
	1977	807 units
	1978	911 units
	1979	653 units
	1980	38 units
	total	4,266 units

Model 350SE (1972-1980)

S = Super, E (Einspritzung) = fuel injection

The 350SE was the third of the newly designed cars of the S-class which made their debut at the Paris Auto Show in 1972. It was the eight-cylinder edition of this new body style automobile. With the 3.5-liter displacement engine of 200 DIN horsepower and a weight of 1,675 kilograms (3,685 pounds), the car achieved a maximum speed of 205 kilometers (127 miles) per hour and accelerated to 100 kilometers in 11.5 seconds, a fine performance figure. (Torque was rated at 32 mkg or 321 ft/lb. at 4,200 rpm.)

That these newly styled and improved cars were well accepted by the automobile-buying public is indicated by the production figures. For 1972 it was about 4,000 units (of each of the three new models) and for the first full year of manufacture it reached nearly 15,000 units.

Model 350SEL (1973-1980)

SE L (Lang) = long wheelbase chassis

The 350SEL was the other of the two new models shown first to the public at the Geneva Auto Show in 1974. It was, if anything, a more luxurious version of the other longer wheelbase sedan exhibited at the Salon. With the 3.5-liter eight-cylinder engine, identical to that of the 350SE model, developing 200 (DIN) horsepower, it had a slightly better maximum speed (205 kilometers per hour) than that of the six-cylinder 280SEL model.

With other models of the S-class, the new 350SEL sedan shared all of the newest safety and technical features of this top line of cars.

The 350SEL sedan, 1974

Specifications

	350SE	350SEL
Engine type	V-8 cyl overhead camshafts (M 116)	V-8 cyl overhead camshafts (M 116)
Bore and stroke	92 x 65.8mm (3.62 x 2.59 in)	92 x 65.8mm (3.62 x 2.59 in)
Displacement	3499 cc (213.5 cu in)	3499 cc (213.5 cu in)
Power output	200 hp (DIN) @ 5800 rpm (230 hp SAE @ 6050 rpm); 1977: 195 hp (DIN)	200 hp (DIN) @ 5800 rpm (230 hp SAE @ 6050 rpm); 1977: 195 hp (DIN)
Compression ratio	9.5:1	9.5:1
Torque	29.2 mkg @ 4000 rpm (32 mkg @ 4200 rpm 231.5 ft/lb)	29.2 mkg @ 4000 rpm (32 mkg @ 4200 rpm 231.5 ft/lb)
Fuel injection	Bosch electronic	Bosch electronic
Engine speed at 100 km/hr	2945 rpm; by 1976 (automatic optional): 3295 rpm	2945 rpm; by 1976 (automatic optional): 3295 rpm
Gear ratios	I. 3.90:1 1976: I. 3.96:1 I. 2.31:1 automatic (optional) II. 2.30:1 II. 2.34:1 II. 1.46:1 III. 1.41:1 III. 1.43:1 III. 1.00:1 IV. 1.00:1 IV. 1.00:1	I. 3.90:1 1976: I. 2.31:1 automatic II. 2.30:1 II. 1.46:1 III. 1.41:1 III. 1.00:1 IV. 1.00:1
Rear axle ratio	3.46	3.46
Chassis	unit frame and body	unit frame and body
Suspension	independent front and rear, double wishbones, diagonal-pivot swing axle	independent front and rear, double wishbones, diagonal-pivot swing axle, anti-sway bars
Brakes and area	disc, front vented, rear solid, 278/279mm (10.9/11.0 in)	disc, power assisted, two circuit hydraulic, 278/279mm (10.9/11.0 in)
Wheelbase	2865mm (112.8 in)	2965mm (116.7 in)
Track, front/rear	1525/1505mm (60.0/59.3 in)	1525/1505mm (60/59.3 in)
Length	4960mm (195.3 in)	5060mm (199.2 in)
Width	1865mm (73.4 in)	1865mm (73.4 in)
Height	1425mm (56.1 in)	1430mm (56.3 in)
Ground clearance	150mm (5.9 in)	147mm (5.8 in)
Tires	205/70 HR 14	205/70 HR 14
Turning circle	11.4 meters (37.4 ft)	11.9 meters (39 ft)
Steering type and ratio	recirculating ball (2.7 turns); servo assisted 15.6:1	recirculating ball (3.0 turns), servo assisted
Weight	1675 kg (3685 lbs)	1700 kg (3740 lbs)
Maximum speed	205 km/hr (127 mph); 1977: 200 km/hr (124 mph)	205 km/hr (127 mph); 200 km/hr (124 mph)
Acceleration	11.5 sec 0-100 km/hr	11.5 sec 0-100 km/hr
Fuel consumption	13 liters/100 km (18 mpg)	13 liters/100 km (18 mpg)
Fuel tank capacity	96 liters (25.4 gallons)	96 liters (25.4 gallons)

The 230/4 sedan, 1973

Model 230/4 (1972-1976)

The 230/4 model was one of the two new passenger car models first introduced at the Frankfurt Auto Show in 1973. It replaced the 220 sedan which had been manufactured since 1967. The new four-cylinder engine with a stroke of 83.6 milimeters and bore of 93.75 millimeters developed 110 horsepower and gave the sedan a maximum speed of 170 kilometers (106 miles) per hour against the 161 of the former. Acceleration was the same. However, the new engine used less effort to accomplish this.

The new body had a wider radiator grille and was slightly lower in front and was similar to those of the current S-class models. With these eleven larger models the four-cylinder car shared the suspension and other, modern advanced design and safety features. A total of 24 different models of passenger cars were offered that year.

The 230 model, as it was designated for the United States market, was the lowest priced gasoline-engined Mercedes sedan, and was a good, dependable, and economical car. The roadability of this four-cylinder sedan was excellent, although it did not, of course, have the performance of the top line, the eight-cylinder models.

Prices and Production

The 230/4 four-door sedan sold in 1973 for	DM 15,210
in 1974 for	DM 15,875
in 1975 for	DM 17,505
Power steering	DM 515
Automatic transmission	DM 1,440

In the United States the 230 sedan sold
in November 1973 for (with automatic transmission)

(East coast)	$ 8,420
(West coast)	$ 8,530
in September 1974 (East coast)	$ 9,357
in October 1975 (East coast)	$ 10,497

Production of the 230/4 model [115 V23] (from January/August 1973 until December 1976)

was in	1972	7 units
	1973	9,568 units
	1974	30,013 units
	1975	35,073 units
	1976	13,104 units
	total	87,765 units

The 230/4 sedan, 1973

Specifications

	230/4
Engine type	4 cyl overhead camshaft (M 115)
Bore and stroke	93.75 x 83.6mm (3.69 x 3.29 in)
Displacement	2277 cc (140.8 cu in)
Power output	110 hp (DIN) @ 4800 rpm; (U.S.: 95 hp SAE @ 4800 rpm) 1975: 93 hp SAE @ 4800 rpm 1975 California: 85 hp SAE @ 4500 rpm
Compression ratio	9:1 U.S. 8:1
Torque	19 mkg @ 2500 rpm (137.5 ft/lb); U.S.: 17.7 mkg @ 2500 rpm 128 ft/lb 1975: 125 ft/lb, California: 122 ft/lb
Carburetion	Crossdraft carburetor Stromberg 175 CDT
Engine speed at 100 km/hr	3180 rpm
Gear ratios	I. 3.90:1 II. 2.30:1 III. 1.41:1 IV. 1.00:1
Rear axle ratio	3.69 U.S. 3.92
Chassis	unit frame and body
Suspension	independent front and rear, double wishbones, diagonal-pivot swing axle, anti- sway bars
Brakes and area	disc, hydraulic dual circuit, 273/279mm (10.8/11.0 in)
Wheelbase	2750mm (108.3 in)
Track, front/rear	1448/1.440mm (57.0/56.7 in)
Length	4680mm (184.3 in) U.S.: 195.5 in
Width	1770mm (69.7 in)
Height	1440mm (56.7 in)
Ground clearance	175mm (6.9 in)
Tires	175 SR 14
Turning circle	11 meters (36.1 ft)
Steering type and ratio	recirculating ball (3.0 turns), servo assisted
Weight	1350 kg (2970 lbs) U.S.: 1470 kg (3234 lbs)
Maximum speed	170 km/hr (106 mph)
Acceleration	13.7 sec 0-100 km/hr
Fuel consumption	11.4 liters, super/100 km (20.5 mpg) (U.S.: no lead fuel)
Fuel tank capacity	65 liters (17.2 gallons)

Front view of the 230/4 sedan, 1973

Rear view of the 230/4 sedan, 1973

Model 240D (1973-1976)

D = Diesel

The 240D sedan was one of two new models first shown to the public at the Frankfurt Auto Show in 1973. It was an addition to the fast-selling diesel-engined passenger cars of the 200D and 220D models. With a larger displacement, the four-cylinder engine developed 65 horsepower (against the 55 and 60 of the other two models). It shared with the new 230.4 engine other advancements in engine design.

In the customary tradition, the body style of these two cars was exactly alike. All of the new features of the gasoline-engined model were available to those who preferred the fantastic economy of the diesel-engined car. With the cylinder dimensions of the 240D, engineers believed that they had achieved the ultimate in passenger car development, for the 600 cubic centimeter displacement seemed the very ideal size.

The 240D engine ran slower than the others (at 3,180 revolutions against 3,375 at 100 kilometers per hour) and maximum speed was increased to 138 kilometers per hour against the 130 and 135 of the smaller engined cars.

In August 1973 the long chassis diesel limousine had the 240D engine installed instead of the former 220D. All of the specifications of the earlier model applied to this one except for the maximum speed (now 135 km/hr; automatic: 130 km/hr.) and the fuel consumption (now 11.5 liters; automatic: 12.5 liters per 100 kilometers). The overall weight had also increased slightly (by 15 kg) to 1,555 kg (3,421 lbs.).

The 240D sedan, 1974, U.S. version

Prices and Production

The 240D four-door sedan sold in 1973 for	DM 15,985
in 1974 for	DM 16,710
in 1975 for	DM 18,425
Power steering	DM 515
Automatic transmission	DM 1,440
The 240D long-wheelbase limousine sold in 1973 for	DM 22,590
but the price increased gradually until it reached in 1975	DM 26,075
In the United States the 240D sedan sold in November 1973 for (East coast)	$ 8,140
(West coast)	$ 8,250
and with automatic transmission (East coast)	$ 8,715
(West coast)	$ 8,825
in September 1974 (East coast)	$ 8,862
and with automatic transmission	$ 9,479
in October 1975 (East coast)	$ 9,930
and with automatic transmission	$ 10,621

Production of the 240D model [115 D24] (from February/August 1973 until December 1976)

was in	1973	16,512 units
	1974	60,928 units
	1975	38,019 units
	1976	15,860 units
	total	131,319 units

The 240D sedan, 1975, U.S. version

Specifications

	240D
Engine type	4 cyl diesel overhead camshaft (OM 616)
Bore and stroke	91 x 92.4mm (3.58 x 3.64 in)
Displacement	2376 cc (146.7 cu in)
Power output	65 hp (DIN) @ 4200 rpm (62 hp SAE @ 4000 rpm)
Compression ratio	21:1
Torque	14 mkg @ 2400 rpm (13.4 mkg 97 ft/lb @ 2400 rpm)
Fuel injection	Bosch four plunger pump
Engine speed at 100 km/hr	3180 rpm
Gear ratios	I. 3.90:1 II. 2.30:1 III. 1.41:1 IV. 1.00:1
Rear axle ratio	3.69
Chassis	unit frame and body
Suspension	independent front and rear, double wishbones, diagonal-pivot swing axle, anti- sway bars
Brakes and area	disc, hydraulic dual circuit, 273/279mm (10.8/11.0 in)
Wheelbase	2750mm (108.3 in)
Track, front/rear	1448/1440mm (57.0/56.7 in)
Length	4680mm (184.3 in) U.S.: 195.5 in
Width	1770mm (69.7 in)
Height	1440mm (56.7 in)
Ground clearance	175mm (6.9 in)
Tires	175 SR 14
Turning circle	11 meters (36.1 ft)
Steering type and ratio	recirculating ball (3.0 turns), servo assisted
Weight	1390 kg (3058 lbs) U.S.: 1457 kg (3205 lbs)
Maximum speed	138 km/hr (85.7 mph)
Acceleration	24.6 sec 0-100 km/hr
Fuel consumption	9.5 liters/100 km (24.75 mpg)
Fuel tank capacity	65 liters (17.2 gallons) 1976: 80 liters (20.6 gallons)

Longitudinal and cross section of the OM 616 engine, 1973

Installation of the diesel engine, 1973

The 280SEL sedan, 1974

Model 280SEL (1973-1980)

SE L (Lang) = long wheelbase chassis

The 280SEL was first shown at the Geneva Salon in early 1974. In the true tradition of the company, it was a stretched version of the 280SE model sedan. The wheelbase was, as before on these long models, ten centimeters longer than that of the regular sedan, all of which benefitted the passengers in the rear seat. With the same engine of 2.8 liters displacement and 185 horsepower (DIN), the performance was equal to that of the shorter car. Maximum speed was calculated at 200 kilometers (124 miles) per hour.

The 280SEL model was one of 24 different passenger car models offered that year by Mercedes-Benz and fulfilled the specific needs of a wide range of preference by the motorists.

The 280SEL was meant to be a car for the executive, to travel in style, for it was a most comfortable long distance touring sedan. With the extra space for the passengers in the rear seats, easier entry and exit, the greater leg room, this sedan filled a certain need in the passenger car program of the company.

Prices and Production

The 280SEL four-door sedan sold in 1974 for . . . . .DM 30,680
    in 1975 for . . . . .DM 33,340
    in 1977 for . . . . .DM 34,854

Production of the 280SEL model [116 E28] (from October 1973/ April 1974 until May 1980)

was in		
1973	1 unit
1974	535 units
1975	716 units
1976	1,042 units
1977	1,295 units
1978	1,622 units
1979	1,551 units
1980	270 units
total	7,032 units

The 280SEL sedan, 1974

Specifications

	280SEL
Engine type	6 cyl double overhead camshafts (M 110)
Bore and stroke	86 x 78.8mm (3.41 x 3.10 in)
Displacement	2746 cc (168 cu in)
Power output	185 hp (DIN) @ 6000 rpm (205 hp SAE); 1977: 177 hp (DIN)
Compression ratio	9:1
Torque	24.3 mkg @ 4500 rpm (175.8 ft/lb)
Fuel injection	Bosch electronic
Engine speed at 100 km/hr	3140 rpm; 3375 rpm
Gear ratios	I. 3.90:1 1976: I. 3.98:1 automatic (optional) II. 2.30:1 II. 2.39:1 III. 1.41:1 III. 1.46:1 IV. 1.00:1 IV. 1.00:1
Rear axle ratio	3.69
Chassis	unit frame and body
Suspension	independent front and rear, double wishbones, diagonal-pivot swing axle, anti-sway bars
Brakes and area	disc, power assisted, two circuit hydraulic, 278/279mm (10.9/11.0 in)
Wheelbase	2965mm (116.7 in)
Track, front/rear	1525/1505mm (60/59.3 in)
Length	5060mm (199.2 in)
Width	1865mm (73.4 in)
Height	1430mm (56.3 in)
Ground clearance	147mm (5.8 in)
Tires	185 HR 14
Turning circle	11.9 meters (39 ft)
Steering type and ratio	recirculating ball (3.0 turns), servo assisted
Weight	1645 kg (3619 lbs)
Maximum speed	200 km/hr (124 mph); 195 km/hr (121 mph)
Acceleration	12 sec 0-100 km/hr
Fuel consumption	12.5 liters/100 km (18.75 mpg)
Fuel tank capacity	96 liters (25.4 gallons)

The 280SEL sedan, 1974

The 280SEL sedan, 1974

Front view of the 450SE sedan, 1974

Model 450SE (1972-1980)

S = Super, E (Einspritzung) = fuel injection

The 450SE sedan was introduced to the public at the Geneva Salon in March 1973. Along with the 450SEL, 450SLC, these cars represented the top of the S-class and included all of the newest technological and safety features developed by the engineers. These incorporated design features of the C111 experimental car, such as the front axle geometry and design first tested on that amazing vehicle, and increased lateral and roll-over protection, distinct crumble zones and other safety features first tested with the experimental safety vehicles ESF 5, 13 and 22.

The 450SE was quickly recognized as one of the finest cars ever produced by Daimler-Benz and the group of forty-five European automotive journalists voted it the Car of the Year. The basic criteria were overall engineering concept with special regard to safety, aesthetic impression, styling and design, and price in relation to value offered.

While the 450SE had the 225 horsepower (DIN) engine and three- or four-speed torque converter, the U.S. version had a detuned unit which developed 190 SAE horsepower and had the three-speed automatic transmission only. Still, *Road & Track* considered the car the Best Sedan in the World.

In Europe the car was also judged Car of the Year by the automotive journalists representing six leading publications: Auto Visie of Holland, Stern of Germany, Daily Telegraph Magazine of Britain, L'Equipe of France, Quattroruote of Italy and ViBilägare of Sweden.

Prices and Production

The 450SE four-door sedan sold in 1973 for . . . . .DM 33,970
  in 1974 for . . . . .DM 35,500
  in 1975 for . . . . .DM 39,150
  in 1977 for . . . . .DM 40,925

The 450SE four-door sedan sold in the United States in March 1973 (fully equipped) for
  (East coast) $13,396
  (West coast) $13,491
  in November 1973 (East coast) $15,820
  in September 1974 (East coast) $17,713
  in October 1975 (East coast) $19,989

Production of the 450SE model [116 E45] (from August/December 1972 until April 1980)

was in	1972	52 units
	1973	13,400 units
	1974	7,579 units
	1975	4,672 units
	1976	5,188 units
	1977	4,223 units
	1978	3,570 units
	1979	2,746 units
	1980	174 units
	total	41,604 units

The 450SE sedan, 1974, U.S. version

Specifications

	450SE
Engine type	V-8 cyl overhead camshafts (M 117)
Bore and stroke	92 x 85mm (3.62 x 3.35 in)
Displacement	4520 cc (275.8 cu in)
Power output	225 hp (DIN) @ 5000 rpm; U.S.: 190 hp SAE @ 4750 rpm; 1977: 217 hp (DIN) 1975 California: 180 hp SAE
Compression ratio	8.8:1 U.S.: 8:1
Torque	38.5 mkg @ 3000 rpm (278.5 ft/lb) U.S.: 33.0 mkg @ 3000 rpm (238.8 ft/lb); 1975 California: 232 ft/lb
Fuel injection	Bosch electronic
Engine speed at 100 km/hr	2865 rpm U.S.: 2700 rpm
Gear ratios	I. 3.98:1 U.S. automatic I. 2.31:1 II. 2.39:1 II. 1.46:1 III. 1.46:1 III. 1.00:1 IV. 1.00:1
Rear axle ratio	3.07
Chassis	unit frame and body
Suspension	independent front and rear, double wishbones, diagonal-pivot swing axle
Brakes and area	disc, front vented, rear solid, 278/279mm (10.9/11.0 in)
Wheelbase	2860mm (112.6 in)
Track, front/rear	1525/1505mm (60.0/59.3 in)
Length	4960mm (195.3 in) U.S.: 205.5 in
Width	1870mm (73.6 in)
Height	1425mm (56.1 in)
Ground clearance	150mm (5.9 in)
Tires	205/70 VR 14
Turning circle	11.4 meters (37.4 ft)
Steering type and ratio	recirculating ball (2.7 turns); servo assisted 15.6:1
Weight	1740 kg (3828 lbs) U.S.: 4070 lbs
Maximum speed	210 km/hr (130 mph) U.S.: 205 km/hr (127 mph)
Acceleration	9.3 sec 0-100 km/hr U.S.: 10.8 sec 0-100 km/hr
Fuel consumption	14.5 liters/100 km (16 mpg) (U.S.: no lead fuel)
Fuel tank capacity	96 liters (25.4 gallons)

The console of the 450SE sedan, 1977

The 450SE sedan, 1974

The 450SEL sedan, 1973

Prices and Production

The 450SEL four-door sedan sold in 1973 for........DM 38,575
   in 1974 for..............................DM 40,300
   in 1975 for..............................DM 44,450
   in 1977 for..............................DM 45,798

The 450SEL four-door sedan sold in the United States
   in March 1973 (fully equipped) for
     (East coast)................................$14,605
     (West coast)................................$14,698
   in November 1973 (East coast)..................$17,400
   in September 1974 (East coast).................$19,106
   in October 1975 (East coast)...................$21,709
   in March 1977 (East coast).....................$24,506
   in February 1979 (East coast)..................$32,858

Production of the 450SEL model [116 E45] (from December 1972 until June 1980)

was in	1972	24 units
	1973	6,930 units
	1974	8,350 units
	1975	6,167 units
	1976	9,650 units
	1977	10,042 units
	1978	8,505 units
	1979	8,217 units
	1980	1,690 units
	total	59,575 units

Model 450SEL (1972-1980)

SE L (Lang) = long wheelbase chassis

The 450SEL sedan, also first shown at the Geneva Auto Show in 1973, was basically the same car as the regular length 450SE. With a fifteen-centimeter longer wheelbase, only the rear passenger benefited from that change. The interior was nearly the same as that of the SE model, with headrest, safety belts, electrically operated windows, center locking system, and such safety features as standard equipment. Velour carpeting and leather upholstery were some of the finer appointments over the 450E model.

The rear diagonal swing axle had been further developed for the 450 models because of the high torque and fitted with an anti-squat device, eliminating entirely rear end dipping when aggressively accelerating from a standstill. The hydraulic dual circuit brake with vacuum booster and disc brakes on all four wheels was, of course, standard on these models as on the other S-class cars.

In the United States, the 450SEL had the same detuned engine as the regular sedan and shared all other alterations with it to comply with the more stringent emission controls and regulations on safety.

The 450SEL sedan, 1979, U.S. version

Specifications

	450SEL
Engine type	V-8 cyl overhead camshafts (M 117)
Bore and stroke	92 x 85mm (3.62 x 3.35 in)
Displacement	4520 cc (275.8 cu in)
Power output	225 hp (DIN) @ 5000 rpm; 1977: 217 hp (DIN) U.S.: 190 hp SAE @ 4750 rpm; 1975 California: 180 hp SAE; 1977: 180 hp SAE @ 4750 rpm; 1980: 160 hp SAE @ 4200 rpm
Compression ratio	8.8:1 U.S. 8:1
Torque	38.5 mkg @ 3000 rpm (278.5 ft/lb); U.S.: 33.0 mkg @ 3000 rpm (240 ft/lb); 1975 California: 232 ft/lb U.S. 1977: 32.25 mkg @ 3000 rpm (220 ft/lb); 1979: 31.9 mkg @ 2500 rpm (230 ft/lb)
Fuel injection	Bosch electronic
Engine speed at 100 km/hr	2865 rpm U.S.: 2700 rpm
Gear ratios	I. 3.98:1 U.S. automatic I. 2.31:1 II. 2.39:1 II. 1.46:1 III. 1.46:1 III. 1.00:1 IV. 1.00:1
Rear axle ratio	3.07; U.S. 1979: 3.06; 1980: 2.65
Chassis	unit frame and body
Suspension	independent front and rear, double wishbones, diagonal-pivot swing axle
Brakes and area	disc, front vented, rear solid, 278/279mm (10.9/11.0 in)
Wheelbase	2965mm (116.7 in)
Track, front/rear	1525/1505mm (60.0/59.3 in); U.S. 1977 front: 1521mm (59.9 in)
Length	5060mm (199.2 in) U.S.: 209.4 in (5320mm)
Width	1870mm (73.6 in)
Height	1430mm (56.3 in)
Ground clearance	150mm (5.9 in)
Tires	205/70 VR 14
Turning circle	11.8 meters (38.4 ft) U.S.: 11.9 meters (39 ft)
Steering type and ratio	recirculating ball (2.7 turns); servo assisted 15.6:1
Weight	1740 kg (3828 lbs) U.S.: 4100 lbs (1864 kg); 1977: 4080 lbs (1850 kg); 1980: 3975 lbs (1800 kg)
Maximum speed	210 km/hr (130 mph) U.S.: 205 km/hr (127 mph)
Acceleration	9.3 sec 0-100 km/hr U.S.: 10.8 sec 0-100 km/hr
Fuel consumption	14.5 liters/100 km (16 mpg) (U.S.: no lead fuel)
Fuel tank capacity	96 liters (25.4 gallons)

The 240D 3.0 sedan, 1974

Model 240D 3.0/300D
(1974-1976)

D = Diesel

The 240D 3.0 made its appearance in July 1974. It was a radical and startling solution to the problem of increasing the available horsepower in a diesel-engined car and still maintain its size. Designated as the 300D in the United States, it was a luxury sedan (as was the 280) and was priced only slightly under that of the 280 sedan ($11,782 against $12,325), fully equipped with radio, air conditioning, power steering, power brakes, et al.

The five-cylinder diesel engine was basically the same as the four-cylinder unit of the 240D, except that another cylinder had been added. All dimensions and essential construction features were alike, but the Bosch injection pump was entirely redesigned. A centrifugal governor operated the metering rack and regulated the power output. The starting of the cold engine was decidedly easier than on previous diesel models, taking but a short time for the glow plug to heat up. Cylinder crank head and housing, head gasket, and the six main bearing crankshaft and oil pan were also new. Developing 80 DIN horsepower (U.S.: 77 SAE) and 17.5 mkg (U.S.: 115 ft/lb.) of torque, it gave the amazingly economical sedan a maximum speed of 92 miles (148 kilometers) per hour with the 3.46:1 rear axle ratio. The 240D, with the 3.69:1 rear axle ratio, had a maximum speed of 85.7 miles (138 kilometers) per hour.

Prices and Production

The 240D 3.0 four-door sedan sold in 1974 for . . . . . . .DM 18,815
   in 1975 for. . . . . .DM 19,915
In the United States the 300D sedan sold
   in September 1974 for (fully equipped)
      (East coast) . . . .$ 11,782
      (West coast) . . . .$ 11,921
   in October 1975 (East coast). . . . .$ 13,582

Production of the 240D 3.0 four-door sedan [115 D30] (from May 1974 until November 1976)

was in	1974	7,650 units
	1975	34,420 units
	1976	11,620 units
	total	53,690 units

Rear view of the 300D sedan, 1974

Specifications

	240D 3.0 / (300D)
Engine type	5 cyl diesel, overhead camshaft (OM 617)
Bore and stroke	91 x 92.4mm (3.58 x 3.64 in)
Displacement	2971 cc (183.4 cu in)
Power output	80 hp (DIN) @ 4000 rpm (77 hp SAE @ 4000 rpm)
Compression ratio	21:1
Torque	17.5 mkg @ 2400 rpm (16 mkg @ 2400 rpm 115.7 ft/lb)
Fuel injection	Bosch injector pump
Engine speed at 100 km/hr	2980 rpm
Gear ratios	I. 3.98:1 (13.77) II. 2.39:1 (8.27) III. 1.46:1 (5.05) IV. 1.00:1 (3.46)
Rear axle ratio	3.46
Chassis	unit frame and body
Suspension	independent front and rear, double wishbones, diagonal-pivot swing axle
Brakes and area	disc, front vented, rear solid, 273/279mm (10.8/11.0 in)
Wheelbase	2750mm (108.3 in)
Track, front/rear	1448/1440mm (57.0/56.7 in)
Length	4680mm (184.3 in) U.S.: 195.5 in
Width	1770mm (69.7 in)
Height	1440mm (56.7 in)
Ground clearance	175mm (6.9 in)
Tires	175 SR 14
Turning circle	11 meters (36.1 ft)
Steering type and ratio	recirculating ball (3.0 turns), servo assisted
Weight	1430 kg (3146 lbs) U.S.: 3450 lbs
Maximum speed	148 km/hr (92 mph) U.S.: 89 mph (143 km/hr)
Acceleration	20.6 sec 0-100 km/hr
Fuel consumption	10.8 liters/100 km (21.5 mpg)
Fuel tank capacity	65 liters (17.2 gallons); 1976: 80 liters (20.6 gallons)

Cutaway of the OM 617 diesel engine

Five-cylinder arrangement of the OM 617 engine

Model 450SEL 6.9 (1975-1980)

SE L (Lang) = long wheelbase chassis

The 450SEL 6.9 model was first publicly shown in 1974. It was a fast, powerful luxury sedan in the manner of the 300SEL 6.3 of 1968-1972. The sedan utilized the same body and chassis of the larger S-class, but had a hydropneumatic suspension system with four spring units carrying the weight of the vehicle. A constant self-leveling device kept the car at an even level under all road or load conditions, giving it a superb roadability. All of the technological improvements of the time were incorporated in the construction, making it truly an excellent automobile in every respect.

The 6.9-liter V-8 engine was an enlarged version of the tested powerplant used so successfully in the former 6.3 model and currently in the large 600 models. Many improvements had been accomplished since the time it was first introduced in the 6.3 sedan. With greater torque (405 ft/lb. against 369) and an increase in actual DIN horsepower to 286 from 250 formerly, the new 450SEL 6.9 car had a maximum speed of 140 miles (225 kilometers) per hour, although the new car weighed about 400 pounds more than the 6.3 model. The final drive had been reduced to 2.65:1 (against 2.85:1) which gave it a slightly greater maximum speed (about 3 mph), but reduced the acceleration somewhat.

In the words of *Road & Track* magazine, it was "the fastest, best sedan in the world."

The 450SEL 6.9 sedan, 1975

Prices and Production

The 450SEL 6.9 four-door sedan sold in 1975 for . . . . .DM 70,000
in 1977 for . . . . .DM 73,093
In the United States the 450SEL 6.9 four-door sedan sold
in February (East coast) for. $50,190
(West coast). $50,417

Production of the 450SEL 6.9 four-door sedan [116 E69] (from February/September 1975 until May 1980)

was in	1975	474 units
	1976	1,475 units
	1977	1,798 units
	1978	1,665 units
	1979	1,839 units
	1980	129 units
	total	7,380 units

The 450SEL 6.9 sedan, 1976, U.S. version

Specifications

	450SEL 6.9	
Engine type	V-8 cyl overhead camshafts (M 100)	
Bore and stroke	107 x 95mm (4.21 x 3.74 in)	
Displacement	6834 cc (417 cu in)	
Power output	286 hp (DIN) @ 4250 rpm	U.S.: 250 hp SAE @ 4000 rpm
Compression ratio	8.8:1	U.S.: 8.0:1
Torque	56 mkg @ 3000 rpm (405 ft/lb)	U.S.: 51.6 mkg @ 2500 rpm (360 ft/lb)
Fuel injection	Bosch electronic (K-Jetronic)	
Engine speed at 100 km/hr	2595 rpm	
Gear ratios	automatic I. 2.31:1 II. 1.46:1 III. 1.00:1	
Rear axle ratio	2.65	
Chassis	unit frame and body	
Suspension	independent front and rear, double wishbones, diagonal-pivot swing axle, hydropneumatic, self-leveling, torsion bar stabilizers	
Brakes and area	disc, vented front, solid rear, 278/279mm (10.9/11.0 in)	
Wheelbase	2960mm (116.5 in)	
Track, front/rear	1525/1505mm (60.0/59.3 in)	U.S.: 1521/1505mm (59.9/59.3 in)
Length	5060mm (199.2 in)	U.S.: 5335mm (210.0 in)
Width	1410mm (40mm with level adjustment) (57.1 in)	U.S.: 1425mm (56.1 in)
Height	1410mm (40mm with level adjustment) (57.1 in)	
Ground clearance	150mm (5.9 in)	
Tires	215/70 VR 14	
Turning circle	11.8 meters (38.7 ft)	U.S.: 12.18 meters (40 ft)
Steering type and ratio	recirculating ball (2.7 turns); servo assisted 15.6:1	
Weight	1935 kg (4257 lbs)	U.S.: 1990 kg (4390 lbs); 1979: 2010 kg (4435 lbs)
Maximum speed	225 km/hr (140 mph)	
Acceleration	7.4 sec 0-100 km/hr	
Fuel consumption	16 liters, super/100 km (14.75 mpg)	
Fuel tank capacity	96 liters (25.4 gallons)	

The instrument panel of the 6.9, 1976

The M 100 engine of the 450SEL 6.9, 1976

The 280SL roadster, 1974

# Model 280SL (1974-1981)
S = Sports, L (Leicht) = light

The 280SL was introduced in late 1974 as a less powerful (and consequently more economical) version of the larger engined sports cars. It shared the body and all appointments with the 350SL and 450SL fast touring models.

The engine specifications were exactly those of the other 280 cars, using the identical twin overhead camshaft six-cylinder powerplant of 185 horsepower. The 280SL weighed 45 kilograms (99 pounds) less than the 350SL and 85 kilograms (187 pounds) less than the 450SL. This still gave the smallest of the three sports cars a respectable acceleration of 9.5 seconds for the 0-100 km/hr. against the 8.8 for the 350SL and 8.5 for the 450SL. Maximum speed of the 280SL was 205 kilometers per hour (127 miles). Fuel consumption was 12.5 liters per 100 kilometers.

The 280SL model was available with the regular four-speed or five-speed transmission and the fully automatic transmission, while the other two larger-engined models had the automatic transmission and only the three-speed automatic transmission. (The 350SL had a four-speed transmission until July 1972.)

Prices and Production

The 280SL model sold in 1974 for . . . . .DM 32,445
in 1975 for . . . . .DM 34,335
in 1977 for . . . . .DM 35,619
in 1980 for . . . . .DM 44,522

Production of the 280SL model [107 E28] (from May/August 1974)

was in	1974	297 units
	1975	1,020 units
	1976	1,099 units
	1977	1,347 units
	1978	1,536 units
	1979	2,155 units
	1980	2,429 units

The 280SLC model sold in 1974 for . . . . .DM 37,200
in 1975 for . . . . .DM 39,385
in 1977 for . . . . .DM 41,196
in 1980 for . . . . .DM 49,155

Production of the 280SLC coupe [107 E28] (from May/August 1974 until September 1981)

was in	1974	300 units
	1975	1,312 units
	1976	1,508 units
	1977	1,624 units
	1978	1,553 units
	1979	1,741 units
	1980	1,510 units
	1981	1,118 units
total		10,666 units

# Model 280SLC (1974-1981)
S = Sports, L = Light, C = Coupe

The 280SLC was brought out at the same time as the 280SL, in late 1974. As in the sports car line, this smaller engined version of the SLC model was the most economical of the three sizes available. In all appointments as well as body style and specifications, it was identical to the 350SLC and the 450SLC models.

Performance was, of course, not as brisk as that of the other two larger engined versions of the luxury coupe line, but to customers concerned with the fuel shortage and ever-increasing prices, it seemed the right answer. Weight differentials and performance figures were the same as those cited on the SL models. (The 280SLC weighed 1,550 kilograms (3,410 pound), and still attained the same maximum speed as the SL model.)

As the 280SL, this coupe also came equipped with the four- or five-speed transmission or the fully automatic transmission, while the other larger engined SLCs had only the three-speed manual and the automatic three-speed transmission.

Specifications

	280SL	280SLC
Engine type	6 cyl double overhead camshafts (M 110)	
Bore and stroke	86 x 78.8mm (3.41 x 3.10 in)	
Displacement	2746 cc (168 cu in)	
Power output	185 hp (DIN) @ 6000 rpm; 1977: 177 hp (DIN); 1979: 185 hp (DIN) @ 5800 rpm	
Compression ratio	9:1	
Torque	24.3 mkg @ 4500 rpm (175.8 ft/lb)	
Fuel injection	Bosch electronic; 1979: mechanical, with air flow sensor	
Engine speed at 100 km/hr	3140 rpm; automatic: 3380 rpm	
Gear ratios	I. 3.98:1 (14.69) or I. 3.96:1 1976: I. 3.90:1 automatic: I. 3.98:1 1979: I. 3.98:1 automatic: I. 3.98:1 II. 2.39:1 (8.82) II. 2.34:1 II. 2.30:1 II. 2.39:1 II. 2.29:1 II. 2.39:1 III. 1.46:1 (5.39) III. 1.43:1 III. 1.41:1 III. 1.46:1 III. 1.45:1 III. 1.46:1 IV. 1.00:1 (3.69) IV. 1.00:1 IV. 1.00:1 IV. 1.00:1 IV. 1.00:1 IV. 1.00:1 V. 0.88:1	
Rear axle ratio	3.69 (for 5-speed 3.92)	
Chassis	unit frame and body	
Suspension	independent front and rear, double wishbones, diagonal-pivot swing axle	
Brakes and area	disc, front vented, rear solid, 278/279mm (10.9/11.0 in)	
Wheelbase	2460mm (96.9 in)	2820mm (111.0 in)
Track, front/rear	1452/1440mm (57.2/56.7 in)	
Length	4390mm (172.8 in)	4750mm (187 in)
Width	1790mm (70.5 in)	
Height	1300mm (51.2 in)	1330mm (52.4 in)
Ground clearance	140mm (5.5 in)	
Tires	185 HR 14	
Turning circle	10.34 meters (33.9 ft)	11.55 meters (36.9 ft)
Steering type and ratio	recirculating ball (3.0 turns); servo assisted 15.6:1	
Weight	1500 kg (3300 lbs)	1550 kg (3410 lbs)
Maximum speed	205 km/hr (127 mph); automatic: 200 km/hr (124 mph); 1977: 200 km/hr; automatic: 195 km/hr (121 mph)	
Acceleration	9.5 sec 0-100 km/hr; 1979: 10.1 sec; automatic: 11.0 sec	10.1 sec 0-100 km/hr; automatic: 11.0 sec
Fuel consumption	12.5 liters, super/100 km (18.75 mph); 1979: at 120 km/hr, 11.8 liters; automatic: 12.6 liters	
Fuel tank capacity	90 liters (23.8 gallons)	

The 200 sedan, 1979

Prices and Production

The 200 four-door sedan sold in 1976 for . . . . .DM 18,381
   in 1979 for. . . . . .DM 20,260
   in 1980 (M102) for. . . . . .DM 22,554
   In 1982 for. . . . . .DM 25,815

Production of the 200 model [123 V20] (from July 1975/February 1976 until August 1980)

was in	1975	5 units
	1976	26,374 units
	1977	39,112 units
	1978	35,884 units
	1979	34,190 units
	1980	23,207 units
	total	158,772 units

Production of the 200 (M102) model [123 V20] from October 1979/August 1980)

was in	1979	37 units
	1980	17,606 units
	1981	54,780 units
	1982	60,670 units

Model 200 (1975-   )

The 200 Sedan — W123 — was first introduced at the Geneva Auto Show in March 1976. It was the least powerful of the entire line of nine middle range sedans with the new body style, and was quite similar to the other existing models. The 200 through 250 models had round headlights, but otherwise the bodies were alike.

The new cars incorporated many new engineering features and high technical standards of the more expensive models. Some details will be mentioned in the descriptive text of subsequent models which shared these W123 body styles.

Because of the unusually high demands for the cars, production of the older W115 style 200 model, begun in 1967, was maintained and over 13,000 units were actually sold that first year when the new model was also available to the purchaser of a 200 sedan. However, production of the new 123 style was about twice that number during 1976.

In June 1980 an entirely new M102 four-cylinder carburetor engine was introduced. This new design had achieved improved fuel consumption, increased power output and smoother operation than the previous engine, the well proven M115.

Outwardly the car was the same as before, with no changes in the W123 chassis or body. Substantial changes were made, however, in the power unit and other mechanical parts. The 16% increase in power output, from 94 DIN horsepower to 109 horsepower for the new 1,997 cubic centimeter engine, allowed a longer rear axle ratio and with the 25% lighter new mechanical four-speed transmission a saving of from 9 to 13% of gasoline was accomplished.

The urban fuel consumption was rated at 13.3 liters with the manual transmission and 13.0 liters for the automatic for 100 kilometers, while the 120 kilometers per hour speed gave 10.7 and 10.9 liters, respectively, or an average of 21.5 miles per gallon, compared with the 18.3 average for the former 1,987 cc four-cylinder engine.

Production of the 200 sedan with the M102 engine began in March 1980 — although 37 units were built for exhaustive testing in October 1979 — and manufacture of the old engined models ceased in August of that year.

Specifications

	200	
Engine type	4 cyl overhead camshaft (M115)	4 cyl overhead camshaft (M102)
Bore and stroke	87 x 83.6 mm (3.43 x 3.29 in)	89 x 80.25 mm (3.50 x 3.16 in)
Displacement	1987 cc (121.27 cu in); 1979: 1988 cc	1997 cc (121.72 cu in)
Power output	94 hp (DIN) @ 4800 rpm (105 hp SAE)	109 hp (DIN) @ 5200 rpm
Compression ratio	9.0:1	9.0:1
Torque	16.1 mkg @ 3000 rpm (116.5 ft/lb)	17.3 mkg @ 3000 rpm (125.2 ft/lb)
Carburetion	Stromberg crossdraft 175 CD	Stromberg sidedraft 175 CDT
Maximum engine speed	6000 rpm	
Engine speed at 100 km/hr	3395 rpm; automatic: 3470 rpm	
Gear ratios	I. 3.90:1 I. 3.98:1 (automatic) II. 2.30:1 II. 2.39:1 III. 1.41:1 III. 1.46:1 IV. 1.00:1 IV. 1.00:1	I. 3.91:1 II. 2.52:1 (1982: 2.32:1) III. 1.42:1 IV. 1.00:1
Rear axle ratio	3.92	
Chassis	unit frame and body	
Suspension	independent front and rear, with coil springs; diagonal swing axle, coil springs, anti-roll bar. Optional level control; standard in 1979	
Brakes and area	dual circuit discs, power assisted, front brake pad wear indicator, 278/279 mm (10.9/11.0 in)	
Wheelbase	2795 mm (110.0 in)	
Track, front/rear	1488/1446 mm (58.6/56.9 in)	
Length	4725 mm (186.0 in)	
Width	1786 mm (70.3 in)	
Height	1438 mm (56.5 in)	
Tires	175 SR 14	
Turning circle	11.25 meters (36.9 feet); 1979: 11.29 meters (37 feet)	
Steering type and ratio	recirculating ball (4.0 turns), servo assisted	
Weight	1340 kg (2948 lbs)	
Maximum speed	160 km/hr (99 mph); automatic: 155 km/hr (96 mph)	168 km/hr (104 mph); automatic: 163 km/hr (101 mph)
Acceleration	15.2 sec 0-100 km/hr; automatic: 16.3 sec	14.4 sec 0-100 km/hr; automatic: 15.4 sec 0-100 km/hr
Fuel consumption	11.1 liters/100 km (21.3 mpg) 1979: at 120 km/hr: 12.5 liters; automatic: 13.2 liters	at 120 km/hr: 10.7 liters/100 km; automatic: 10.9 liters
Fuel tank capacity	65 liters (17.2 gallons)	

The 200D sedan, 1976

Model 200D (1975-   )

D = Diesel

The 200D model was, as usual, exactly as the gasoline-engined version and only different in the engine installation. The diesel power unit had been only slightly altered from that widely proven OM615 engine in the previous 200D line. Specifications were practically the same, but the engine speed at 100 kilometers per hour was now 3,395 revolutions per hour instead of 3,375. The maximum speed remained the same despite a 25-kilogram increase in total weight. Acceleration of the new style sedan was 31.0 seconds, just 1 second slower than before. Fuel consumption, always extremely miserly, was 8.3 liters for 100 kilometers, up 0.2 from the previous 29 miles per gallon.

All of the diesel engines had the oil filters placed so that it could be changed from above, saving time and effort. And the new type cylinder head gaskets required no maintenance.

The older model was still produced during the first year of availability of the 123 body style, but production was only slightly over 21,000 units against the nearly 39,000 built of the newer model.

Despite its relatively low power and consequently unexciting performance, this model was one of the most desired cars built by Daimler-Benz. The smallest of the diesel models had always found a huge number of enthusiastic buyers over the years, and with this latest body style, it was not different.

The fact that production was nearly twice as large as that of its gasoline-engined counterpart indicated its immense popularity. The fantastic economy of operation — and especially its miserly fuel consumption at this time when supplies were critical and rapidly becoming more expensive — this diesel model made great sense to the thousands of satisfied owners.

Over the five-year period from 1976 to 1980 a total of over 25,000 cars were manufactured, more than of any other diesel model made by Daimler-Benz.

Prices and Production

The 200D four-door sedan sold in 1976 for . . . . .DM 18,870
    in 1979 for. . . . . .DM 21,347
    in 1982 for. . . . . .DM 26,369

Production of the 200D model [123 D22] (from July 1975/February 1976)

was in	1975	5 units
	1976	36,894 units
	1977	56,378 units
	1978	49,359 units
	1979	52,834 units
	1980	56,435 units
	1981	51,152 units
	1982	44,661 units

Specifications	200D
Engine type	4 cyl diesel, overhead camshaft (OM 615)
Bore and stroke	87 x 83.6mm (3.43 x 3.29 in)
Displacement	1988 cc (121.27 cu in)
Power output	55 hp (DIN) @ 4200 rpm; 1979: 60 hp (DIN) @ 4400 rpm
Compression ratio	21:1
Torque	11.5 mkg @ 2400 rpm (83.2 ft/lb)
Fuel injection	Bosch four plunger pump
Maximum engine speed	5300 rpm
Engine speed at 100 km/hr	3395 rpm automatic: 3470 rpm
Gear ratios	I. 3.90:1 automatic: I. 3.98:1 II. 2.30:1 II. 2.39:1 III. 1.41:1 III. 1.46:1 IV. 1.00:1 IV. 1.00:1
Rear axle ratio	3.92
Chassis	unit frame and body
Suspension	independent front and rear, with coil springs; diagonal swing axle, coil springs, anti-roll bar. Optional level control; standard in 1979
Brakes and area	dual circuit discs, power assisted, front brake pad wear indicator, 278/279mm (10.9/11.0 in)
Wheelbase	2795mm (110.0 in)
Track, front/rear	1488/1466mm (58.6/56.9 in)
Length	4725mm (186.0 in)
Width	1786mm (70.3 in)
Height	1438mm (56.6 in)
Ground clearance	
Tires	175 SR 14
Turning circle	11.25 meters (36.9 ft); 1979: 11.29 meters (37 ft)
Steering type and ratio	recirculating ball (4.0 turns); servo assisted
Weight	1375 kg (3025 lbs)
Maximum speed	130 km/hr (81 mph); automatic: 125 km/hr (78 mph) 1979: 135 km/hr (84 mph) automatic: 130 km/hr (81 mph)
Acceleration	31 sec 0–100 km/hr; automatic: 33.2 sec; 1979: 27.4 sec; automatic: 29.4 sec
Fuel consumption	8.3 liters/100 km (28 mpg); 1979: at 120 km/hr 10.2 liters, automatic: 11.7 liters
Fuel tank capacity	65 liters (17.2 gallons)

Instrument panel of the 200D, 1976

The 220D sedan, 1976

Prices and Production

The 220D four-door sedan sold in 1976 for . . . . .DM 19,588
   in 1977 for. . . . . .DM 20,346

Production of the 220D model [123 D22] (from July 1975/February 1976 until March 1979)

was in 1975	4 units
1976	16,733 units
1977	19,323 units
1978	19,230 units
1979	1,446 units
total	56,736 units

Model 220D (1975-1979)

D = Diesel

The 220D model was undistinguishable outwardly from the smaller-engined diesel sedan. This intermediate model, between the 200D and 240D, had actually been the best selling of all the diesel-powered automobiles, with over 420,000 units being sold of the W115 body style (the 200D sold nearly 340,000 and the 240D over 131,000).

But sales of this new model with the W123 body — and perhaps the increasing popularity of the five-cylinder diesel-engined 3-liter sedan — did never even challenge the other available models and the 220D was discontinued early in 1979.

The 2,197-cubic centimeter diesel engine developed only five more horsepower than the 2-liter unit, and the curb weight of both models was within five kilograms of each other. Acceleration figures for the 220D were 28.1 seconds for the 0-100 kilometers per hour, about 3 seconds faster, and the top speed was 5 kilometers faster. Fuel consumption of this larger engined diesel was 9 liters against the 8.3 liters per 100 kilometers for the 200D. The critical power-to-weight ratio for the 200D was 25 kilograms per horsepower but that of the 220D was 23 kilograms.

Offered to satisfy the buyer of a most economic sedan, yet also giving him a slightly more powerful car than the 2-liter model, this 220D had lost popularity over the past years. Ever since the introduction of the 123 line of body styles, only about half as many of the smaller size were built, and it was only because the sales department believed that it should offer the largest possible choice of model sizes to its prospective customers that this 220D was kept in production. Its demise was clearly indicated long before manufacture of the model was stopped. Still, a production run of 56,736 units during the lifetime of this 220D was not too insignificant.

Specifications

	220D
Engine type	4 cyl diesel, overhead camshaft (OM 615)
Bore and stroke	87.0 x 92.4mm (3.43 x 3.64 in)
Displacement	2197 cc (134 cu in)
Power output	60 hp (DIN) @ 4200 rpm
Compression ratio	21:1
Torque	12.8 mkg @ 2400 rpm (92.6 ft/lb)
Fuel injection	Bosch four plunger pump
Engine speed at 100 km/hr	3395 rpm automatic: 3470 rpm
Gear ratios	I. 3.90:1 automatic: I. 3.98:1 II. 2.30:1 II. 2.39:1 III. 1.41:1 III. 1.46:1 IV. 1.00:1 IV. 1.00:1
Rear axle ratio	3.92
Chassis	unit frame and body
Suspension	independent front and rear, with coil springs; diagonal swing axle, coil springs, anti-roll bar. Optional level control; standard in 1979
Brakes and area	dual circuit discs, power assisted, front brake pad wear indicator, 278/279mm (10.9/11.0 in)
Wheelbase	2795mm (110.0 in)
Track, front/rear	1488/1466mm (58.6/56.9 in)
Length	4725mm (186.0 in)
Width	1786mm (70.3 in)
Height	1438mm (56.6 in)
Ground clearance	
Tires	175 SR 14
Turning circle	11.25 meters (36.9 ft)
Steering type and ratio	recirculating ball (4.0 turns); servo assisted
Weight	1380 kg (3036 lbs)
Maximum speed	135 km/hr (84 mph); automatic: 130 km/hr (81 mph)
Acceleration	28.1 sec 0-100 km/hr; automatic: 29.1 sec
Fuel consumption	9.0 liters/100 km (26 mpg)
Fuel tank capacity	65 liters (17.2 gallons)

Instrument panel and console of the 220D

Injection part of OM 615 engine

The 230 sedan, 1976

Prices and Production

The 230 four-door sedan sold in 1976 for . . . . .DM 19,203
    in 1979 for. . . . . .DM 21,336
    in 1980 (M102) for. . . . . .DM 25,221

Production of the 230 model [123 V23] (from July 1975/February 1976 until September 1981)

was in	1975	9 units
	1976	32,060 units
	1977	49,426 units
	1978	42,270 units
	1979	47,739 units
	1980	23,549 units
	1981	1,132 units
	total	196,185 units

Production of the 230E (M102) model [123 E23] (from October 1979/July 1980)

was in	1979	37 units
	1980	24,997 units
	1981	62,125 units
	1982	60,777 units

Model 230 (1975-1981)

The 230 model, the middle range of the smaller sedans, was also first shown at the Geneva Auto Show in 1976. It shared the body style with the 200 and 250 models, and as in those cars, it was outwardly recognizable by the round headlights.

Some of the features of these new bodies were that the entire roof frame and the front, center and rear pillars had a profile of a closed cross section for greater roll-over resistance. Lateral strength had also been improved over the old body style.

The front axle required no maintenance. The fuel tank, holding 65 liters (17.2 gallons), was positioned above the rear axle and the spare wheel was laid down horizontally to absorb tail end impact energy.

For the U.S. market and in the 1977 model year, this 230 sedan had gained 100 kilograms in weight (1450 kg or 3195 lbs) and 123 millimeters (to 109.0 in) in length over the European version. It was sold for another year and then dropped.

Again, production of the previous 230 model remained with over 13,000 cars built, but of the new style, more than 32,000 were produced that first year.

Model 230E (1979 -   )

E (Einspritzung) = fuel injection

The 230E sedan, introduced in June 1980, also had a brand new M102 four-cylinder fuel injected engine. Similar to the 2-liter unit, this mechanical fuel injection type displayed 2,299 cubic centimeters and developed 136 DIN horsepower at 5,100 revolutions per minute.

Fuel economy was considerably improved, and developing greater power, lower revolutions were sufficient for the same performance with consequently less stress on engine and driver than previously with the carburetor model. Urban cycle fuel consumption was rated at 13.6 liters for 100 kilometers with manual transmission (14.7 for the M115) and 13.5 with automatic transmission. At 120 kilometers per hour, fuel consumption was 10.4 and 11.0 liters, respectively, which gave an average of 22 miles per gallon (12.5 and 12.8 liters for the M115).

Over 25,000 units were built the first year, including the 37 cars for testing constructed the previous year, and it seemed that the regular 230 sedan would soon be phased out. For 1981 a greatly curtailed official manufacturing schedule was listed.

Specifications

	230		230E
Engine type	4 cyl overhead camshaft (M115)		4 cyl overhead camshaft (M102)
Bore and stroke	93.75 x 83.6 mm (3.69 x 3.29 in)		95.5 x 80.25 mm (3.74 x 3.16 in)
Displacement	2307 cc (140.8 cu in)		2299 cc (140.12 cu in)
Power output	109 hp (DIN) @ 4800 rpm; U.S. 1977: 86 hp SAE @ 4600 rpm		136 hp (DIN) @ 5100 rpm
Compression ratio	9.0:1	U.S. 1977: 8:1	9.0:1
Torque	18.9 mkg @ 3000 rpm (136.7 ft/lb) U.S. 1977: 16.8 mkg @ 3000 rpm (116 ft/lb)		20.9 mkg @ 3500 rpm (151.2 ft/lb)
Carburetion	Stromberg crossdraft 175 CD		Bosch mechanical (fuel injection)
Maximum engine speed	6000 rpm		6000 rpm
Engine speed at 100 km/hr	3195 rpm	automatic: 3275 rpm	
Gear ratios	I. 3.90:1 II. 2.30:1 III. 1.41:1 IV. 1.00:1	I. 3.98:1 (automatic) II. 2.39:1 III. 1.46:1 IV. 1.00:1	I. 3.91:1 II. 2.32:1 III. 1.42:1 IV. 1.00:1
Rear axle ratio	3.69		3.58
Chassis	unit frame and body		
Suspension	independent front and rear, with coil springs; diagonal swing axle, coil springs, anti-roll bar. Optional level control; standard in 1979		
Brakes and area	dual circuit discs, power assisted, front brake pad wear indicator, 278/279 mm (10.9/11.0 in)		
Wheelbase	2795 mm (110.0 in)		
Track, front/rear	1488/1446 mm (58.6/56.9 in)		
Length	4725 mm (186.0 in)	U.S. 1977: 4848 mm (190.9 in)	
Width	1786 mm (70.3 in)		
Height	1438 mm (56.5 in)		
Tires	175 SR 14		175 HR 14
Turning circle	11.25 meters (36.9 feet); 1979: 11.29 meters (37 feet) U.S. 1977: 11.29 meters (37 feet)		11.29 meters (37 feet)
Steering type and ratio	recirculating ball (4.0 turns), servo assisted; U.S. 1977: 2.7 turns		recirculating ball
Weight	1350 kg (2970 lbs)	U.S. 1977: 1450 kg (3195 lbs)	1360 kg (2992 lbs)
Maximum speed	170 km/hr (106 mph); automatic: 165 km/hr (103 mph)		180 km/hr (112 mph); automatic: 175 km/hr (109 mph)
Acceleration	13.7 sec 0-100 km/hr; automatic: 13.9 sec 0-100 km/hr		11.5 sec 0-100 km/hr; automatic: 12.3 sec 0-100 km/hr
Fuel consumption	11.7 liters/100 km (20.6 mpg) 1979: at 120 km/hr: 12.5 liters; automatic: 12.8 liters		at 120 km/hr: 10.4 liters/100 km; automatic: 11 liters
Fuel tank capacity	65 liters (17.2 gallons); U.S. 1977: 80 liters (21.1 gallons)		

Model 240D (1975-   )

D = Diesel

The 240D sedan, 1976

The 240D, the third diesel sedan with the same new body style of the other middle class models, also went into full production in January 1976. The older style was still built to ease the demand for these most economical cars.

The wheelbase of all of the W123 bodies was 45 millimeters longer than on the previous models and the front axle track 40 millimeters wider to give improved comfort and better roadhandling.

The bumpers had rubber guards and side strips with rubber inlets to protect the body from negligent and careless opening of doors. Windshield wipers were parallel running instead of the former butterfly style and were black to prevent reflections. Seat belts had been repositioned for improved comfort and safety. The heating and ventilating system was simplified and made more efficient and the easy-to-read panel with round instruments had a heavily inclined glass plate which eliminated glare and was easier to keep clean. A key-operated starter was available by 1977.

Acceleration figures for the 0 to 100 kilometers per hour were 24.6 seconds with the manual, and 27.4 seconds with the automatic transmission. In 1980 the figures were 22 seconds and 24.7, respectively. However, for that year the power output in the cars in the United States was raised to 67 SAE horsepower, but the weight of the sedan had increased to 1,415 kilograms (3,120 pounds).

The Environmental Protection Agency rating for the 240D for 1979 was 30 miles per gallon for city driving and 34 miles per gallon for the highway cycle. In 1980 this was changed to 28 mpg for city and 34 for highway, or a combined average rating of 30 miles per gallon of fuel. With the automatic transmission the figures were 26 and 29, or 27 combined. The 1981 figures were 29 and 33 for manual and 27 and 31 for the automatic.

The longer wheelbase (LW) model also became available in 1979 in the new body style. The rear suspension of that long limousine had a leveling control devise as standard equipment.

Prices and Production

The 240D four-door sedan sold in 1976 for . . . . .DM 20,146
in 1979 for. . . . . .DM 22,825
in 1982 for. . . . . .DM 28,109
The 240D sedan sold in the United States
in February 1979 for (East Coast). $15,068
with automatic transmission. $16,313
in November 1980 (East Coast) $19,312
with automatic transmission. $20,558
in October 1981 (East Coast). $20,989
in September 1982 (East Coast) $22,470
with automatic transmission. $23,800

Production of the 240D model [123 D24] (from July 1975/February 1976)

was in	1975	7 units
	1976	21,247 units
	1977	40,382 units
	1978	42,816 units
	1979	62,678 units
	1980	69,908 units
	1981	73,162 units
	1982	74,627 units

Specifications

	240D	240D (LW)
Engine type	4 cyl diesel, overhead camshaft (OM 616)	In 1979 the 240D model became also available with a longer wheelbase as an eight-passenger limousine. The basic specifications were as those of the regular model, but with the following exceptions:
Bore and stroke	91 x 92.4mm (3.58 x 3.64 in) 1979: 90.9 x 92.4mm	
Displacement	2402 cc (146.7 cu in) 1979: 2399 cc (146.4 cu in)	
Power output	65 hp (DIN) @ 4200 rpm; 1977: 64 hp 1979: 72 hp (DIN) @ 4400 rpm U.S. 1977: 62 hp SAE @ 4000 rpm U.S. 1980: 67 hp (SAE) @ 4000 rpm	
Compression ratio	21:1	
Torque	14 mkg @ 2400 rpm (101.3 ft/lb) U.S. 1977: 13.4 mkg @ 2400 rpm (97 ft/lb) 1982: 13.5 mkg (97 lb/ft)	
Fuel injection	Bosch four plunger pump	
Maximum engine speed	5400 rpm; 1979: 5300 rpm; U.S. 1977: 4350 rpm U.S. 1980: 4000 rpm	
Engine speed at 100 km/hr	3195 rpm; automatic: 3275 rpm 1980: 4000rpm, 1982: 4600 rpm	
Gear ratios	I. 3.90:1 automatic: I. 3.98:1 1980: I. 3.91:1 II. 2.30:1 II. 2.39:1 II. 2.32:1 III. 1.41:1 III. 1.46:1 III. 1.42:1 IV. 1.00:1 IV. 1.00:1	
Rear axle ratio	3.69	
Chassis	unit frame and body	
Suspension	independent front and rear, with coil springs; diagonal swing axle, coil springs, anti-roll bar. Optional level control; standard in 1979	
Brakes and area	dual circuit discs, power assisted, front brake pad wear indicator, 278/279 mm (10.9/11.0 in)	
Wheelbase	2795mm (110.0 in)	3425mm (134.8 in)
Track, front/rear	1488/1466mm (58.6/56.9 in)	1477/1430mm (58.1/56.3 in)
Length	4725mm (186.0 in) U.S. 1977: 4848mm (190.9 in)	5355mm (210.8 in)
Width	1786mm (70.3 in)	
Height	1438mm (56.6 in)	1480mm (58.3 in)
Ground clearance		
Rear suspension		level control standard
Tires	175 SR 14	
Turning circle	11.25 meters (36.9 ft) 1979: 11.29 meters (37 ft) U.S. 1977: 11.29 meters (37 ft)	13.35 meters (43.8 ft)
Steering type and ratio	recirculating ball (4.0 turns); servo assisted U.S. 1977: 2.7 turns; U.S. 1980: 3.2 turns	
Weight	1385 kg (3047 lbs) U.S. 1977: 1455 kg (3210 lbs) U.S. 1980: 1415 kg (3120 lbs)	1565 kg (3443 lbs)

The 240D sedan, 1981, U.S. version

Regular and long wheelbase 240D sedans

	240D	240D (LW)
Maximum speed	138 km/hr (86 mph) automatic: 133 km/hr (83 mph) 1979: 143 km/hr (89 mph) automatic: 138 km/hr (86 mph)	
Acceleration	24.6 sec 0-100 km/hr; automatic: 27.4 sec 1979: 22.0 sec; automatic: 24.7 sec	0-100 km/hr: 24.6 sec automatic: 27.2 sec
Fuel consumption	9.5 liters/100 km (24.75 mpg); 1979: at 120 km/hr: 10.9 liters; automatic: 11.4 liters	at 120 km/hr: 11.1 liters automatic: 12.2 liters
Fuel tank capacity	65 liters (17.2 gallons) U.S. 1977: 80 liters (21.1 gallons) U.S. 1980: 65 liters (17.2 gallons)	

The 250 sedan, 1976

The M 123 2.5-liter engine

Prices and Production

The 250 four-door sedan sold in 1976 for . . . . .DM 21,767
in 1979 for. . . . . .DM 24,662

Production of the 250 model [123 V25] (from July 1975/April 1976)
was in 1975   5 units
       1976   14,915 units
       1977   25,183 units
       1978   23,306 units
       1979   21,758 units
       1980   17,447 units
       1981   8,029 units
       1982   5,392 units

Model 250 (1975-   )

The 250 model was the third of the newly introduced cars at the Geneva Auto Show in 1976, having the identical 123 style body as the 200 and 230 models with the round headlights.

It replaced the 250 model, in production since 1967 and built until 1972, when the designated 250 sedan, built from 1970 until 1976, actually had a 2.8-liter engine. The six-cylinder 230.6 model (1973-1976) was perhaps closer to the true 250, with the 2.3-liter engine of 120 horsepower, and it was really considered a replacement for that model.

But the engine for this W123 model style was a newly designed 2.5-liter six-cylinder unit developing 129 (DIN) horsepower at 5,500 revolutions per minute. It was a high performance engine built for economical operation. The four-bearing crankshaft had nine counterweights for improved balance, while the 2.3-liter engine had only three. Overhead camshaft with single roller chain drive, hydraulic chain tensioner and a Solex four-barrel carburetor were other features of the new power unit.

As in all of these new models, the oil change for the engine was simplified by the use of a sucking-out method, thus eliminating the need for a hoist, and making for quicker service.

This new 250 sedan, the smallest of the six-cylinder line of cars, was a lively performer and promised to be a good choice in the wide range of 30 models then offered to the public by Daimler-Benz. Still, the smaller four-cylinder 230 model outsold it by about two to one over the next five years and the 250 sedan sold as well as the larger six-cylinder 280 and 280E models combined.

Specifications

	250			250 (LW)
Engine type	6 cyl overhead camshaft (M123)			
Bore and stroke	86 x 72.45 mm (3.38 x 2.85 in)			
Displacement	2525 cc (154.1 cu in)			
Power output	129 hp (DIN) @ 5500 rpm; 1979: 140 hp (DIN) @ 5500 rpm			
Compression ratio	8.7:1; 1979: 9:1			
Torque	20 mkg @ 3500 rpm (144.7 ft/lb)			
Carburetion	Solex dual-compound downdraft 4A1			
Maximum engine speed	6000 rpm			
Engine speed at 100 km/hr	3195 rpm		automatic: 3275 rpm	
Gear ratios	I. 3.90:1 II. 2.30:1 III. 1.41:1 IV. 1.00:1	I. 3.98:1 (automatic) II. 2.39:1 III. 1.46:1 IV. 1.00:1	I. 3.98:1 (1979: manual transmission) II. 2.29:1 III. 1.45:1 IV. 1.00:1	
Rear axle ratio	3.92			
Chassis	unit frame and body			
Suspension	independent front and rear, with coil springs; diagonal swing axle, coil springs, anti-roll bar. Optional level control; standard in 1979			
Brakes and area	dual circuit discs, power assisted, front brake pad wear indicator, 278/279 mm (10.9/11.0 in)			
Wheelbase	2795 mm (110.0 in)			3425mm (134.8 in)
Track, front/rear	1488/1446 mm (58.6/56.9 in)			1477/1430mm (58.1/56.3 in)
Length	4725 mm (186.0 in)			5355mm (210.8 in)
Width	1786 mm (70.3 in)			
Height	1438 mm (56.6 in)			1480mm (58.3 in)
Tires	175 SR 14			
Turning circle	11.25 meters (36.9 feet); 1979: 11.29 meters (37 feet)			13.35 meters (43.8 feet)
Steering type and ratio	recirculating ball (4.0 turns), servo assisted			
Weight	1360 kg (2992 lbs); 1979: 1375 kg (3025 lbs)			1540 kg (3388 lbs)
Maximum speed	180 km/hr (112 mph); automatic: 175 km/hr (109 mph)			
Acceleration	11.5 sec 0-100 km/hr; automatic: 12.4 sec			0-100 km/hr: 12.4 sec.; automatic: 13.3 sec
Fuel consumption	11.8 liters/100 km (20.5 mpg); 1979: at 120 km/hr: 12.1 liters; automatic: 12.9 liters			at 120 km/hr: 11.9 liters; automatic: 13.1 liters
Fuel tank capacity	65 liters (17.2 gallons)			

The 250 sedan, 1976

In 1979 the 250 model became also available with a longer wheelbase as an eight-passenger limousine, but with the following exceptions:

The 280 sedan, 1975

The 280 sedan, 1975

Prices and Production

The 280 four-door sedan sold in 1976 for . . . . .DM 24,997
   in 1979 for. . . . . .DM 27,899

Production of the 280 model [123 V28] (from July/December 1975 until July 1981)

was in	1975	957 units
	1976	12,821 units
	1977	7,530 units
	1978	4,103 units
	1979	3,139 units
	1980	3,477 units
	1981	1,179 units
	total	33,206 units

Model 280 (1975-1981)

The 280 model, also first shown at the Geneva Auto Show in 1976, was distinguishable from the smaller engined cars by the halogen headlights. Otherwise, the W123 body style was the same.

The reflector surface of the main headlights was increased by 13%, standard with halogen lamps, signifying a definite safety contribution to the 280 and 280E models. Fog lights were also standard equipment and these had a 40% larger reflector surface on these models.

Interior appointments also incorporated many new safety features, such as recessed and easier to read instruments, improved padding of roof frame, relocated mounting seat belts, newly arranged combination switches stalk mounted on left of steering column, and redesigned heating and cooling systems, among others.

The front seats had better lateral support at hip height and had seat height control adjustments as standard equipment. It also extended the seat adjustment to the rear by 86 millimeters, a feature especially appreciated by long-legged drivers and normal body size who did not need the height adjustment.

The new exhaust system on all 123 models used an improved corrosion resistant material which extended its service life. The cars also had a hydraulic two-circuit braking system with vacuum brake booster and, of course, disc brakes on all four wheels, as all previous models. A brake pad wear indicator, up to then only used on the S-class cars, was included in all models. The foot-operated parking brake needed 30% less pressure to achieve the same effect as before.

The 280 was powered by the double overhead camshaft six-cylinder engine of 2,746 cubic centimeter displacement and developed 156 DIN horsepower.

Specifications

	280
Engine type	6 cyl double overhead camshafts (M110)
Bore and stroke	86 x 78.8 mm (3.39 x 3.10 in)
Displacement	2746 cc (167.6 cu in)
Power output	156 hp (DIN) @ 5500 rpm
Compression ratio	8.7:1
Torque	22.7 mkg @ 4000 rpm (164.2 ft/lb)
Carburetion	Solex dual-compound downdraft 4A1
Maximum engine speed	6500 rpm
Engine speed at 100 km/hr	3065 rpm automatic: 3155 rpm
Gear ratios	I. 3.90:1 I. 3.98:1 (automatic) I. 3.98:1 (1979: manual transmission) II. 2.30:1 II. 2.39:1 II. 2.29:1 III. 1.41:1 III. 1.46:1 III. 1.45:1 IV. 1.00:1 IV. 1.00:1 IV. 1.00:1
Rear axle ratio	3.54
Chassis	unit frame and body
Suspension	independent front and rear, with coil springs; diagonal swing axle, coil springs, anti-roll bar. Optional level control; standard in 1979
Brakes and area	dual circuit discs, power assisted, front brake pad wear indicator, 278/279 mm (10.9/11.0 in)
Wheelbase	2795 mm (110.0 in)
Track, front/rear	1488/1446 mm (58.6/56.9 in)
Length	4725 mm (186.0 in)
Width	1786 mm (70.3 in)
Height	1438 mm (56.6 in)
Tires	175 SR 14; 1979: 195/70 HR 14
Turning circle	11.25 meters (36.9 feet); 1979: 11.29 meters (37 feet)
Steering type and ratio	recirculating ball (4.0 turns), servo assisted
Weight	1455 kg (3201 lbs)
Maximum speed	190 km/hr (118 mph) automatic: 185 km/hr (115 mph)
Acceleration	10.6 sec 0-100 km/hr; automatic: 11.3 sec
Fuel consumption	12.5 liters/100 km (18.75 mph); 1979: at 120 km/hr: 12.7 liters; automatic: 13.5 liters
Fuel tank capacity	65 liters (17.2 gallons); 1979: 80 liters (21.1 gallons)

The 280 sedan, 1976

The 280E sedan, 1976

Instrument panel of the 280E, 1976

Prices and Production

The 280E four-door sedan sold in 1976 for . . . . .DM 26,895
   in 1979 for. . . . . .DM 30,016
The 280E sedan sold in the United States
  (with automatic transmission)
  in February 1979 for (East Coast). $22,318
  in November 1980 (East Coast) $26,848

Production of the 280E model [123 E28] (from July/December 1975)
was in	1975	607 units
	1976	17,638 units
	1977	17,651 units
	1978	14,904 units
	1979	18,383 units
	1980	17,703 units
	1981	12,723 units
	1982	10,757 units

Model 280E (1975-   )

E (Einspritzung) = fuel injection)

The 280E model, resembling in every detail the 280, was also first introduced at the Geneva Auto Show in 1976. It was, of course, the fuel-injection engine (E for Einspritzung) which made it different from the 280 model.

Fuel injection was by means of a mechanically controlled unit (Bosch K-Jetronic) with air volume control instead of the electronic system used previously. This improved type had been employed to a certain extent in the S-class models and had been introduced first in the 6.9-liter engine of the 450 SEL.

The optional sunroof on the 123 bodied models, where available, had an automatically operating wind deflector which popped up when the sunroof was opened. It was a most desirable feature.

The earlier 280E sedan (of the 114 body style) was gradually phased out. Only 344 units were built during the first year of production of this new model style when nearly 18,000 units of the 123 bodied 280E sedan were built.

As the least expensive six-cylinder model in the United States, this 280E was offered fully equipped. Many optional and extra cost items were, as was customary in this country, included in the price. The car had the four-wheel power disc brakes, variable assisted power steering, quartz clock, central locking system, fog lights, tinted windshield, heated rear window, electric window lifts, cruise control, arm rests front and rear, and radio as standard equipment.

Because of stringent emission controls and safety devices, the 280E was quite different from the regular European version. The engine developed only 137 SAE horsepower, instead of the 177 DIN, and the weight of the sedan was 1,600 kilograms (or 3,530 pounds), instead of 1,460 kilograms (or 3,212 pounds) for the other version. In 1977 a total of 4,166 units were imported into the U.S., outselling the more expensive and larger 280SE model by a small margin. Sales dropped the following years, and by 1980, 8,551 units had been brought to this country, against the 8,080 for the 280SE model sedan.

Specifications

	280E
Engine type	6 cyl double overhead camshafts (M110)
Bore and stroke	86 x 78.8 mm (3.39 x 3.10 in)
Displacement	2746 cc (167.6 cu in)
Power output	177 hp (DIN) @ 6000 rpm; 1979: 185 hp (DIN) @ 5800 rpm; U.S. 1977: 142 hp SAE @ 5750 rpm; 1980: 140 hp SAE @ 5500 rpm California: 137 hp SAE @ 5750 rpm
Compression ratio	8.7:1 1979: 9:1 U.S. 1977: 8:1
Torque	23.8 mkg @ 4500 rpm (172 ft/lb); U.S. 1977: 21.4 mkg @ 4600 rpm (149 ft/lb); 1980: 20.1 mkg California: 20.5 mkg @ 4600 rpm (142 ft/lb)
Fuel injection	Bosch mechanical with air metering device
Maximum engine speed	6500 rpm; US 1980: 6650 rpm
Engine speed at 100 km/hr	3065 rpm
Gear ratios	I. 3.90:1 I. 3.98:1 (automatic) I. 3.98:1 (1979: manual transmission) II. 2.30:1 II. 2.39:1 II. 2.29:1 III. 1.41:1 III. 1.46:1 III. 1.45:1 IV. 1.00:1 IV. 1.00:1 IV. 1.00:1
Rear axle ratio	3.54; 1982: 3.58 U.S. 1980: 3.58
Chassis	unit frame and body
Suspension	independent front and rear, with coil springs; diagonal swing axle, coil springs, anti-roll bar. Optional level control; standard in 1979
Brakes and area	dual circuit discs, power assisted, front brake pad wear indicator, 278/279 mm (10.9/11.0 in)
Wheelbase	2795 mm (110.0 in)
Track, front/rear	1488/1446 mm (58.6/56.9 in)
Length	4725 mm (186.0 in); U.S. 1977: 4848 mm (190.9 in)
Width	1786 mm (70.3 in)
Height	1438 mm (56.6 in)
Tires	175 SR 14; 1979: 195/70 HR 14
Turning circle	11.25 meters (36.9 feet); 1979: 11.29 meters (37 feet)
Steering type and ratio	recirculating ball (4.0 turns), servo assisted U.S. 1977: 2.7 turns
Weight	1460 kg (3212 lbs) U.S. 1977: 1600 kg (3530 lbs); 1980: 1570 kg
Maximum speed	200 km/hr (124 mph); automatic: 195 km/hr (121 mph)
Acceleration	9.9 sec 0-100 km/hr; automatic: 10.8 sec
Fuel consumption	12.5 liters/100 km (18.75 mpg); 1979: at 120 km/hr: 12.1 liters; automatic: 13 liters
Fuel tank capacity	65 liters (17.2 gallons); 1979: 80 liters (21.1 gallons)

The 280E sedan, 1977, U.S. version

Model 300D (1975-)

D = Diesel

The 300D sedan, 1976

Prices and Production

The 300D four-door sedan sold in 1976 for . . . . .DM 22,311
   in 1979 for. . . . . .DM 24,897
   in 1982 for. . . . . .DM 30,465
The 300D sedan sold in the United States
   (with automatic transmission)
   in February 1979 for (East Coast). $20,911
   in November 1980 (East Coast) $25,640
   in October 1981 (East Coast). $28,483
   in September 1982 (East Coast) $30,530

Production of the 300D model [123 D30] (from July 1975/February 1976)

was in	1975	9 units
	1976	28,996 units
	1977	48,605 units
	1978	49,908 units
	1979	52,296 units
	1980	50,197 units
	1981	38,858 units
	1982	30,720 units

Production of the 300D (turbo) model [123 D30A] (from July/September 1981)

was in	1981	4,505 units
	1982	20,178 units

The 300D, the five-cylinder diesel-engined sedan, shared with the other eight models the same body style introduced at the Geneva Auto Show in 1976.

Over 53,000 of these sedans had been produced since their introduction in 1974 as the 240D 3.0 models, attesting to the enormous popularity of this larger diesel engine with buyers who valued the economy of a diesel.

The W123 body had, as the others mentioned earlier, the synchronized four-speed transmission with floor shift or, as an optional extra, the automatic four-speed with torque converter. It had an improved, more rigid clutch bell housing and transmission case, which reduced the bending vibration and made for smoother running.

The front had individual wheel suspension by means of double control arms, two coil springs with additional rubber springs, hydraulic telescopic shock absorbers and anti-roll bar. The rear had a diagonal pivot swing axle, two coil springs with additional rubber springs, hydraulic shock absorbers and anti-roll bar. Level control was an optional extra item.

The fuel injection pump for this diesel was entirely redesigned. A centrifugal governor operated the metering rack and regulated the power output. Cylinder crankhead and housing, head gasket, and the six main bearing crankshaft and oil pan were also new.

Automatic transmission was standard on this 300D model. Acceleration was 19.9 seconds for the 0 to 100 kilometers per hour, and with the rear axle ratio of 3.46 to 1, maximum speed was 89 miles per hour in the United States version, but 92 miles per hour for the European model.

The Environmental Protection Agency rating for 1979 and 1980 was 23 miles per gallon for city and 28 miles per gallon for the highway cycle, for an average of 25 miles per gallon fuel consumption. For 1981 the rating was 24 and 28 miles per gallon.

The 300D LW (long wheelbase) model was also available with the new body style.

The 300D outsold the 240D in the United States for the five-year period from 1979 to 1980 with 39,075 units against 38,777; but for the last two years the four-cylinder diesel had topped it.

For the 1982 model year the OM617A turbo-charged diesel engine replaced the regularly aspirated version. With the significant increase in power (45%), fuel economy was actually improved.

Specifications

	300D	300D (LW)	300D (turbo)
Engine type	5 cyl diesel, overhead camshaft (OM 617)	In 1979 the 300D model became also available with a longer wheelbase as an eight-passenger limousine. The basic specifications were as those of the regular model, but with the following exceptions:	5 cyl diesel, overhead camshaft, with turbo-charger (OM 617A)
Bore and stroke	91 x 92.4mm (3.58 x 3.64 in) 1979: 90.9 x 92.4mm		91 x 92.4mm (3.58 x 3.64 in)
Displacement	3055 cc (183.4 cu in) U.S. 1979: 2998 cc (183.0 cu in)		2998 cc (182.9 cu in)
Power output	80 hp (DIN) @ 4000 rpm 1979: 88 hp (DIN) @ 4400 rpm U.S. 1977: 77 hp (SAE) @ 4000 rpm U.S. 1980: 83 hp (SAE) @ 4200 rpm		125 hp (DIN) @ 4350 rpm U.S.: 120 hp (SAE)
Compression ratio	21:1		21.5:1
Torque	17.5 mkg @ 2400 rpm (126.6 ft/lb) U.S. 1977: 15.9 mkg @ 2400 rpm (115 ft/lb) U.S. 1980: 16.7 mkg @ 2400 rpm (120 ft/lb)		25.5 mkg @ 2400 rpm U.S.: 23.6 mkg (170 ft/lb)
Fuel injection	Bosch five plunger pump		Bosch five plunger pump w/injection timer
Maximum engine speed	5100 rpm; 1979: 5300 rpm U.S. 1977: 4350 rpm; U.S. 1980: 4200 rpm		5100 rpm; U.S.: 4350 rpm 1982: 4500 rpm, 1983: 4640 rpm
Engine speed at 100 km/hr			
Gear ratios	I. 3.90:1 II. 2.30:1 III. 1.41:1 IV. 1.00:1	automatic I. 3.98:1 II. 2.39:1 III. 1.46:1 IV. 1.00:1	I. 3.90:1 II. 2.30:1 III. 1.41:1 IV. 1.00:1
Rear axle ratio	3.46		3.07
Chassis	unit frame and body		
Suspension	independent front and rear, with coil springs; diagonal swing axle, coil springs, anti-roll bar. Optional level control; standard in 1979		
Brakes and area	dual circuit discs, power assisted, front brake pad wear indicator (278/279mm (10.9/11.0 in)		
Wheelbase	2795mm (110.0 in)	3425mm (134.8 in)	
Track, front/rear	1488/1466mm (58.6/56.9 in)	1477/1430mm (58.1/56.3 in)	
Length	4725mm (186.0 in) U.S. 1977: 4848mm (190.9 in)	5355mm (210.8 in)	
Width	1786mm (70.3 in)		
Height	1438mm (56.6 in)	1480mm (58.3 in)	
Ground clearance			
Rear suspension		level control standard	
Tires	175 SR 14		1982: 195/70 SR-14
Turning circle	11.25 meters (36.9 ft) 1979: 11.29 meters (37 ft) U.S. 1977: 11.29 meters (37 ft)	13.35 meters (43.8 ft)	
Steering type and ratio	recirculating ball (4.0 turns), servo assisted U.S. 1977: 2.7 turns; U.S. 1980: 3.2 turns		
Weight	1445 kg (3179 lbs) U.S. 1977: 1595 kg (3515 lbs) U.S. 1978: 1600 kg (3530 lbs) U.S. 1980: 1555 kg (3430 lbs)	1615 kg (3553 lbs)	1982: 1625 kg (3585 lbs)
Maximum speed	148 km/hr (92 mph) automatic: 143 km/hr (89 mph) 1979: 155 km/hr automatic: 150 km/hr (93 mph)		
Acceleration	19.9 sec 0-100 km/hr automatic: 20.8 sec; 1979: 17.8 sec automatic: 19.2 sec	19.4 sec 0-100 km/hr automatic: 20.8 sec	
Fuel consumption	10.8 liters/100 km (21.5 mpg) 1979: at 120 km/hr 11.5 liters automatic: 12.4 liters	at 120 km/hr: 12.4 liters automatic: 12.0 liters	
Fuel tank capacity	65 liters (17.2 gallons) U.S. 1977: 80 liters (21.1 gallons)		

The 300D sedan, 1976

Model 240TD (1978-   )

T (Touristik und Transport) = station wagon, D = Diesel

The 240TD station wagon, 1977

The 240TD, as the entire range of T models — the five different engined station wagons but with identical bodies — were first shown at the Frankfurt Auto Show in 1977. Regular production was scheduled to begin in the Bremen factory in April 1978, but actually started a month earlier than planned.

The T stood for Tourism and Transport, and the figures in that designation indicated the engine type.

Two diesel-engined and three gasoline-engined models were built, affording a great variety and satisfying nearly every conceivable preference.

It was the first time that Daimler-Benz manufactured a station wagon, although such type vehicles had been made available over the years, beginning with the 180/180D, by body building specialists, such as Christian Miesen of Bonn and Binz & Co. of Lorch, and the Belgium IMA assembly plant.

The station wagons were based on the 123 sedan line of passenger cars and shared many components used in those vehicles. The roof line had been harmoniously integrated into the body shape, retaining the character of the sedan, but at the same time dramatically increasing the usable space. Other description details will be mentioned in connection with the following models.

The 240TD was powered by a 2.4-liter four-cylinder engine of 65 (DIN) horsepower. The 1,485-kilogram (3,267-pound) station wagon had a maximum speed of 138 kilometers per hour with manual transmission and 133 km/hr (83 miles per hour) with the automatic. Fuel consumption was rated at 9.5 liters per 100 kilometers (24.75 miles per gallon).

This diesel-powered model proved the best selling station wagon, except for the five-cylinder diesel sold also in the United States. The reliability and economy of the diesel engine proved irresistible to many buyers.

Prices and Production

The 240TD station wagon sold in 1977 for..........DM 25,052
    in 1980 for...............................DM 28,159

Production of the 240TD station wagon [123 D24] (from February/May 1978)

was in	1978	3,003 units
	1979	6,387 units
	1980	5,820 units
	1981	5,078 units
	1982	5,881 units

Specifications

	240TD
Engine type	4 cyl diesel, overhead camshaft (OM 616)
Bore and stroke	91 x 92.4mm (3.58 x 3.64 in) 1979: 90.9 x 92.4mm
Displacement	2404 cc (146.7 cu in) 1979: 2399 cc (146.4 cu in)
Power output	65 hp (DIN) @ 4200 rpm 1979: 72 hp @ 4400 rpm
Compression ratio	21:1
Torque	14 mkg @ 2400 rpm (101.3 ft/lb) 1979: 13.9 mkg @ 2400 rpm
Fuel injection	Bosch four plunger pump
Maximum engine speed	5300 rpm
Gear ratios	I. 3.90:1 automatic: I. 3.98:1 1980: I. 3.91:1 II. 2.30:1 II. 2.39:1 II. 2.32:1 III. 1.41:1 III. 1.46:1 III. 1.42:1 IV. 1.00:1 IV. 1.00:1
Rear axle ratio	3.69
Chassis	unit frame and body
Suspension	independent front and rear, coil springs; diagonal swing axle, coil springs, torsion bar stabilizer, standard level control
Brakes and area	dual circuit discs, front brake pad wear indicator, 278/279mm (10.9/11.0 in)
Wheelbase	2795mm (110.0 in)
Track, front/rear	1488/1453mm (58.6/57.2 in)
Length	4725mm (186.0 in)
Width	1786mm (70.3 in)
Height	1425mm (56.1 in) 1979: 1470mm (57.9 in)
Tires	195 SR 14
Turning circle	11.29 meters (37 ft)
Steering type and ratio	recirculating ball (3.2 turns), power assisted
Weight	1485 kg (3267 lbs) 1979: 1505 kg (3311 lbs)
Maximum speed	138 km/hr (86 mph) automatic: 133 km/hr (83 mph) 1979: 143 km/hr; automatic: 138 km/hr
Acceleration	24.6 sec 0-100 km/hr automatic: 27.4 sec 1979: 23.2 sec; automatic: 26.1 sec
Fuel consumption	9.5 liters/100 km (24.75 mpg) 1979: at 120 km/hr — 11.0 liters; automatic: 11.6
Fuel tank capacity	70 liters (18.5 gallons)

Rear lid open of 240TD, 1977

Front view of 240TD, 1977

The 300TD station wagon, 1978, U.S. version

Prices and Production

The 300TD station wagon sold in 1977 for . . . . .DM 27,317
   in 1980 for. . . . . .DM 30,736
The 300TD station wagon sold in the United States
   (with automatic transmission)
   in February 1979 for (East Coast). $23,900
   in November 1980 (East Coast) $31,373

Production of the 300TD station wagon [123 D30] (from September 1977/May 1978)

was in	1977	1 unit
	1978	3,144 units
	1979	11,180 units
	1980	7,523 units
	1981	3,308 units
	1982	3,712 units

Model 300TD (1977-   )

T (Touristik und Transport) = station wagon, D = Diesel

The 300TD was the other of diesel-engined and another of the same bodied station wagons introduced at the Frankfurt Auto Show in 1977.

It was the only model destined for sale in the United States market and would have the identical mechanical specifications as the 300D sedans.

The interior was the very same as that of the sedan, with the instrument panel, console and gear shift exactly alike. A sunroof was available, but only the manual operated kind was offered because of lack of space for the electrical mechanism.

The wide opening rear door of the vehicle gave easy access to the normal loading area of 1.23 meters long and 1.48 meters wide. With the rear seat-back folded down, this could be extended to 1.78 meters, giving a volume of 525 or 879 liters (45.9 cubic feet). And by removing the rear seat, the floor length could be increased to 2.03 meters, or with the passenger seat folded down another 2.86 meters could be gained. There appeared to be almost no limit to the various loading possibilities available to suit practically every purpose. The load-carrying capacity was increased to 700 kilograms (1,540 pounds). An automatic self-leveling device on the rear axle was standard on these station wagons.

The 300TD was powered by the 3,005 cubic centimeter diesel engine of 80 (DIN) horsepower. The 1,545 kilogram (3,090 pound) vehicle had a maximum speed of 148 kilometers (92 miles) per hour with manual transmission and 143 km/hr (89 mph) with the automatic. Fuel consumption was rated at 10.8 liters per 100 kilometers (21.5 miles per gallon).

The 300TD became available first in the United States in March 1979. Specifications were consequently different from the regular version, with the 77SAE horsepower engine and a curb weight of 1,715 kilograms (3,780 pounds). The Environmental Protection Agency fuel consumption rate was 23 miles per gallon for city driving and 28 miles per gallon for the highway cycle, the same as for the 300D sedan, for an average of 25 miles per gallon.

Specifications

300TD

Engine type	5 cyl diesel, overhead camshaft (OM 617)	Wheelbase	2795mm (110.0 in)
Bore and stroke	91 x 92.4mm (3.58 x 3.65 in) 1979: 90.9 x 92.4mm	Track, front/rear	1488/1453mm (58.6/57.2 in)
		Length	4725mm (186.0 in) U.S.: 4848mm (190.9 in)
Displacement	3005 cc (183.4 cu in) 1979: 2998 cc (183 cu in)	Width	1786mm (70.3 in)
Power output	80 hp (DIN) @ 4000 rpm 1979: 88 hp @ 4400 rpm; U.S.: 77 hp SAE @ 4000 rpm U.S. 1980: 83 hp (SAE) @ 4200 rpm	Height	1425mm (56.1); 1979: 1470mm (57.9 in)
		Tires	195 SR 14
		Turning circle	11.29 meters (37 ft)
Compression ratio	21:1	Steering type and ratio	recirculating ball (3.2 turns), power assisted
Torque	17.5 mkg @ 2400 rpm (126.6 ft/lb) 1979: 17.5 mkg @ 2400 rpm U.S.: 15.9 mkg (115 ft/lb); U.S. 1980: 16.7 mkg @ 2400 rpm (120 ft/lb)	Weight	1545 kg (3399 lbs); 1979: 1565 kg (3443 lbs); U.S.: 1715 kg (3773 lbs) U.S. 1980: 1635 kg (3597 lbs)
Fuel injection	Bosch five plunger pump	Maximum speed	148 km/hr (92 mph) automatic: 143 km/hr (89 mph) 1979: 155 km/hr; automatic: 150 km/hr
Maximum engine speed	5300 rpm; U.S.: 4350 rpm U.S. 1980: 4200 rpm		
Gear ratios	I. 3.90:1 automatic: I. 3.98:1 II. 2.30:1 II. 2.39:1 III. 1.41:1 III. 1.46:1 IV. 1.00:1 IV. 1.00:1	Acceleration	19.9 sec 0-100 km/hr; automatic: 20.8 sec 1979: 18.9 sec; automatic: 20.4 sec
		Fuel consumption	10.8 liters/100 km (21.5 mpg) 1979: at 120 km/hr: 11.3 liters; automatic: 13.0
Rear axle ratio	3.46		
Chassis	unit frame and body	Fuel tank capacity	70 liters (18.5 gallons)
Suspension	independent front and rear, coil springs; diagonal swing axle, coil springs, torsion bar stabilizer, standard level control		
Brakes and area	dual circuit discs, front brake pad wear indicator, 278/279mm (10.9/11.0 in)		

Schematic drawing of station wagon

The 230T station wagon, 1979

Hydraulic self-leveling device

Prices and Production

The 230T station wagon sold in 1977 for . . . . .DM 23,976
    in 1979 for. . . . . .DM 25,704

Production of the 230T station wagon [123 V23] (from February/May 1978 until April 1980)

was in	1978	1,793 units
	1979	3,829 units
	1980	1,262 units
	total	6,884 units

The 230TE station wagon sold in 1980 for . . . . .DM 28,781

Production of the 230TE station wagon [123 E23] (from October 1979/April 1980)

was in	1979	2 units
	1980	3,750 units
	1981	5,655 units
	1982	7,158 units

Model 230T (1978-1980)

T (Touristik und Transport) = station wagon

The 230T was the same bodied station wagon as the others shown first at the Frankfurt Auto Show in 1977. It had the smallest gasoline engine of the three vehicles so powered.

The entire range of station wagons had available a large assortment of special equipment which was especially developed for these vehicles, which were meant also for leisure driving, as well as for light commercial purposes. Special rails were built into the roof, able to take roof racks with aerodynamically styled luggage containers, or ski and ski boot cases, and protect them from possible inclement weather and potential thieves. In addition, various racks were offered for the convenient carrying of boats, surfboards, bicycles, and such recreation equipment.

The 230T was powered by the regular 2,307 cubic centimeter four-cylinder engine of 109 (DIN) horsepower, giving the 1,450 kilogram (3,190 lb) station wagon a top speed of about 170 kilometers per hour with manual or 165 km/hr (102 mph) with the automatic transmission. Fuel consumption was rated at 11.7 liters per 100 kilometers (20 miles per gallon).

Model 230TE (1979-   )

T = station wagon, E = fuel injection

The 230TE model station wagon with the newly designed M102 fuel-injection engine appeared in early 1980 when the regular carburetor engined model was phased out in April of that year.

These 2,299 cubic centimeter four-cylinder engines with better fuel consumption and greater smoothness of operation developed 136 DIN horsepower, actually 25% more power than the carburetor units they replaced.

The 230TE had a maximum speed of 180 kilometers per hour, and acceleration of 0-100 kilometers per hour was 12.2 seconds with manual and 13.1 seconds with the automatic transmission. Fuel consumption was rated at 14.2 liters with manual and 13.8 liters with automatic transmission for the urban cycle, and for the 120 kilometers per hour speed, the figures were 10.6 and 11.5, respectively.

Specifications

	230T	230TE
Engine type	4 cyl overhead camshaft (M115)	4 cyl overhead camshaft (M102)
Bore and stroke	93.75 x 83.6 (3.69 x 3.29 in)	95.5 x 80.25 mm (3.74 x 3.16 in)
Displacement	2307 cc (140.8 cu in)	2299 cc (140.12 cu in)
Power output	109 hp (DIN) @ 4800 rpm	136 hp (DIN) @ 5100 rpm
Compression ratio	9.0:1	9.0:1
Torque	18.9 mkg @ 3000 rpm (136.7 ft/lb) 1979: 18.9 mkg @ 3000 rpm	20.9 mkg @ 3500 rpm (151.2 ft/lb)
Carburetion	Stromberg crossdraft 175 CD	Bosch mechanical (fuel injection)
Maximum engine speed	6000 rpm	6000 rpm
Gear ratios	I. 3.90:1　　　I. 3.98:1 (automatic) II. 2.30:1　　II. 2.39:1 III. 1.41:1　　III. 1.46:1 IV. 1.00:1　　IV. 1.00:1	I. 3.91:1 II. 2.32:1 III. 1.42:1 IV. 1.00:1
Rear axle ratio	3.69	
Chassis	unit frame and body	
Suspension	independent front and rear, with coil springs; diagonal swing axle, coil springs, torsion bar stabilizer, standard level control	
Brakes and area	dual circuit discs, front brake pad wear indicator, 278/279 mm (10.9/11.0 in)	
Wheelbase	2795 mm (110.0 in)	
Track, front/rear	1488/1453 mm (58.6/57.2 in)	
Length	4725 mm (186.0 in)	
Width	1786 mm (70.3 in)	
Height	1425 mm (56.1 in)　　1979: 1470 mm (57.9 in)	1470 mm (57.9 in)
Tires	195 SR 14	195/70 HR 14
Turning circle	11.29 meters (37 feet)	
Steering type and ratio	recirculating ball (3.2 turns), power assisted	
Weight	1450 kg (3190 lbs)　　1979: 1470kg (3234 lbs)	1455 kg (3205 lbs)
Maximum speed	170 km/hr (106 mph); automatic: 165 km/hr (103 mph)	168 km/hr (105 mph); automatic: 163 km/hr (102 mph)
Acceleration	13.7 sec 0-100 km/hr; automatic 13.9 sec 1979: 14.4 sec 0-100 km/hr; automatic: 14.8 sec	11.5 sec 0-100 km/hr; automatic: 12.3 sec 0-100 km/hr
Fuel consumption	11.7 liters/100 km (20.6 mph) 1979: at 120 km/hr: 12.5 liters; automatic 12.8	at 120 km/hr: 10.7 liters/100 km; automatic: 11.4 liters
Fuel tank capacity	70 liters (18.5 gallons)	70 liters (18.5 gallons)

Model 250T (1977-   )

Rear view of the 280TE, 1977

Prices and Production

The 250T station wagon sold in 1977 for . . . . .DM 26,751
   in 1980 for . . . . .DM 30,600

Production of the 250T station wagon [123 V25] (from September 1977/May 1978)

was in	1977	1 unit
	1978	1,382 units
	1979	2,946 units
	1980	2,761 units
	1981	402 units
	1982	213 units

The 280TE station wagon sold in 1977 for . . . . .DM 32,056
   in 1980 for . . . . .DM 35,798

Production of the 280TE station wagon [123 E28] (from September 1977/May 1978)

was in	1977	3 units
	1978	1,260 units
	1979	4,059 units
	1980	3,614 units
	1981	1,956 units
	1982	2,545 units

T (Touristik und Transport) = station wagon

The 250T was the fourth of the five station wagons shown first at the Frankfurt Auto Show in 1977. This medium powered vehicle actually proved to be the slowest selling model of the whole range of these utility vehicles.

The entire line of the station wagons shared the same body style and features of this utilitarian wagon. The interior design was a fine example of the most ingenious use of space. Built to carry five adult persons in comfort, with either all or some of the seats folded down, it offered an immense variety of space to carry a vast diversity of objects.

When raising the tailgate, the hinges and shock absorber units were discreetly tucked into the roof, allowing an absolutely smooth inner roof surface so that bulky packages would not snag on outjutting hinges.

The 250T was powered by the 2,525 cubic centimeter six-cylinder engine of 129 (DIN) horsepower. This 1,460 kilogram (3,212 pound) heavy station wagon had a maximum speed of about 180 kilometers per hour with standard transmission and 175 km/hr (109 mph) with automatic transmission. Fuel consumption was rated at 11.8 liters per 100 kilometers (20 miles per gallon).

Model 280TE (1977-   )

T = station wagon, E = fuel injection

The 280TE was the last and fastest of the five differently powered station wagons, introduced publicly at the Frankfurt Auto Show in 1977.

The interior outfitting compared in practically every detail to the sedans, including carpeting for the entire loading area.

The specifications for this line of vehicles was the same as those of the sedans — wheelbase, length and width. The fuel tank had a capacity of 70 liters (18.2 gallons). The regular manual four-speed Mercedes-Benz transmission was standard equipment, with the automatic transmission as an optional choice.

The 280TE had the 2,746 cubic centimeter six-cylinder fuel injection engine of 177 (DIN) horsepower to give it a maximum speed of 200 kilometers per hour with the manual and 195 km/hr (121 mph) with the automatic transmission. Fuel consumption was rated at 12.5 liters per 100 kilometers (18.75 miles per gallon).

Specifications

	250T	280 TE
Engine type	6 cyl overhead camshaft (M123)	6 cyl double overhead camshafts (M110)
Bore and stroke	86 x 72.45 mm (3.38 x 2.85 in)	86 x 78.8 mm (3.39 x 3.10 in)
Displacement	2525 cc (154.1 cu in)	2746 cc (167.6 cu in)
Power output	129 hp (DIN) @ 5500 rpm 1979: 140 hp (DIN) @ 5500 rpm	177 hp (DIN) @ 6000 rpm 1979: 185 hp (DIN) @ 5800 rpm
Compression ratio	8.7:1 1979: 9:1	8.7:1 1979: 9.0:1
Torque	20 mkg @ 3500 rpm (144.7 ft/lb) 1979: 20 mkg @ 3500 rpm	23.8 mkg @ 4500 rpm (172.2 ft/lb) 1979: 24.4 mkg
Carburetion	Solex dual-compound downdraft 4A1	Bosch mechanical with air metering device (fuel injection)
Maximum engine speed	6000 rpm	6500 rpm
Gear ratios	I. 3.90:1 I. 3.98:1 (automatic) I. 3.98:1 (1979: manual transmission) II. 2.30:1 II. 2.39:1 II. 2.29:1 III. 1.41:1 III. 1.46:1 III. 1.45:1 IV. 1.00:1 IV. 1.00:1 IV. 1.00:1	I. 3.90:1 II. 2.30:1 III. 1.41:1 IV. 1.00.1
Rear axle ratio	3.69	3.58
Chassis	unit frame and body	
Suspension	independent front and rear, with coil springs; diagonal swing axle, coil springs, torsion bar stabilizer, standard level control	
Brakes and area	dual circuit discs, front brake pad wear indicator, 278/279 mm (10.9/11.0 in)	
Wheelbase	2795 mm (110.0 in)	
Track, front/rear	1488/1453 mm (58.6/57.2 in)	
Length	4725 mm (186.0 in)	
Width	1786 mm (70.3 in)	
Height	1425 mm (56.1 in) 1979: 1470 mm (57.9 in)	
Tires	195 SR 14	
Turning circle	11.29 meters (37 feet)	
Steering type and ratio	recirculating ball (3.2 turns), power assisted	
Weight	1460 kg (3212 lbs) 1979: 1495 kg (3289 lbs)	1525 kg (3355 lbs) 1979: 1545 kg (2542 lbs)
Maximum speed	180 km/hr (112 mph); automatic: 175 km/hr (109 mph) 1979: 185 km/hr; automatic: 180 km/hr	200 km/hr (124 mph); automatic: 195 km/hr (121 mph)
Acceleration	11.5 sec 0-100 km/hr; automatic: 12.4 sec 1979: 11.9 sec; automatic: 12.9 sec	9.9 sec 0-100 km/hr; automatic: 10.8 sec 1979: 10.2 sec; automatic: 11.2 sec
Fuel consumption	11.8 liters/100 km (20.5 mpg) 1979: at 120 km/hr: 12.1 liters automatic: 12.9 liters	12.5 liters/100 km (18.75 mpg) 1979: at 120 km/hr: 12.2 liters automatic: 13.4 liters
Fuel tank capacity	70 liters (18.5 gallons)	

Model 450SLC 5.0 (1977-1981)

S = Sports, L = Light, C = Coupe

The 450SLC 5.0 coupe was first shown to the general public at the Frankfurt Auto Show in September 1977. It was equipped with a new light-alloy V-8 gasoline fuel injection engine of 240 (DIN) horsepower.

Mainly urged by the desire to improve fuel consumption efficiency, this new engine was based on the existing V-8 units. The improved power output reduced the noise level and gave the car the finest performance of any model built then.

In addition to the lighter engine (by 43 kilograms or 94.6 pounds), the wheels, hood and trunk lid were also of light alloy, thus achieving a weight reduction of over 100 kg (220 lbs), or 7% over the former 450SLC. By the installation of front and rear spoilers, wind resistance was reduced by 9%. The car had a maximum speed of 225 kilometers (140 miles) per hour. Fuel consumption was rated at only 14.5 liters per 100 kilometers (16 miles per gallon).

The 450SLC 5.0 was a rather limited production model and never reached the sales figures of the 6.9 model, except for the 1980 year of manufacture. It seemed that it rather afforded a glimpse of future models with lighter engines and lighter bodies and greater fuel economy.

This new coupe was a car for driving enthusiasts, offering high performance and great driving comfort. It was quite suitable for sporting events and the use in rallies by private entries was apparently not disapproved of by the factory.

In fact, eventually some factory-prepared cars — 450SLC 5.0 and 280E models — participated in several selected rally events over the years, but the cars were never able to win the coveted world's rally championships. Although occasionally they won the first several places in a rally, their weight and power were not suited to all twelve of the international events rallies, which counted toward the championship.

The 450SLC 5.0 coupe, 1977

Front view of the 450SLC 5.0 coupe, 1977

Prices and Production

The 450SLC 5.0 coupe sold in 1977 for............DM 58,841

Production of the 450SLC 5.0/500SLC coupe [107 E50] (from September 1977/May 1978 until September 1981)

was in	1977	9 units
	1978	524 units
	1979	937 units
	1980	816 units
	1981	483 units
	total	2,769 units

Specifications

	450SLC 5.0	
Engine type	V-8 cyl overhead camshafts (M117)	
Bore and stroke	97 x 85 mm (3.82 x 3.35 in)	1979: 96.5 x 85 mm (3.80 x 3.35 in)
Displacement	4990 cc (304.5 cu in)	1979: 4973 cc (303.5 cu in)
Power output	240 hp (DIN) @ 5000 rpm	
Compression ratio	8.8:1	
Torque	41 mkg @ 3200 rpm (296.6 lb/ft)	
Fuel injection	Bosch mechanical with air flow sensor	
Maximum engine speed	5800 rpm	
Gear ratios	I. 2.31:1 (automatic, standard) II. 1.46:1 III. 1.00:1	
Rear axle ratio	4.08	
Chassis	unit frame and body	
Suspension	independent front and rear, with coil springs, anti-roll bar; diagonal swing axle, coil springs, anti-roll bar, level control	
Brakes and area	dual circuit discs, power assisted, brake pad wear indicator, 278/279 mm (10.9/11.0 in)	
Wheelbase	2815 mm (110.8 in)	
Track, front/rear	1452/1440 mm (57.2/56.7 in)	
Length	4750 mm (187 in)	
Width	1790 mm (70.5 in)	
Height	1330 mm (52.3 in)	
Tires	205/70 VR 14	
Turning circle	11.55 meters (37.9 feet)	
Steering type and ratio	recirculating ball (3.0 turns), servo assisted	
Weight	1515 kg (3333 lbs)	
Maximum speed	225 km/hr (140 mph)	
Acceleration	8.5 sec 0-100 km/hr	
Fuel consumption	14.5 liters/100 km (16 mpg) 1979: at 120 km/hr: 13.3 liters/100 km	
Fuel tank capacity	90 liters (23.8 gallons)	

Rear view of the 450SLC 5.0 coupe, 1977

Instrument panel of the 450SLC 5.0 coupe, 1977

The 300SD sedan, 1978, U.S. version

The 300SD sedan, 1979, U.S. version

Prices and Production

The 300SD sedan sold in the United States
(with automatic transmission)
in February 1979 for (East Coast) $26,265

Production of the 300SD model [116D 30A] (from February 1977/
May 1978 until September 1980)
was in	1977	51 units
	1978	5,970 units
	1979	13,194 units
	1980	9,419 units
	total	28,634 units

Model 300SD (1977-1980)

S = turbo charged, D = Diesel

The 300SD sedan, the first turbo-charged diesel-engined passenger car, was introduced at the Frankfurt Auto Show in September 1977. However, at that time it was intended for the United States market only, beginning in the spring of 1978.

The body style was that of the S-class cars, the larger displacement gasoline models (die Oberklasse), with a 2,865 millimeter (112.8 inch) wheelbase and overall length of 5,220 millimeters (205.5 inches). The turbo-charged five-cylinder diesel engine of 2,998 cubic centimeters, with the Garrett turbo charger unit, developed 115 (DIN) horsepower, an increase of 44% of power over the naturally aspirated 300D 80 horsepower unit. Torque was increased by 37%, and fuel economy was actually improved by 9%.

Turbo-charging was, of course, a long tradition with Daimler-Benz, having begun in the 1940s with airplane engines, then large industrial units and finally truck engines. The new engine had been widely tested, and installed in somewhat modified trim — to develop 200 horsepower — in the experimental coupe C 111, it established on the track at Nardo absolute long distance world records at continuous speeds of more than 250 kilometers (156 miles) per hour.

In 1979 the 300SD was the best selling diesel sedan in the United States, leading the second place 240D (11,066 units sold) with sales of 11,067 cars. In fact, that year, diesels sold constituted 67.4% of total of all cars sold in this country by Mercedes-Benz. (In 1980 diesels were 73% of all cars sold.) The Environmental Protection Agency rating was 24 for city and 29 for highway, with an average of 26 miles per gallon fuel consumption, — the best of the entire diesel line, and beating by 1 mile per gallon the five-cylinder regularly aspirated diesel models. This becomes an even greater feat when considering that the 300D sedan weighed (in the U.S.) 1,600 kilograms (3,530 pounds) and the 300SD 1,745 kilograms (3,850 pounds).

Specifications

	300SD
Engine type	5 cyl diesel, overhead camshaft, with turbo-charger (OM 617A)
Bore and stroke	90.9 x 92.4mm (3.58 x 3.64 in)
Displacement	2998 cc (182.9 cu in)
Power output	115 hp (DIN) @ 4200 (110 SAE hp); U.S. 1980: 120 hp (SAE) @ 4350 rpm
Compression ratio	21.5:1
Torque	23.2 mkg @ 2400 rpm (168 ft/lb); U.S. 1980: 23.6 mkg @ 2400 rpm (170 ft/lb)
Maximum engine speed	4350 rpm
Fuel injection	Bosch five plunger pump with injection timer
Engine speed at 100 km/hr	2580 rpm
Gear ratios	automatic, standard: I. 3.98:1 / II. 2.39:1 / III. 1.46:1 / IV. 1.00:1
Rear axle ratio	3.07
Chassis	unit frame and body
Suspension	independent front and rear, coil springs, anti-roll bar; diagonal swing axle, coil springs, anti-roll bar, standard level control
Brakes and area	dual circuit discs, power assisted, brake pad wear indicator, 278/279mm (10.9/11.0 in)
Wheelbase	2865mm (112.8 in)
Track, front/rear	1521/1505mm (59.9/59.3 in)
Length	5220mm (205.5 in)
Width	1870mm (73.6 in)
Height	1425mm (56.1 in)
Tires	185 HR 14
Turning circle	11.59 meters (38 feet)
Steering type and ratio	recirculating ball (2.7 turns); servo assisted
Weight	1765 kg (3883 lbs); U.S.: 1745 kg (3839 lbs); 1980: 1715 kg (3773 lbs)
Maximum speed	165 km/hr (103 mph)
Acceleration	12.7 sec 0-100 km/hr
Fuel consumption	10.6 liters/100 km (22 mph)
Fuel tank capacity	82 liters (21.7 gallons)

The OM 617A engine for the 300SD, 1979

The short-lived insignia for the turbo-diesel

Model 280CE (1976-   )

C = Coupe, E (Einspritzung) = fuel injection

The 280CE coupe was first shown at the Geneva Auto Show in March 1977. This new body style was based on the W123 sedan body, introduced just a year before at the same exhibition.

The wheelbase of the coupe was actually 2,710 millimeters (106.7 inches), or 85 millimeters (3.3 inches), shorter than that of the sedans, but the resemblance to the new style was unmistakable. It was to replace the C114 line of coupes originally introduced in late 1968 as the 250C and four years later as the 280C coupe. Now the coupes were available as the 230C, 280C, and 280CE.

The 280CE had the double overhead camshaft six-cylinder engine of 2,746 cubic centimeters (168 cubic inches), the very same as the 280SE sedan, and it was the most spirited performer of the trio. In overall appearance and in the rather elegant distinct interior appointments, all of the coupes were alike.

The 185 DIN horsepower fuel injected engine gave the coupe a good acceleration, from 0 to 100 kilometers per hour in 9.9 seconds with the manual transmission and 10.8 seconds with the automatic. Maximum speed was an even 200 kilometers (124 miles) per hour, and 195 kilometers with the manual transmission, the same figures as the sedan which actually weighed 10 kilograms more than the 1,450 kilograms given for the coupe.

For the United States market, the engine for the 280CE developed 142 SAE horsepower (California: 137 hp), and the coupe weighed 1,590 kilograms (3,510 lbs) when it was first introduced for the 1978 model year. For 1980 these specifications had changed to a weight of 1,560 kilograms (3,440 pounds), and the engine developed 140 SAE horsepower at 5,500 revolutions per minute. Torque was 145 feet/pounds, or 20.1 mkg at 4,500 revolutions.

The 280CE coupe, 1978, U.S. version

Prices and Production

The 280CE coupe sold in 1977 for . . . . DM 31,834
   in 1980 for. . . . . DM 36,566
The 280CE coupe sold in the United States
   (with automatic transmission)
   in February 1979 for (East Coast). $24,951
   in November 1980 (East Coast) $30,314

Production of the 280CE coupe [123 E28] (from October 1976/ April 1977)

was in	1976	2 units
	1977	6,413 units
	1978	6,958 units
	1979	5,091 units
	1980	4,013 units
	1981	2,774 units
	1982	2,509 units

Specifications

	280CE
Engine type	6 cyl double overhead camshafts (M110)
Bore and stroke	86 x 78.8 mm (3.39 x 3.10 in)
Displacement	2746 cc (167.6 cu in)
Power output	177 hp (DIN) @ 6000 rpm 1979: 185 hp (DIN) @ 5800 rpm U.S. 142 hp SAE @ 5750 rpm 1980: 140 hp @ 5500 rpm California: 137 hp SAE @ 2750 rpm
Compression ratio	8.7:1 1979: 9:1 U.S.: 8:1
Torque	23.8 mkg @ 4500 rpm (172.2 ft/lb) U.S.: 21.4 mkg @ 4600 rpm (149 ft/lb; California: 142 ft/lb)
Fuel injection	Bosch mechanical with air metering device
Maximum engine speed	6500 rpm U.S. 1980: 6650 rpm
Engine speed at 100 km/hr	3065 rpm automatic: 3155 rpm
Gear ratios	I. 3.90:1 I. 3.98:1 (automatic) I. 3.98:1 (1979: manual transmission) II. 2.30:1 II. 2.39:1 II. 2.29:1 III. 1.41:1 III. 1.46:1 III. 1.45:1 IV. 1.00:1 IV. 1.00:1 IV. 1.00:1
Rear axle ratio	3.58 U.S. 3.54 1978: 3.58
Chassis	unit frame and body
Suspension	independent front and rear, with coil springs; diagonal swing axle, coil springs, anti-lift control, stabilizer bar
Brakes and area	dual circuit discs, power assisted, 278/279 mm (10.9/11.0 in)
Wheelbase	2710 mm (106.7 in)
Track, front/rear	1488/1446 mm (58.6/56.9 in)
Length	4640 mm (182.6 in) U.S.: 4763 mm (187.5 in)
Width	1786 mm (70.3 in)
Height	1395 mm (54.9 in)
Tires	175 SR 14 1979: 195/70 HR 14 U.S. 195/70 HR 14
Turning circle	11 meters (36.1 feet)
Steering type and ratio	recirculating ball (3.2 turns), servo assisted
Weight	1450 kg (3190 lbs) U.S.: 1590 kg (3510 lbs) 1980: 1570 kg 1981: 1565 kg
Maximum speed	200 km/hr (124 mph); automatic: 195 km/hr (121 mph)
Acceleration	9.9 sec 0-100 km/hr; automatic: 10.8 sec
Fuel consumption	12.5 liters/100 km (18.75 mpg); 1979: at 120 km/hr: 11.8 liters; automatic: 13.2 liters
Fuel tank capacity	80 liters (21.1 gallons)

The 280CE coupe, 1979, U.S. version

Model 280C (1976-1980)

C = Coupe

The 280C coupe was another variation of that introduced at the Geneva Auto Show in 1977. The new body style of the 123, with a graceful arc of the roofline and pillarless design, gave the cars a rakish shape.

The front suspension linked the zero offset front axle with a sway bar to provide unusual tracking and superb roadability on any surface. The rear suspension, fully independent, incorporated a patented design with parallel constant velocity couplings and another sway bar. Power-assisted disc brakes were standard equipment, as were radial tires.

The 2,746 cubic centimeter six-cylinder engine had a Solex dual downdraft carburetor and developed 156 (DIN) horsepower at 5,500 revolutions per minute in that form. The 280C weighed 1,445 kilograms (3,179 pounds) and maximum speed was 190 kilograms (118 miles) per hour with the manual transmission.

Prices and Production

The 280C coupe sold in 1977 for . . . . .DM 29,847

Production of the 280C coupe [123 V28] (from November 1976/ April 1977 until March 1980)

was in	1976	2 units
	1977	1,577 units
	1978	1,243 units
	1979	757 units
	1980	125 units
	total	3,704 units

The 230C coupe sold in 1977 for . . . . .DM 25,063

Production of the 230C coupe [123 V23] (from November 1976/ June 1977 until June 1980)

was in	1976	1 unit
	1977	3,484 units
	1978	7,049 units
	1979	6,538 units
	1980	1,603 units
	total	18,675 units

The 230CE coupe sold in 1980 for . . . . .DM 30,837

Production of the 230CE coupe [123 E23] (from February/April 1980)

was in	1980	4,818 units
	1981	7,192 units
	1982	6,734 units

Model 230C (1976-1980)

C = Coupe

The 230C was the third version of the coupe first shown at the Geneva Auto Show in 1977. In outward appearance it was just as the other two models.

The interior was as sumptious as the more powerful cars, except that it had the 2,307 cubic centimeter four-cylinder engine of 109 horsepower (DIN) installed. The curb weight of the coupe was 1,375 kilograms (3,025 lbs), giving it a power-to-weight ratio of 12.6. The others had a ratio of 9.3 and 8.2, respectively. Still, the acceleration of the 230C was 13.7 seconds for the 0-100 kilometers per hour, and maximum speed was 170 kilometers (106 miles) per hour. Of course, it was the most economical of the elegant coupes, using only 12.1 liters of gasoline for 100 kilometers (over 19 miles per gallon), driving at 120 kilometers per hour.

Model 230CE (1980 -   )

C = Coupe

The 230CE coupe with the same body style but with the newly designed M102 four-cylinder engine went into production in April 1980. The 230C model was phased out in June.

It was in keeping with the policy of replacing the older 2-liter and 2.3-liter gasoline engines in sedans and station wagons as well. The 230CE had improved acceleration times and top speed was bettered by 10 km/hr. Fuel consumption was also greatly improved.

The 230CE coupe, 1980

Specifications

	280C	230C	230CE
Engine type	6 cyl double overhead camshafts (M110)	4 cyl overhead camshaft (M115)	4 cyl overhead camshaft (M102)
Bore and stroke	86 x 78.8 mm (3.39 x 3.10 in)	93.75 x 83.6 mm (3.69 x 3.29 in)	95.5 x 80.25 mm (3.74 x 3.16 in)
Displacement	2746 cc (167.6 cu in)	2307 cc (140.8 cu in)	2299 cc (140.12 cu in)
Power output	156 hp (DIN) @ 5500 rpm	109 hp (DIN) @ 4800 rpm	136 hp (DIN) @ 5100 rpm
Compression ratio	8.7:1	9.0:1	9.0:1
Torque	22.7 mkg @ 4000 rpm (164.2 ft/lb)	18.9 mkg @ 3000 rpm (136.7 ft/lb)	20.9 mkg @ 3500 rpm (151.2 ft/lb)
Carburetion	Solex dual compound downdraft 4A1	Stromberg crossdraft 175 CD	Bosch mechanical (fuel injection)
Maximum engine speed	6500 rpm	6000 rpm	6000 rpm
Engine speed at 100 km/hr	3065 rpm automatic: 3155 rpm	3195 rpm automatic: 3275 rpm	
Gear ratios	automatic 1979: manual transmission I. 3.90:1 I. 3.98:1 I. 3.98:1 II. 2.30:1 II. 2.39:1 II. 2.29:1 III. 1.41:1 III. 1.46:1 III. 1.45:1 IV. 1.00:1 IV. 1.00:1 IV. 1.00:1		I. 3.91:1 II. 2.32:1 III. 1.42:1 IV. 1.00:1
Rear axle ratio	3.54		
Chassis	unit frame and body		
Suspension	independent front and rear, with coil springs; diagonal swing axle, coil springs, anti-lift control, stabilizer bar		
Brakes and area	dual circuit discs, power assisted, 278/279 mm (10.9/11.0 in)		
Wheelbase	2710 mm (106.7 in)		
Track, front/rear	1488/1446 mm (58.6/56.9 in)		
Length	4640 mm (182.6 in)		
Width	1786 mm (70.3 in)		
Height	1395 mm (54.9 in)		
Tires	175 SR 14; 1979: 195/70 HR 14		
Turning circle	11 meters (36.1 feet)		
Steering type and ratio	recirculating ball (3.2 turns), servo assisted		
Weight	1445 kg (3179 lbs)	1375 kg (3025 lbs)	1390 kg (3060 lbs)
Maximum speed	190 km/hr (118 mph); automatic: 185 km/hr (115 mph)	170 km/hr (106 mph) automatic: 165 km/hr (103 mph)	180 km/hr (112 mph) automatic: 175 km/hr (109 mph)
Acceleration	10.6 sec 0-100 km/hr; automatic: 11.3 sec	13.7 sec 0-100 km/hr automatic: 13.9 sec 0-100 km/hr	11.5 sec 0-100 km/hr automatic: 12.3 sec 0-100 km/hr
Fuel consumption	12.5 liters/100 km (18.75 mpg) 1979: at 120 km/hr: 12.8 liters; automatic: 14.0 liters	11.7 liters/100 km (20.6 mpg) 1979: at 120 km/hr: 12.1 liters automatic: 13.7 liters	at 120 km/hr: 10.4 liters/100 km automatic: 11.9 liters
Fuel tank capacity	80 liters (21.1 gallons)		65 liters (17.2 gallons)

The 300CD coupe, 1981, U.S. version

Instrument panel of the 300CD, 1980

Prices and Production

The 300CD coupe sold in the United States
(with automatic transmission)
in February 1979 for (East Coast).................$23,619
in November 1980 (East Coast) $29,231
in October 1981 (East Coast)...................$31,541
in September 1982 (East Coast) $33,750

Production of the 300CD coupe [123 D30] (from May/September 1977 until August 1981)

was in	1977	1,078 units
	1978	2,485 units
	1979	1,834 units
	1980	1,770 units
	1981	335 units
	total	7,502 units

Production of the 300CD (turbo) coupe [123 D30A] (from July/September 1981)

was in	1981	777 units
	1982	1,985 units

Model 300CD (1977-   )

C = Coupe, D = Diesel

The 300CD became available by August 1977 when 98 units were produced, although a single unit had been built in May of that year. (Another one was manufactured in July.) It shared the body style with the other three coupes introduced at the Geneva Auto Show in March 1977.

This diesel coupe, using the 3-liter five-cylinder OM617 engine of 77 SAE horsepower, was as luxuriously appointed as any of the high-line automobiles of previous years, and was fitted with the latest and most advanced technological concepts. The climate control and radio were positioned in the center console and the instruments were logically arranged, all graced generously with real burled walnut trim. Cruise control, centrally locking system, and such items were standard equipment on this model sold in the United States. In fact, the diesel-engined coupe was built expressly for sales in the North American market.

The 1,585 kilogram (3,495 pound) coupe, weighing 20 pounds less than the sedan, had a maximum speed of about 150 kilometers (93 miles) per hour and, of course, the outstanding economy of that five-cylinder diesel engine. The rated Environmental Protection Agency mileage was 23 for the city and 28 for highway, giving the 300CD a combined rating of 25 miles per gallon for 1979.

This luxury diesel-engined coupe was quite similar to the gasoline-engined 280CE coupe, also sold in the United States. The performance of the diesel was naturally considerably less spirited, but it compared favorably with that of the 300D sedan. Apparently production of the 300CD was clearly justified by sales in the United States over a four-year period compared with the CE coupe.

As all five-cylinder diesel models in this country, the coupe also had the turbo-charged engine for 1982. The EPA mileage rating was 27 miles per gallon for city and 33 for highway driving. This welcome change was reflected in the production figures, which showed an increase of nearly 100% in 1982 over the previous year.

Specifications

	300CD	(turbo)
Engine type	5 cyl diesel, overhead camshaft (OM 617)	5 cyl diesel, overhead camshaft, with turbo-charger (OM 617A)
Bore and stroke	91 x 92.4mm (3.58 x 3.64 in)	91 x 92.4mm (3.58 x 3.64 in)
Displacement	3005 cc (183.4 cu in); 1979: 2998 cc (183 cu in)	2998 cc (182.9 cu in)
Power output	80 hp (DIN) @ 4000 rpm; 1979: 88 hp (DIN) @ 4400 rpm; U.S. 1977: 77 hp (SAE) @ 4000 rpm; 1980: 83 hp (SAE) @ 4200 rpm	125 hp (DIN) @ 4350 rpm U.S.: 120 hp (SAE)
Compression ratio	21:1	21.5:1
Torque	17.5 mkg @ 2400 rpm (126.6 ft/lb); 1979: 17.5 mkg @ 2400 rpm; U.S. 1977: 15.9 mkg (110.0 ft/lb); U.S. 1980: 16.7 mkg @ 2400 rpm (120 ft/lb)	25.5 mkg @ 2400 rpm U.S.: 23.6 mkg (170 ft/lb)
Fuel injection	Bosch five plunger pump	Bosch five plunger pump w/injection timer
Maximum engine speed	5300 rpm; U.S. 1980: 4200 rpm	5100 rpm; U.S.: 4350 rpm 1983: 4640 rpm
Engine speed at 100 km/hr	2995 rpm; automatic: 3090 rpm	
Gear ratios	I. 3.90:1 automatic: I. 3.98:1 II. 2.30:1 II. 2.39:1 III. 1.41:1 III. 1.46:1 IV. 1.00:1 IV. 1.00:1	I. 3.90:1 II. 2.30:1 III. 1.41:1 IV. 1.00:1
Rear axle ratio	3.46	3.07
Chassis	unit frame and body	
Suspension	independent front and rear, with coil springs; diagonal swing axle, coil springs, anti-lift control, stabilizer bar	
Brakes and area	dual circuit discs, power assisted, 278/279mm (10.9/11.0 in)	
Wheelbase	2710mm (106.7 in)	
Track, front/rear	1488/1446mm (58.6/56.9 in)	
Length	4640mm (182.6 in); U.S.: 4763mm (187.5 in)	
Width	1786mm (70.3 in)	
Height	1395mm (54.9 in)	
Tires	175 SR 14; 1979: 195/70 HR 14; U.S.: 195/70 HR 14	
Turning circle	11 meters (36.1 ft)	
Steering type and ratio	recirculating ball (3.2 turns), servo assisted	
Weight	1445 kg (3179 lbs); U.S.: 1585 kg (3487 lbs); U.S. 1978: 1575 kg (3465 lbs); U.S. 1980: 1545 kg (3399 lbs)	U.S. 1981: 1550 kg (3420 lbs) 1625 kg (3583 lbs)
Maximum speed	148 km/hr (92 mph); automatic: 143 km/hr (89 mph); 1979: 155 km/hr; automatic: 150 km/hr (93 mph)	
Acceleration	19.9 sec 0-100 km/hr; automatic: 20.8 sec; 1979: 17.8 sec; automatic: 19.2 sec	
Fuel consumption	10.8 liters/100 km (21.5 mpg); 1979: at 120 km/hr: 11.5 liters; automatic: 12.4 liters	
Fuel tank capacity	80 liters (21.1 gallons)	

The 280S sedan, 1979

The 280S sedan, 1979

Prices and Production

The 280S four-door sedan sold in 1981 for.........DM 40,511

Production of the 280S model [126 W28] (from April/December 1979)

	was in	1979	408 units
		1980	6,348 units
		1981	7,212 units
		1982	8,761 units

Model 280S (1979-   )

S = Super

The 280S sedan of the new S-class was introduced to the public at the Frankfurt Auto Show in 1979. It was one of seven models which had the new W126 body style.

By redesigning and completely reconstructing the body, with a lower and rather wedge-shaped hood line, recessing the windshield wipers, and such refinements, this new aerodynamic design resulted in a drag coefficient improvement of 14% over the previous W116 S-class bodies. The use of lighter material in construction resulted in a considerable saving of weight also, thus greatly contributing to superior economy of operation.

Actually, work on the design of this new S-class of model had begun some seven years previously, long before the oil shortage and ever escalating fuel cost was a known factor. Yet the Daimler-Benz engineers concentrated on the creation of a vehicle which would use considerably less gasoline because of lighter body weight and vastly improved engine design.

The 280S model was the least expensive of the new luxury line (Oberklasse) of sedans, and as such would find many anxious buyers who desired the top line car even if only the least powerful one of that type, which was still the most economical one as well.

The proven six-cylinder carburetor engine was improved to give better elasticity and combustion efficiency. The 2,746 cubic centimeter engine now developed 156 (DIN) horsepower at 5,500 revolutions per minute, giving the 1,560 kilogram (3,432 pound) sedan a top speed of 200 kilometers (124 miles) per hour with the manual transmission, and 195 km/hr with the automatic. (The old 280S weighed 1,610 kilograms (3,542 pounds) and had a maximum speed of 190 kilometers (118 miles) per hour.)

Specifications

	280S
Engine type	6 cyl double overhead camshafts (M110)
Bore and stroke	86 x 78.8 mm (3.39 x 3.10 in)
Displacement	2746 cc (167.6 cu in)
Power output	156 hp (DIN) @ 5500 rpm
Compression ratio	9:1
Torque	22.6 mkg @ 4000 rpm (164 ft/lb)
Carburetion	Solex dual compound downdraft 4A1
Maximum engine speed	6500 rpm
Gear ratios	I. 3.98:1 I. 3.68:1 (automatic) II. 2.29:1 II. 2.41:1 III. 1.45:1 III. 1.44:1 IV. 1.00:1 IV. 1.00:1
Rear axle ratio	3.46
Chassis	unit frame and body
Suspension	independent front and rear, with coil springs, anti-roll bar; diagonal swing axle, coil springs, anti-roll bar, level control
Brakes and area	dual circuit discs, power assisted, brake pad wear indicator, 278/279 mm (10.9/11.0 in)
Wheelbase	2935 mm (115.5 in)
Track, front/rear	1545/1517 mm (60.8/59.7 in)
Length	4995 mm (196.6 in)
Width	1820 mm (71.6 in)
Height	1430 mm (56.3 in)
Tires	195/70 HR 14
Turning circle	11.80 meters (38.7 feet)
Steering type and ratio	recirculating ball (2.75 turns), servo assisted
Weight	1560 kg (3432 lbs)
Maximum speed	200 km/hr (124 mph); automatic: 195 km/hr (121 mph)
Acceleration	10.8 sec 0-100 km/hr; automatic: 12 sec
Fuel consumption	at 120 km/hr: 11.1 liters/100 km (21 mpg); automatic: 11.6 liters (20.6 mpg)
Fuel tank capacity	90 liters (23.8 gallons)

Dimensions of the S-Class cars, 1979

Drawing of the S-Class sedans, 1979

Model 280SE/SEL (1979-)

S = Super, E (Einspritzung) = fuel injection

SE L (Lang) = long wheelbase chassis

The 280SE and 280SEL, introduced at the Frankfurt Auto Show in 1979, were the other six-cylinder sedans which shared the new W126 bodies. As in all of the models, the bodies were actually 3.5 centimeters (1.4 inches) longer and 5 centimeters (1.97 inches) wider than the previous W116 S-class bodies. The drag coefficient was only 0.38, considerably less than that of the modern sedans then being offered by the competitive automobile manufacturers. The new body style car was, of course, easily recognized as a Mercedes. By using newly developed materials and new body structures, the weight of the body shell was reduced by about 50 kilograms (110 pounds) and yet considerably improved in resistance in crash tests.

The 280SE offered the same driving performance of the former 350SE model which it replaced. The 280SEL was, of course, the longer wheelbase (121.1-inch) version of the 116.4-inch SE car. By changing the front wheel suspension and further reducing engine and wind noise, smoother running and handling were achieved.

The fuel-injected 280 engine, using mechanical fuel injection (K-Jetronic) with air flow metering device, developed 185 (DIN) horsepower at 5,800 revolutions per minute. The 280SE weighed 1,560 kilograms (3,432 pounds), while the longer SEL weighed 1,590 kg (3,498 lbs). Maximum speed was 210 kilometers (130 miles) per hour with manual transmission and 205 km/hr with automatic transmission. The 350SE weighed 1,675 kg (3,685 lbs) and had a top speed of 205 km/hr (127 mph).

The 280SE and 280SEL models were good touring cars with the characteristic features expected of this upper class line of cars, but with their six-cylinder fuel-injection engines they were still economical to operate, using about 11.3 liters of fuel for 100 kilometers, driving at 120 kilometers per hour, thus averaging about 20.5 miles per gallon with the manual transmission. The power-to-weight ratio of these models was 11.5 and 11.7 kilograms per horsepower, while the more powerful V-8 engined 380SE and 380SEL models had a 9.96 and 10.09 kilograms ratio, respectively, with consequently better acceleration and a 10 miles per hour higher maximum speed.

The 280SE sedan, 1979

Prices and Production

The 280SE four-door sedan sold in 1981 for.........DM 43,980

Production of the 280SE model [126 E28] (from February/December 1979)

was in	1979	812 units
	1980	22,482 units
	1981	26,654 units
	1982	23,287 units

The 280SEL four-door sedan sold in 1981 for.........DM 57,174

Production of the 280SEL model [126 E28] (from December 1979/June 1980)

was in	1979	1 unit
	1980	887 units
	1981	2,423 units
	1982	3,843 units

Specifications

	280SE/SEL	
Engine type	6 cyl double overhead camshafts (M110)	
Bore and stroke	86 x 78.8 mm (3.39 x 3.10 in)	
Displacement	2746 cc (167.6 cu in)	
Power output	185 hp (DIN) @ 5800 rpm	
Compression ratio	9:1	
Torque	24.4 mkg @ 4500 rpm (176.5 ft/lb)	
Fuel injection	Bosch mechanical with air flow sensor	
Maximum engine speed	6500 rpm	
Gear ratios	I. 3.98:1 II. 2.29:1 III. 1.45:1 IV. 1.00:1	I. 3.68:1 (automatic) II. 2.41:1 III. 1.44:1 IV. 1.00:1
Rear axle ratio	3.46	
Chassis	unit frame and body	
Suspension	independent front and rear, with coil springs, anti-roll bar; diagonal swing axle, coil springs, anti-roll bar, level control	
Brakes and area	dual circuit discs, power assisted, brake pad wear indicator, 278/279 mm (10.9/11.0 in)	
Wheelbase	2935 mm (115.5 in)	SEL: 3075 mm (121 in)
Track, front/rear	1545/1517 mm (60.8/59.7 in)	
Length	4995 mm (196.6 in)	SEL: 5135 mm (202.1 in)
Width	1820 mm (71.6 in)	
Height	1430 mm (56.3 in)	SEL: 1434 mm (56.4 in)
Tires	195/70 VR 14	
Turning circle	11.80 meters (38.7 feet)	SEL: 12.26 meters (40.2 feet)
Steering type and ratio	recirculating ball (2.75 turns), servo assisted	
Weight	1560 kg (3432 lbs)	SEL: 1590 kg (3498 lbs)
Maximum speed	210 km/hr (130 mph); automatic: 205 km/hr (127 mph)	
Acceleration	9.8 sec 0-100 km/hr; automatic: 11.1 sec	
Fuel consumption	at 120 km/hr: 11.3 liters/100 km (20.8 mpg); automatic: 11.7 liters (20.5 mpg)	
Fuel tank capacity	90 liters (23.8 gallons)	

The 280SE sedan, 1979

The SE sedans of 1979

The 380SE sedan, 1979

Prices and Production

The 380SE four-door sedan sold in 1980 for ....DM 48,510

Production of the 380SE model [126 E38] (from May 1979/January 1980)

was in	1979	217 units
	1980	7,935 units
	1981	8,603 units
	1982	7,423 units

The 380SEL four-door sedan sold in 1980 for ....DM 50,974
The 380SEL sedan sold in the United States
  (with automatic transmission)
    in November 1980 for (East Coast)................$44,298
    in September 1982 (East Coast).................$47,870

Production of the 380SEL model [126 E38] (from October 1979/June 1980)

was in	1979	1 unit
	1980	1,648 units
	1981	6,726 units
	1982	8,496 units

Model 380SE/SEL (1979-   )

S = Super, E (Einspritzung) = fuel injection

SE L (Lang) = long wheelbase chassis

The 380SE and 380SEL, with the new S-class body style, were also first shown at the Frankfurt Auto Show in 1979. This line of cars was to replace the previous 450 line of sedans, and with the smaller displacement engines and lighter bodies, appeared to be worthy successors to the 450 line of sedans.

With the newly designed lighter V-8 engines of 218 (DIN) horsepower and favorable body weight of 1,595 kilograms (3,509 pounds), and 1,615 kilograms (3,553 lbs), respectively, they were spirited performers. Acceleration from 0 to 100 kilometers per hour was 8.9 seconds and maximum speed was 215 kilometers (133.5 miles) per hour with the automatic transmission. The 450SE sedan (1,740 kg or 3,828 lbs) had posted acceleration figures of 9.3 seconds and a top speed of 210 kilometers (130 miles) per hour. Fuel consumption was reduced by 10%, partly due to the new four-speed automatic transmission.

The 380SEL model became available in the United States for the 1981 model year. It was, however, a greatly altered car and, because of strict emission control and safety standards, appreciably different from the European version.

The engine, with a bore of 88 millimeters and stroke of 78.9 millimeters, displaced 3,839 cubic centimeters instead of the 3,818 and developed only 155 SAE horsepower at 4,750 revolutions per minute instead of 218. Torque was 196 lb/ft (27.1 mkg) at 2,750 rpm. Compression ratio was 8.3:1 instead of 9:1. The weight of the sedan had increased by 90 kilograms (110 pounds) to 1,685 kg (3,715 lbs). With the rear axle ratio of 2.47:1 (3.27:1 in Europe), the car had a maximum speed of about 115 miles per hour. The power-to-weight ratio of this model was 25.5 pounds per horsepower against the 16.28 for the European version.

Despite all of these changes, the character of the car had not changed much, and the 380SEL was still a most desirable automobile, and in the words of a most prestiguous reviewer magazine, *Road & Track*, "the best four-door sedan in the world today" (January 1981).

Specifications

	380SE/SEL		
Engine type	V-8 cyl overhead camshafts (M116)		
Bore and stroke	92 x 71.8 mm (3.62 x 2.83 in)	1981: 88 x 78.9 mm (3.46 x 3.10 in)	
Displacement	3818 cc (233 cu in)	1981: 3839 cc (234 cu in)	
Power output	218 hp (DIN) @ 5500 rpm	1981: 204 hp (DIN) @ 5250 rpm	SEL U.S. 1981: 155 hp SAE @ 4750 rpm
Compression ratio	9:1	1981: 9.4:1	SEL U.S. 1981: 8.3:1
Torque	31 mkg @ 4000 rpm (224.3 ft/lb)	1981: 32 mkg @ 3250 rpm (230.0 ft/lb)	SEL U.S. 1981: 27.1 mkg @ 2750 rpm
Fuel Injection	Bosch mechanical with air flow sensor		
Maximum engine speed	6600 rpm		SEL U.S. 1981: 5300 rpm; 1983: 5500 rpm
Gear ratios	I. 3.68:1 (automatic, standard) II. 2.41:1 III. 1.44:1 IV. 1.00:1		
Rear axle ratio	3.27		SEL U.S. 1981: 2.47
Chassis	unit frame and body		
Suspension	independent front and rear, with coil springs, anti-roll bar; diagonal swing axle, coil springs, anti-roll bar, level control, hydropneumatic, optional		
Brakes and area	dual circuit discs, power assisted, brake pad wear indicator, 278/279 mm (10.9/11.0 in)		
Wheelbase	2935 mm (115.5 in)		SEL: 3075 mm (121 in)
Track, front/rear	1545/1517 mm (60.8/59.7 in)		
Length	4995 mm (196.6 in)		SEL: 5135 mm (202.1 in); U.S.: 5285 mm (208 in)
Width	1820 mm (71.6 in)		
Height	1436 mm (56.5 in)		SEL: 1440 mm (56.7 in)
Tires	205/70 VR 14		
Turning circle	11.80 meters (38.7 feet)		SEL: 12.26 meters (40.2 feet)
Steering type and ratio	recirculating ball (2.75 turns), servo assisted		
Weight	1595 kg (3509 lbs)		SEL: 1615 kg (3553 lbs) SEL U.S.: 1685 kg (3715 lbs) SEL 1982: 1715 kg (3780 lbs)
Maximum speed	215 km/hr (134 mph)		SEL 1981: 210 km/hr
Acceleration	8.9 sec 0-100 km/hr		SEL 1981: 9.8 sec 0-100 km/hr
Fuel consumption	at 120 km/hr: 13.3 liters/100 km (17.6 mpg)		SEL 1981: 10.8 liters/100 km
Fuel tank capacity	90 liters (23.8 gallons)		

The 500SE sedan, 1979

Front view of the 500SE sedan, 1979

Prices and Production

The 500SE four-door sedan sold in 1980 for . . . . .DM 52,680

Production of the 500SE model [126 E50] (from September 1979/ January 1980)

was in	1979	149 units
	1980	5,312 units
	1981	3,308 units
	1982	3,349 units

The 500SEL four-door sedan sold in 1980 for . . . . . . .DM 58,364

Production of the 500SEL model [126 E50] (from September 1979/ June 1980)

was in	1979	2 units
	1980	2,206 units
	1981	5,942 units
	1982	8,966 units

Model 500SE/SEL (1979-   )

S = Super, E (Einspritzung) = fuel injection

SE L (Lang) = long wheelbase chassis

The 500SE and 500SEL were the top of the line cars of the new S-class shown first at the Frankfurt Auto Show in 1979. They were the most luxurious sedans built by Daimler-Benz.

The newly bodied sedans replaced the former star performer, the 450SEL 6.9. The light allow 4,973-cubic centimeter engine, already used in the 450SLC 5.0 since its debut in 1977, developed 240 (DIN) horsepower at 4,750 revolutions per minute in the new sedans. (The SLC engine ran at 5,000 revolutions per minute.)

This engine was not only widely tested in the former luxury coupe, but also in a number of highly competitive rally events under most trying conditions. As an example, in the 1979 Bandama Rally in December 1979, four factory-prepared coupes, weighing 1,350 kilograms and their engines developing 300 horsepower, won the first four places of this 5,600-kilometer long and extremely brutal rally event.

All of these new models with the V-8 engines had the newly designed four-speed automatic transmission and showed improved fuel economy. At a speed of 90 kilometers (56 miles) per hour, the 2,175-kilogram (4,785-pound) car used 11.3 liters per 100 kilometers and at 120 kilometers (75 miles) per hour it used 13.5 liters, or 17.4 miles per gallon. Acceleration was 7.7 seconds for the 0 to 100 kilometers (0-62 miles) per hour and maximum speed for the 500SE and SEL was 225 kilometers (140 miles) per hour. For the 6.9 sedan, weighing 1,935 kilograms (4,257 pounds), the acceleration figures had been 7.4 seconds, and top speed achieved by the 500SEL was the same.

At the time of their introduction, Werner Breitschwerdt, Chief of Development at Daimler-Benz, said, "The new 500SE and 500SEL five-liter models are equal or even superior to our 450SEL 6.9 in design and equipment." His and his predecessor's (Hans Scherenberg) team of able designers and engineers had indeed achieved an exceedingly high level of comfort and performance in the new models.

Specifications

	500SE/SEL		
Engine type	V-8 cyl overhead camshafts (M117)		
Bore and stroke	96.5 x 85 mm (3.80 x 3.35 in)		
Displacement	4973 cc (303.5 cu in)		
Power output	240 hp (DIN) @ 4750 rpm	1981: 231 hp (DIN) @ 4750 rpm	
Compression ratio	8.8:1	1981: 9.2:1	
Torque	41 mkg @ 3200 rpm (296.6 ft/lb)		
Fuel injection	Bosch mechanical with air flow sensor		
Maximum engine speed	5950 rpm		
Gear ratios	I. 3.68:1 (automatic, standard) II. 2.41:1 III. 1.44:1 IV. 1.00:1		
Rear axle ratio	2.82	1981: 2.24	
Chassis	unit frame and body		
Suspension	independent front and rear, with coil springs, anti-roll bar; diagonal swing axle, coil springs, anti-roll bar, level control, hydropneumatic, optional		
Brakes and area	dual circuit discs, power assisted, brake pad wear indicator, 278/279 mm (10.9/11.0 in)		
Wheelbase	2855 mm (112.4 in)	1981: 2930 mm	SEL: 2955 mm (116.3 in); 1981: 3070 mm (120.8 in)
Track, front/rear	1545/1517 mm (60.8/59.7 in)		
Length	4995 mm (196.6 in)		SEL: 5135 mm (202.1 in)
Width	1820 mm (71.6 in)		
Height	1436 mm (56.5 in)		SEL: 1440 mm (56.7 in)
Tires	205/70 VR 14		
Turning circle	11.80 meters (38.7 feet)		SEL: 12.26 meters (40.2 feet)
Steering type and ratio	recirculating ball (2.75 turns), servo assisted		
Weight	1620 kg (3564 lbs)		SEL: 1655 kg (3641 lbs)
Maximum speed	225 km/hr (140 mph)		
Acceleration	7.7 sec 0-100 km/hr		
Fuel consumption	at 120 km/hr: 13.5 liters/100 km (17.4 mpg)	1981: 11.4 liters/100 km	
Fuel tank capacity	90 liters (23.8 gallons)		

Instrument panel of the 500SE sedan, 1979

Model 300TD (1979-   )

T = station wagon, D = Diesel

The 300TD turbo-charged diesel-engined station wagon was introduced at the Frankfurt Auto Show in 1979, but was not scheduled to go into production until the middle of 1980.

This newest addition to the line of five differently powered wagons would use up to 10% less fuel, gave superior performance, and had a higher load capacity than the regular five-cylinder diesel-engined vehicle.

The OM617A turbo diesel engine was the same as had been available in the United States only in the SD sedan and developed 125 (DIN) horsepower at 4,350 revolutions per minute. Maximum torque was 25.5 mkg (184.4 pounds/feet) at 2,400 revolutions per minute. In the U.S., this turbo diesel developed 120 SAE horsepower and had a torque of 23.6 mkg (170 lbs/ft).

Appointments of this station wagon, available now in other countries than the United States, were those of the more luxurious 280TE. Automatic transmission was standard, and with over 40% greater output and lower fuel consumption than the regular aspirated five-cylinder diesel, this new model was expected to be a good choice. A new, quicker starting system, available from August 1980, would reduce the starting time to some five seconds at outside temperatures of 0 degrees Centigrade (32 degrees Fahrenheit). At higher temperatures the engine could be started in an even shorter time.

For the model year 1981, the turbo charged diesel-engined station wagon was the only model station wagon sold in the United States market. It replaced the former model with the naturally aspirated OM617 five-cylinder diesel engine, but the old designation of 300TD remained. The body style and appointments were the same as previously, but the performance had, of course, greatly improved. And so had the price.

The Environmental Protection Agency rated for 1981 the 300TD at 26 miles per gallon for the city cycle and 30 miles per gallon for highway travel, or an average fuel consumption of 28 miles per gallon.

The 300TD turbo station wagon, 1980

Prices and Production

The 300TD (turbo) station wagon sold in 1980 for . . . .DM 36,521
   in 1982 for. . . . . .DM 40,940
The 300TD station wagon sold in the United States
   (with automatic transmission)
   in November 1980 for (East Coast). $31,373
   in September 1982 (East Coast) $33,850

Production of the 300TD turbo station wagon [123 D30A] (from November 1979/October 1980)

was in	1979	2 units
	1980	1,852 units
	1981	6,710 units
	1982	6,302 units

Specifications

	300TD (turbo)
Engine type	5 cyl diesel, overhead camshaft, with turbo-charger (OM 617A)
Bore and stroke	91 x 92.4mm (3.58 x 3.64 in)
Displacement	2998 cc (182.9 cu in)
Power output	125 hp (DIN) @ 4350 rpm U.S.: 120 hp (SAE)
Compression ratio	21.5:1
Torque	25.5 mkg @ 2400 rpm U.S.: 23.6 mkg (170 ft/lb)
Fuel injection	Bosch five plunger pump w/injection timer
Maximum engine speed	5100 rpm; U.S.: 4350 rpm, 1982: 4500 rpm; 1983: 4640 rpm
Gear ratios	I. 3.90:1 II. 2.30:1 III. 1.41:1 IV. 1.00:1
Rear axle ratio	3.07
Chassis	unit frame and body
Suspension	independent front and rear, coil springs; diagonal swing axle, coil springs, torsion bar stabilizer, standard level control
Brakes and area	dual circuit discs, front brake pad wear indicator, 278/279mm (10.9/11.0 in)
Wheelbase	2795mm (110.0 in)
Track, front/rear	1488/1453mm (58.6/57.2 in)
Length	4725mm (186.0 in) U.S.: 4848mm (190.9 in)
Width	1786mm (70.3 in)
Height	1470mm (57.9 in)
Tires	195/70 SR 14
Turning circle	11.29 meters (37 ft)
Steering type and ratio	recirculating ball (3.2 turns), power assisted
Weight	1610 kg (3542 lbs) U.S.: 1695 kg (3729 lbs), 1715 kg (3780 lbs)
Maximum speed	automatic: 165 km/hr (103 mph)
Acceleration	automatic: 15 sec 0-100 km/hr
Fuel consumption	at 120 km/hr: 11.1 liters
Fuel tank capacity	70 liters (18.5 gallons)

The 300TD turbo station wagon, 1981, U.S. version

The 200T station wagon, 1980

The M 102 engine for the 200T, 1980

The 200T, 1980

Prices and Production

The 200T station wagon sold in 1980 for . . . . .DM 26,114

Production of the 200T station wagon [123 V20] (from May/November 1980)

was in	1980	648 units
	1981	3,142 units
	1982	3,809 units

Model 200T (1980-   )

T (Touristik und Transport) = station wagon

The 200T station wagon model was built when the newly designed, greatly advanced four-cylinder gasoline engine was created in early 1980. The 200 sedan was the only other model then available with this smoother, fuel-saving, and more powerful M102 engine.

The 200T was like the other station wagons in body style and appointments, and it represented just another addition to the already wide range of those popular utility vehicles first shown in 1977 and enthusiastically received by the public. For buyers who wanted a gasoline-engined version with the greatest economy possible, this new model proved most satisfactory.

Fuel saving was the ultimate concern at that time and this least powerful of station wagon models was in keeping with the times of serious fuel shortages and steadily advancing costs.

Real production began in September, but one unit was produced in May, a month after the manufacture of the 230T model had ceased, with another one following in June, none in July, and two in August. These early units were, of course, used mainly for testing purposes, and sales began with the fall production. By December, 349 units of the 200T were built.

The 1,997-cubic centimeter displacement engine developed 109 DIN horsepower at 5,200 revolutions per minute, had a 9:1 compression ratio, and torque of 17.3 mkg at 3,000 rpm. The acceleration of the 1,455-kilogram heavy 200T wagon was 14.4 seconds for the 0 to 100 kilometers per hour speed with the manual, and 15.4 seconds with the automatic transmission. The maximum speed was 168 kilometers per hour with the manual and 163 kilometers per hour with the automatic transmission.

Fuel consumption was rated at 14.2 liters per 100 kilometers of driving the urban cycle with the manual, and 13.8 liters with the automatic transmission. At a speed of 120 kilometers per hour, consumption was 10.6 liters with manual, and 11.5 liters with the automatic tranmission.

Specifications

	200T
Engine type	4 cyl overhead camshaft (M102)
Bore and stroke	89 x 80.25 (3.50 x 3.16 in)
Displacement	1997 cc (121.72 cu in)
Power output	109 hp (DIN) @ 5200 rpm
Compression ratio	9.0:1
Torque	17.3 mkg @ 3000 rpm (125.2 ft/lb)
Carburetion	Stromberg sidedraft 175 CDT
Maximum engine speed	6000 rpm
Gear ratios	I. 3.91:1 I. 3.98:1 (automatic) II. 2.32:1 II. 2.39:1 III. 1.42:1 III. 1.46:1 IV. 1.00:1 IV. 1.00:1
Rear axle ratio	3.69
Chassis	unit frame and body
Suspension	independent front and rear, with coil springs; diagonal pivot axle; coil springs, anti-roll bar
Brakes and area	dual circuit discs, front brake pad wear indicator, 278/279 mm (10.9/11.0 in)
Wheelbase	2795 mm (110.0 in)
Track, front/rear	1488/1446 mm (58.6/56.9 in)
Length	4725 mm (186.0 in)
Width	1786 mm (70.3 in)
Height	1438 mm (56.6 in)
Tires	195/70 SR 14
Turning circle	11.29 meters (37 feet)
Steering type and ratio	recirculating ball (3.2 turns), power assisted
Weight	1455 kg (3204 lbs)
Maximum speed	168 km/hr (104 mph); automatic: 163 km/hr (101 mph)
Acceleration	15.3 sec 0-100 km/hr; automatic: 16.4 sec 0-100 km/hr
Fuel consumption	at 120 km/hr: 10.2 liters/100 km; automatic: 11.0 liters
Fuel tank capacity	70 liters (18.5 gallons)

Dimensions for the T-models

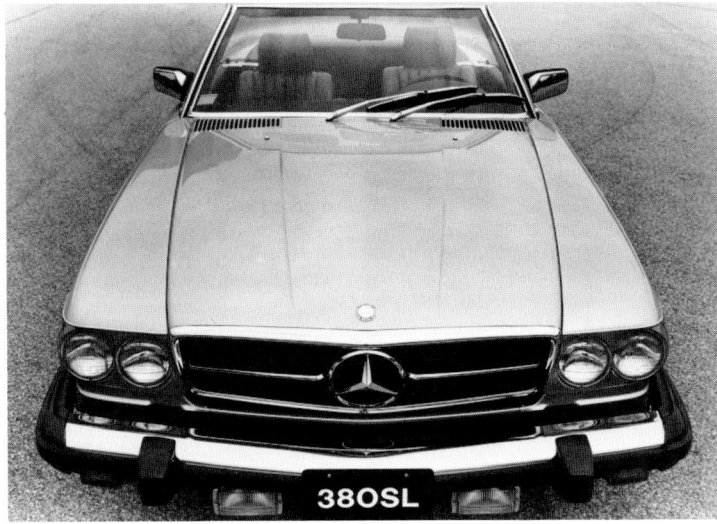

The 380SL roadster, 1981, U.S. version

Prices and Production

The 380SL roadster sold in 1980 for . . . . DM 54,014
The 380SL roadster sold in the United States
  (with automatic transmission)
  in November 1980 for (East Coast) $38,993
  in September 1982 (East Coast) $43,030

Production of the 380SL model [107 E 38] (from February/May 1980)

was in	1980	3,347 units
	1981	9,470 units
	1982	9,926 units

Model 380SL (1980-   )

S = Sports, L = Light, C = Coupe

The 380SL model was first publicly shown in March 1980 at the 50th Geneva Auto Show, the traditional exhibition for the introduction of Mercedes sports models. This sporty roadster was one of the three open cars still being manufactured — the others were the 280SL and 500SL — and considering that since 1971 more than 85,000 of the 107 type roadsters had been produced, it was a sound decision to continue the model with a practically unchanged body.

Since the introduction of the latest S-class sedans, all of these 3.8-liter eight-cylinder models were equipped with the economical new generation light-alloy engines of 3,818 cubic centimeter displacement, producing 160 DIN horsepower.

The 1,540 kilogram (3,396 pounds) heavy 380SL had a maximum speed of 215 kilometers per hour and acceleration of 9.0 seconds for the 0 to 100 kilometers per hour speed. The figures for the older 450SL of 1,585 kilograms, which it replaced, had been 8.5 seconds and also 215 km/hr (133.5 mph) top speed, thus this smaller displacement and lighter engined model was practically the identically performing car.

For the United States market, the 380SL was, like the sedan, altered to conform with the government regulations. The 3,839 cubic centimeter engine had a longer stroke for better emission controls, but aside from the slightly differing size, was constructed of the same weight-saving materials. It developed 155 SAE horsepower, had a compression ratio of only 8.3:1, and a torque of 27.1 mkg (196 lbs/ft). The car weighed 1,635 kilograms (3,605 lbs), and maximum speed was about 120 miles per hour.

Despite the alterations, the 380SL was still a superbly performing car, and a fine replacement for the 450SL (with the considerably larger engine) of which over 57,000 units (including the 350SLs) had been sold in this country over the past ten years. Even during 1980, when the 380SL was first introduced for the 1981 model year, a total of 1,624 cars had already been imported.

Specifications

	380SL		
Engine type	V-8 cyl overhead camshafts (M116)		
Bore and stroke	92 x 71.8 mm (3.62 x 2.83 in)	1981: 88 x 78.9 mm	U.S.: 88 x 78.9 mm (3.46 x 3.11 in)
Displacement	3818 cc (233 cu in)	1981: 3839 cc	U.S.: 3839 cc (234.3 cu in)
Power output	218 hp (DIN) @ 5500 rpm	1981: 204 hp (DIN) @ 5250 rpm	U.S.: 155 hp SAE @ 4750 rpm
Compression ratio	9:1	1981: 9.4:1	U.S.: 8.3:1
Torque	31 mkg @ 4000 rpm (224.3 ft/lb)		U.S.: 27.1 mkg @ 2750 rpm (196 ft/lb)
Fuel injection	Bosch mechanical with air flow sensor		
Maximum engine speed	6600 rpm		U.S.: 5300 rpm; 1983: 5500 rpm
Gear ratios	I. 3.68:1 (automatic, standard) II. 2.41:1 III. 1.44:1 IV. 1.00:1		
Rear axle ratio	3.27		U.S.: 2.47
Chassis	unit frame and body		
Suspension	independent front and rear, coil springs, anti-roll bar; diagonal swing axle, coil springs, anti-roll bar, level control, hydropneumatic, optional		
Brakes and area	dual circuit discs, power assisted, brake pad wear indicator, 278/279 mm (10.9/11.0 in)		
Wheelbase	2455 mm (96.7 in)		
Track, front/rear	1452/1440 mm (57.2/56.7 in)		
Length	4390 mm (172.8 in)		U.S.: 4630 mm (182.3 in)
Width	1790 mm (70.5 in)		
Height	1300 mm (51.2 in)		
Tires	205/70 VR 14		U.S.: 205/70 HR 14
Turning circle	10.74 meters (35.2 ft)		U.S.: 10.48 meters (34.4 ft)
Steering type and ratio	recirculating ball (3.0 turns), servo assisted		
Weight	1540 kg (3392 lbs)		U.S.: 1635 kg (3605 lbs); 1983: 1650 kg
Maximum speed	215 km/hr (134 mph)		
Acceleration	9 sec 0-100 km/hr	1981: 9.8 sec 0-100 km/hr	
Fuel consumption	at 120 km/hr: 13.6 liters/100 km (17.3 mpg); 1981: 11.3 liters		
Fuel tank capacity	90 liters (23.8 gallons)		U.S.: 85 liters (22.4 gallons)

Model 380SLC (1980-1981)

S = Sports, L = Light, C = Coupe

The 380SLC coupe, the companion model to the roadster, was also first shown at the Geneva Auto Show in 1980. Here, too, it was pointed out that these style coupes, with the different engine sizes, were steady sellers with over 54,000 units sold since their inception in 1972, when this 107SCL body type was first produced.

The bodies of the new cars remained as before, but had a front spoiler added, and only the power units were new. Engine specifications were as in the SL models, the usual practice in this line of cars.

These eight-cylinder models had the new four-speed torque converter automatic transmission as standard equipment, while in the six-cylinder 280SL/SLC line it was an optional extra cost item. This new transmission was considered quite suitable for sporty driving as well as for a more fuel-conscious driving style. New brake calipers were fitted with larger brake pads and rear anti-squat suspension linkage was provided.

The fuel consumption of the 380SL/SLC was rated at 18.8 liters per 100 kilometers in urban driving and at 120 kilometers per hour at 13.6 liters for highway driving, again identical with both models.

In the United States the 380SLC was, of course, the true counterpart to the SL. The engine was the very same as in the 380SEL sedan, and practically all essential specifications were identical in all these 380 models. Performance figures of the SLC were also the same as those for the SL, although the weight was 10 kilograms (22 pounds) less for the coupe than for the roadster.

Fuel consumption rated by the Environmental Protection Agency for 1981 was 17 miles per gallon for the city driving cycle and 24 miles per gallon for highway driving, for a combination average rating of 20 miles per gallon.

Over the nine-year period, a total of 13,890 units of the SLC 450 model had been brought to this country (against about 57,000 of the SLs) and in 1980 already 380 cars had been imported by the distributor.

The 380SLC coupe, 1980

Prices and Production

The 380SLC coupe sold in 1980 for . . . . .DM 57,743
The 380SLC coupe sold in the United States
   (with automatic transmission)
   in November 1980 for (East Coast). $46,638

Production of the 380SLC model [107 E38] (from February/May 1980 until September 1981)

was in	1980	1,737 units
	1981	2,052 units
	total	3,789 units

Specifications

	380SLC	
Engine type	V-8 cyl overhead camshafts (M116)	
Bore and stroke	92 x 71.8 mm (3.62 x 2.83 in)	U.S.: 88 x 78.9 mm (3.46 x 3.11 in)
Displacement	3818 cc (233 cu in)	U.S.: 3839 cc (234.3 cu in)
Power output	218 hp (DIN) @ 5500 rpm	U.S.: 155 hp SAE @ 4750 rpm
Compression ratio	9:1	U.S.: 8.3:1
Torque	31 mkg @ 4000 rpm (224.3 ft/lb)	U.S.: 27.1 mkg @ 2750 rpm (196 ft/lb)
Fuel injection	Bosch mechanical with air flow sensor	
Maximum engine speed	6600 rpm	U.S.: 5300 rpm
Gear ratios	I. 3.68:1 (automatic, standard) II. 2.41:1 III. 1.44:1 IV. 1.00:1	
Rear axle ratio	3.27	U.S.: 2.47
Chassis	unit frame and body	
Suspension	independent front and rear, coil springs, anti-roll bar; diagonal swing axle, coil springs, anti-roll bar, level control, hydropneumatic optional	
Brakes and area	dual circuit discs, power assisted, brake pad wear indicator, 278/279 mm (10.9/11.0 in)	
Wheelbase	2820 mm (111 in)	
Track, front/rear	1452/1440 mm (57.2/56.7 in)	
Length	4750 mm (187.0 in)	U.S.: 4990 mm (196.4 in)
Width	1790 mm (70.5 in)	
Height	1330 mm (52.4 in)	
Tires	205/70 VR 14	U.S.: 205/70 RH 14
Turning circle	11.55 meters (37.9 ft)	
Steering type and ratio	recirculating ball (3.0 turns), servo assisted	
Weight	1560 kg (3435 lbs)	U.S.: 1625 kg (3585 lbs)
Maximum speed	215 km/hr (134 mph)	
Acceleration	9 sec 0-100 km/hr	
Fuel consumption	at 120 km/hr: 13.6 liters/100 km (17.3 mpg)	
Fuel tank capacity	90 liters (23.8 gallons)	U.S.: 85 liters (22.4 gallons)

The M 116 engine for the 380SLC, 1980

Model 500SL/SLC (1980-   )

S = Sports, L (Leicht) = light

S = Sports, L = Light, C = Coupe

The 500SL roadster, 1980

The 500SL and 500SLC were nearly identical to the 380SL/SLC sports models introduced also in March at the Geneva Auto Show, except, of course, for the power.

The body style was similar to the old 107 style except that the cars had the rear spoiler, formerly only used on the 450SLC 5.0 model. The front spoiler, also made of dark grey foamed plastic, was a feature of both eight-cylinder SL and SLC models. This innovation definitely improved the handling characteristics at higher speeds because of the great reduction in air resistance. All models also had the light-allow hoods for weight saving.

The running gear was nearly identical with the former models, although some details had been improved, such as the double wishbone axle with coil springs and anti-roll bar in front and the diagonal swing axle with them in the rear, and as the larger brake pads, increasing their serviceable life by about 30%. As an option, the anti-lock braking system was available on all SL and SLC models, which prevented wheel lock-up when braking, particularly under certain road conditions when the car had a tendency to skid. These models also had the anti-squat device on the swing axle which kept the rear end from sagging during fast acceleration.

Acceleration was considerably better than that of the 380 line, taking but 7.8 seconds for the 0 to 100 kilometer per hour speed, with a maximum speed for the 500SL/SLC of 225 kilometers per hour.

Since the cars had a 240 horsepower engine, just as the almost legendary 300SL had almost 30 years ago, comparison with that sports car might be of interest. The 1,330 kilogram 300SL coupe accelerated in 8.7 seconds, the roadster in 8.1 seconds, from 0 to 100 kilometers per hour. (The weight of the 500SL was 1,540 kilograms and that of the 500SLC, strangely, only 1,515 kilograms. However, the 500SL and SLC were quite comfortable sporty cars compared with the real sports characteristics of the 300SL models.) The 500SL and SLC cars were truly splendid performers.

Prices and Production

The 500SL roadster sold in 1980 for . . . . .DM 61,924

Production of the 500SL model [107 E50] (from April 1980)
```
        was in  1980     501 units
                1981     899 units
                1982   1,297 units
```

The 500SLC coupe sold in 1980 for . . . . .DM 67,122

Production of the 500SLC coupe [107 E50] (from February/May 1980 until September 1981)
```
        was in  1980     816 units
                1981     483 units
                total  1,299 units
```

Specifications

	500SL/SLC		
Engine type	V-8 cyl overhead camshafts (M117)		
Bore and stroke	96.5 x 85.0 mm (3.80 x 3.35 in)		
Displacement	4973 cc (303.5 cu in)		
Power output	240 hp (DIN) @ 5000 rpm	1981: 231 hp (DIN) @ 4750 rpm	
Compression ratio	8.8:1	1981: 9.2:1	
Torque	41 mkg @ 3200 rpm (296.6 ft/lb)		
Fuel injection	Bosch mechanical with air flow sensor		
Maximum engine speed	5950 rpm		
Gear ratios	I.　3.68:1 (automatic, standard) II.　2.41:1 III.　1.44:1 IV.　1.00:1		
Rear axle ratio	2.72	1981: 2.24	
Chassis	unit frame and body		
Suspension	independent front and rear, coil springs, anti-roll bar; diagonal swing axle, coil springs, anti-roll bar		
Brakes and area	dual circuit discs, power assisted, brake pad wear indicator, 278/279 mm (10.9/11.0 in)		
Wheelbase	2455 mm (96.7 in)		SLC: 2820 mm (111.0 in)
Track, front/rear	1452/1440 mm (57.2/56.7 in)		
Length	4390 mm (172.8 in)		SLC: 4750 mm (187.0 in)
Width	1790 mm (70.5 in)		
Height	1300 mm (51.2 in)		SLC: 1330 mm (52.4 in)
Tires	205/70 VR 14		
Turning circle	10.74 meters (35.2 ft)		SLC: 11.55 meters (37.9 ft)
Steering type and ratio	recirculating ball (3.0 turns), servo assisted		
Weight	1540 kg (3392 lbs)		SLC: 1515 kg (3336 lbs)
Maximum speed	225 km/hr (140 mph)		
Acceleration	7.8 sec 0-100 km/hr	1981: 8.1 sec 0-100 km/hr	
Fuel consumption	at 120 km/hr: 13.3 liters/100 km (17.6 mpg)	1981: 11.5 liters	
Fuel tank capacity	90 liters (23.8 gallons)		

The 500SLC coupe, 1980

Model 300SD (1979-   )

S = turbo-charged, D = Diesel

The 300SD sedan with the W126 body of the S-class was introduced to the public at the Frankurt Auto Show in 1979. It was one of the four models which shared that upper class body style. The gasoline-engined 280SE/SEL, 380SE/SEL, and 500SE/SEL sedans were the other luxury models.

These lighter cars (by as much as 176 pounds) were indeed "engineered for the future — to meet the demands of today," although development work had begun seven years before when the economic factor was not a dominating concern, but emission and safety received the main emphasis. The lower and smoother hood line gave the W126 bodies a drag coefficient of only .36, an improvement of 14% over the older body style.

Square halogen sealed beam headlights replaced the previous round style. Windshield wipers were recessed. The hood and rear deck lid were of aluminum. Bumpers were redesigned, stronger yet lighter. Climate control was electronically controlled instead of vacuum operated.

The 300SD was available in Europe soon after introduction and production of over 500 units in September, climbing to over 1,500 by November, indicated good sales. In the United States the new 300SD model was first sold in the 1981 model year. That car weighed then 1,705 kilograms (3,760 pounds), fully equipped, and had undergone some changes to comply with government regulations. Alloy wheels were standard, but leather upholstery was an optional extra item.

The Environmental Protection Agency rated the 300SD at 26 miles per gallon for the city cycle of driving and 30 miles per gallon for highway cruising. (The 240D manual got 29/33 mpg, automatic 27/31 mpg.) With the 20.3 gallon fuel tank, the turbo-charged five-cylinder diesel had a driving range of 609 miles, the longest distance of all models then sold in this country. Anticipating an extraordinary demand for this model (quite correctly when using 20/20 hindsight), the distributor brought 2,443 units into this country in 1980 already, just to be prepared for this eventuality.

The 300SD sedan, 1981, U.S. version

The OM 617A engine for the 300SD, 1980

Prices and Production

The 300SD four-door sedan in 1981 sold for . . . . .DM 37,815
The 300SD sedan sold in the United States
  (with automatic transmission)
  in November 1980 for (East Coast). $34,185
  in September 1982 (East Coast) $37,970

Production of the 300SD model [126 D30A] (from September 1979/October 1980)

was in 1979	3 units
1980	4,857 units
1981	16,595 units
1982	18,122 units

Specifications

	300SD
Engine type	5 cyl diesel, overhead camshaft, with turbo-charger (OM 617A)
Bore and stroke	91 x 92.4mm (3.58 x 3.64 in)
Displacement	2998 cc (182.9 cu in)
Power output	125 hp (DIN); U.S.: 120 hp (SAE)
Compression ratio	21.5:1
Torque	25.5 mkg @ 2400 rpm U.S.: 23.6 mkg (170 ft/lb) @ 2400 rpm
Maximum engine speed	5100 rpm; U.S.: 4350 rpm U.S. 1982: 4500 rpm; 1983: 4640 rpm
Fuel injection	Bosch five plunger pump with injection timer
Engine speed at 100 km/hr	
Gear ratios	I. 3.90:1 II. 2.30:1 III. 1.41:1 IV. 1.00:1
Rear axle ratio	3.07
Chassis	unit frame and body
Suspension	independent front and rear, coil springs; diagonal swing axle, coil springs, anti-roll bar, level control standard
Brakes and area	dual circuit discs, power assisted, brake pad wear indicator, 278/279mm (10.9/11.0 in)
Wheelbase	2935mm (115.6 in)
Track, front/rear	1545/1517mm (60.8/59.7 in)
Length	4995mm (196.6 in); U.S.: 5145mm (202.6 in)
Width	1820mm (71.6 in)
Height	1430mm (56.3 in)
Tires	195/70 RS 14
Turning circle	11.80 meters (38.7 ft)
Steering type and ratio	recirculating ball (2.7 turns); servo assisted
Weight	1705 kg (3751 lbs) 1982: 1715 kg (3780 lbs)
Maximum speed	165 km/hr (103 mph) automatic
Acceleration	15 sec 0–100 km/hr
Fuel consumption	11.1 liters at 120 km/hr
Fuel tank capacity	77 liters (20.3 gallons)

The OM 617A engine for the 300SD, 1980

Model 380SEC (1980-   )

S = Super, E (Einspritzung) = fuel injection, C = Coupe

The 380SEC coupe was first shown at the Frankfurt Auto Show in 1981. Developed from the W126 sedan of the S-class of cars introduced two years before, the lines of this coupe showed clearly their heritage. However, the front end had the lower, sportier looking profile of the 380SLC which it replaced.

Air resistance of 0.34 cw of the newer model was actually 14% less than that of the former coupe and 6% less than that of the sedan. Wheelbase was 80 millimeters shorter and the body 30 millimeters lower, but the older 380SLC had been 30 millimeters shorter and 64 millimeters lower, and weighed 25 kilograms less. The new model was indeed a larger car and a coupe with sufficient room for the rear seat passengers.

Rear seats were separate, styled like single seats, and the wide doors made for easier passenger entry. Safety belts were offered by an electrically activated device to the driver and front seat after entering the vehicle to encourage greater use of this safety feature.

The V-8 light alloy gasoline engine was modified to save energy and obtain the highest possible torque at lower engine speeds. The stroke/bore ratio was close to that of the 5-liter unit. Bore was reduced and stroke increased for more compact combustion and less heat losses, and displacement was slightly changed from the previous unit. Compression ratio was also changed and 94% of total torque was available already at 2,000 revolutions per minute. Actually, these dimensions were those of the 3.8-liter engines already used in the U.S. cars two years before. Even the compression ratio and rear axle ratio were the same.

The U.S. version of the 380SEC model was, of course, again a somewhat different car. The 3.8-liter engine was the same as that used in these 380 line cars before, developing 155 horsepower at 4,750 rpm and 196 lb/ft torque at 2,750 rpm. Compression ratio was still 8.3:1. The rear axle ratio was, as on all of these cars, again 2.47:1.

The 380SEC weighed 1,705 kg (3,760 lbs), nearly 100 kilograms more than the European model. It had, consequently, slightly less maximum speed, but was still an excellently performing automobile. And in these days of fuel shortages and higher prices, the average EPA mileage figures of 17 miles per gallon for the city cycle and 22 mpg for highway driving were of definite importance to the buyer of even such a luxury car as this.

There is little doubt that this truly most luxurious 380SEC coupe would be rated, as was the sedan, the best coupe in the world.

Prices and Production

The 380SEC coupe sold in 1981 for . . . . DM 69,495
The 380SEC model sold in the United States
  (with automatic transmission)
  in October 1981 for (East Coast) $49,827
  in September 1982 (East Coast) $53,570

Production of the 380SEC coupe [126 E38] (from September 1980/October 1981)

	was in	1980	3 units
		1981	945 units
		1982	4,393 units

The 380SEC coupe, 1981

Specifications

	380SEC	
Engine type	V-8 cyl overhead camshafts (M116)	
Bore and stroke	88 x 78.9 mm (3.46 x 3.10 in)	
Displacement	3839 cc (234.3 cu in)	
Power output	204 hp (DIN) @ 5250 rpm	U.S.: 155 hp SAE @ 4750 rpm
Compression ratio	9.4:1	U.S.: 8.3:1
Torque	315 Nm @ 3250 rpm (31 mkg, 224.3 ft/lb)	U.S.: 196 lb/ft (27.5 mkg)
Fuel injection	Bosch mechanical with air flow sensor	
Maximum engine speed	5950 rpm	U.S.: 5300 rpm; 1983: 5500 rpm
Gear ratios	I. 3.68:1 (automatic, standard) II. 2.41:1 III. 1.44:1 IV. 1.00:1	
Rear axle ratio	2.47	
Chassis	unit frame and body	
Suspension	double control arm axle, coil springs, anti-roll bar; diagonal swing axle, coil springs, anti-roll bar	
Brakes and area	dual circuit discs, power assisted, brake pad wear indicator, 278/279 mm (10.9/11.0 in)	
Wheelbase	2850 mm (112.2 in)	
Track, front/rear	1545/1517 mm (60.8/59.7 in)	
Length	4910 mm (193.3 in)	U.S.: 5060 mm (199.2 in)
Width	1828 mm (72.0 in)	
Height	1406 mm (55.4 in)	
Tires	205/70 VR 14	
Turning circle	11.53 meters (35.14 feet)	U.S.: 11.62 meters (38.12 feet)
Steering type and ratio	recirculating ball (2.89 turns), servo assisted	
Weight	1585 kg (3487 lbs)	U.S.: 1705 kg (3760 lbs)
Maximum speed	210 km/hr (131 mph)	
Acceleration	9.8 sec 0-100 km/hr	
Fuel consumption	at 120 km/hr: 10.8 liters (21.5 mpg)	
Fuel tank capacity	90 liters (23.8 gallons)	

The 380SEC coupe, 1982, U.S. version

Model 500SEC (1980-   )

S = Super, E (Einspritzung) = fuel injection, C = Coupe

The 500SEC coupe was also introduced to the public at the 1981 Frankfurt Auto Show. It was the identical body style to the 380SEC model, and as in that case, also replaced the former SLC, a body style which had been in production for nine years.

The absolutely best materials went into this top-line coupe, which included all of the safety demands of the S-line sedans, the generously comfortable arrangement of controls and utilization of available space. Longer by 160 mm, wider by 38 mm, and higher by 76 mm, the SEC body also had a 30 mm longer wheelbase than the SLC coupe. The engine hood, trunk lid, and bulk head between tank and trunk were made of light alloy to achieve a curb weight of 1,610 kg, just 25 kg (55 lbs) more than the 3.8-liter coupe.

Besides the luxurious features mentioned for the 380SEC, a choice of eight velour or leather color combinations with matching trim was made available to the buyer. Burl walnut finish of the wood used in the instrument range, center console, and door trim was used (reminiscent of my own 300S coupe of 1957).

The V-8 light alloy fuel-injection gasoline engine was somewhat modified to save energy and to obtain the highest possible torque at low engine speeds. The four-speed converter automatic transmission, first introduced in the S-class sedans, was used. In the 500SEC model, driving off proceeded in second gear when "D" was engaged, but a pedal kickdown resulted in first gear. A new position, "B," used in both coupes, utilized better the engine braking effect, and was especially designed for downhill mountain driving.

The rear axle ratios were changed to obtain lower engine speeds at the same previous vehicle speeds, 18% in the 500SEC and 24% in the 380SEC models. Another new feature was the floating caliper disc brakes in front, reducing the heating-up of brake fluid, thus practically eliminating vapor lock and consequently increasing safety. The ABS (anti-lock breaking system) feature was available as an optional extra.

The fuel mileage figures, according to the German DIN method, showed that the new 500SEC needed 5.5 liters less in the city cycle and 1.8 liters less at 120 km/hr highway driving than did the 500SLC. But acceleration took 8.1 seconds against 7.8 seconds of the former coupe, for the 0-100 km/hr while the maximum speed remained the same for both models at 225 kilometers per hour (140 mph).

Prices and Production

The 500SEC coupe sold in 1981 for . . . . .DM 73,902

Production of the 500SEC coupe [126 E50] (from July 1980/October 1981)

	was in	1980	1 unit
		1981	726 units
		1982	4,059 units

The 500SEC coupe, 1981

Specifications

	500SEC
Engine type	V-8 cyl overhead camshafts (M117)
Bore and stroke	96.5 x 85.0 mm (3.80 x 3.35 in)
Displacement	4973 cc (303.5 cu in)
Power output	231 hp (DIN) @ 4750 rpm
Compression ratio	9.2:1
Torque	405 Nm @ 3000 rpm (41 mkg, 296.6 ft/lb)
Fuel injection	Bosch mechanical with air flow sensor
Maximum engine speed	5950 rpm
Gear ratios	I. 3.68:1 (automatic, standard) II. 2.41:1 III. 1.44:1 IV. 1.00:1
Rear axle ratio	2.24
Chassis	unit frame and body
Suspension	double control arm axle, coil springs, anti-roll bar; diagonal swing axle, coil springs, anti-roll bar
Brakes and area	dual circuit discs, power assisted, brake pad wear indicator, 278/279 mm (10.9/11.0 in)
Wheelbase	2850 mm (112.2 in)
Track, front/rear	1545/1517 mm (60.8/59.7 in)
Length	4910 mm (193.3 in)
Width	1828 mm (72.0 in)
Height	1406 mm (55.4 in)
Tires	205/70 VR 14
Turning circle	11.53 meters (35.14 feet)
Steering type and ratio	recirculating ball (2.89 turns), servo assisted
Weight	1610 kg (3542 lbs)
Maximum speed	225 km/hr (140 mph)
Acceleration	8.1 sec 0-100 km/hr
Fuel consumption	at 120 km/hr: 11.4 liters/100 km (20.5 mpg)
Fuel tank capacity	90 liters (23.8 gallons)

The elegant interior of the 500SEC, 1981

The 190 sedan, 1982

The 190 sedan, 1982

Prices and Production

The 190 four-door sedan sold in 1982 for . . . . .DM 25,538

Production of the 190 four-door sedan [201]
was in 1982   1,635 units

The 190E four-door sedan sold in 1982 for . . . . .DM 27,742

Production of the 190E four-door sedan [201]
was in 1982   2,987 units

Model 190/190E (1982 -   )

E (Einspritzung) = fuel injection

The 190 and 190E models made their debut in early December 1982 near Seville, Spain, where they were shown to representatives of the press. These cars had undergone extensive and exhaustive testing for a long time before their initial production period. This chronicler had seen examples of them already being driven in the factory grounds at Untertuerkheim some three years previously. This new line of cars had the smaller W201 body style, a scaled-down version of the S-class W126 style, and looked as if they were merely a smaller edition of those popular Mercedes models. From the front, the cars looked more like these larger types than the medium range of the current models with the W123 body style.

The sloping front end and integrated headlights resulted in an improved coefficient of aerodynamic drag, and the 190 cars with 0.33 actually bested the 0.36 of the W126 models. Strips of molding placed along the roof conducted rainwater from the windshield, washed by a single arm, double-blade wiper, and away from the side windows.

Despite its smaller size, the interior space was nearly as roomy as that of the larger models. Front leg room was almost identical and headroom and kneeroom in the rear seats was only 0.3 and 0.4 inches less than that in the 240D model. The placement of the driving controls and switches was similar to that of the larger sedans. The seats were all newly designed, combining safety with comfort.

New systems to maintain a high standard of ride, handling, and controllability had been developed. The multi-link rear suspension was a totally new design. Five independent links allowed for a relatively light system which ensured ride comfort and excellent roadhandling. The suspension was new and incorporated anti-squat and anti-dive controls. Gas-filled shock absorber struts with wishbones supported the front wheels. Coil springs were separate from the shocks, unlike the MacPherson strut system. Floating caliper front disc brakes were used, as first found on the 380SEC models, resulting in better front end geometry because of their greater compactness. Disc brakes were also used in the rear, and the entire system was vacuum boosted.

Manual transmission was standard, but a five-speed manual unit with overdrive or an automatic transmission was available as an optional item.

Specifications

	190	190E
Engine type	4 cyl overhead camshaft (M102)	
Bore and stroke	89 x 80.25 mm (3.50 x 3.16 in)	
Displacement	1997 cc (121.72 cu in)	
Power output	90 hp (DIN) @ 5000 rpm	122 hp (DIN) @ 5100 rpm
Compression ratio	9.0:1	9.1:1
Torque	165 Nm @ 2500 rpm	178 Nm @ 3500 rpm
Carburetion/Fuel Injection	175 CDT cross-draught carburetor	mechanically/electronically controlled fuel injection
Engine speed at 100 km/hr	6000 rpm	
Gear ratios	I. 3.91:1 (4 speed) II. 2.32:1 III. 1.42:1 IV. 1.00:1	I. 3.91:1 (5 speed) 4.25:1 (automatic) II. 2.32:1 2.41:1 III. 1.42:1 1.49:1 IV. 1.00:1 1.00:1 V. 0.78:1
Rear axle ratio	3.23	
Chassis	unit frame and body	
Suspension	shock absorber strut with anti-dive control, coil springs, anti-roll bar; multi-link independent rear, anti-dive, anti-squat control, coils, anti-roll bar	
Brakes and area	hydraulic dual circuit, discs; anti-locking system optional	
Wheelbase	2665 mm (104.9 in)	
Track, front/rear	1428/1415 mm (56.2/55.7 in)	
Length	4420 mm (174.0 in)	
Width	1678 mm (66.0 in)	
Height	1383 mm (54.4 in)	
Tires	175/70 R 14 82T	175/70 R 14 82H
Turning circle	10.60 meters (32.3 feet)	
Steering type and ratio	recirculating ball (5 turns); servo-assisted optional	
Weight	1080 kg (2376 lbs)	1100 kg (2420 lbs)
Maximum speed	175 km/hr (109 mph); 167 (5th); automatic 170 km/hr (106 mph)	195 km/hr (120 mph); 187 (5th); automatic 190 km/hr (118 mph)
Acceleration	13.2 sec 0-100 km/hr; automatic 13.8 sec 0-100 km/hr	10.5 sec 0-100 km/hr; automatic 11 sec 0-100 km/hr
Fuel consumption	at 120 km/hr: 8.4 liters/100 km; automatic 8.9 liters	at 120 km/hr: 8.3 liters/100 km; automatic 8.7 liters
Fuel tank capacity	55 liters (14.5 gallons)	

The 190E sedan, 1982

The 190E sedan, 1982

Model Offerings

These random offerings are given merely to emphasize the fact that only carefully selected models of the large variety available from the factory were sold in the United States. For example, in 1976 only 10 models were marketed here while the factory offered a total of 27 models (actually 41 were listed, counting the 2 styles 115/114 and 123 of the smaller cars, the longer wheelbase versions, and three versions of the 600 limousine).

For 1966 Daimler-Benz offered for sale:

200	2.0 liter gasoline	4 cyl	95 hp DIN
200D	2.0 liter diesel	4 cyl	55 hp DIN
230	2.3 liter gasoline	6 cyl	105 hp DIN
230S	2.3 liter gasoline	6 cyl	120 hp DIN
250S	2.5 liter gasoline	6 cyl	130 hp DIN
250SE	2.5 liter gasoline	6 cyl	150 hp DIN
220SE coupe and convertible	2.2 liter gasoline	6 cyl	120 hp DIN
250SE coupe and convertible	2.5 liter gasoline	6 cyl	150 hp DIN
300SEb	3.0 liter gasoline	6 cyl	170 hp DIN
300SEL	3.0 liter gasoline	6 cyl	170 hp DIN
300SE coupe and convertible	3.0 liter gasoline	6 cyl	170 hp DIN
230SL	2.3 liter gasoline	6 cyl	150 hp DIN
600	6.3 liter gasoline	8 cyl	250 hp DIN
600 pullman	6.3 liter gasoline	8 cyl	250 hp DIN

For 1970 the following models were sold in the U.S.

220	2.2 liter gasoline	4 cyl	116 hp SAE
220D	2.2 liter diesel	4 cyl	65 hp SAE
250	2.5 liter gasoline	6 cyl	146 hp SAE
250C	2.8 liter gasoline	6 cyl	157 hp SAE
280S	2.8 liter gasoline	6 cyl	157 hp SAE
280SE	2.8 liter gasoline	6 cyl	180 hp SAE
280SEL	2.8 liter gasoline	6 cyl	180 hp SAE
280SE coupe and convertible	2.8 liter gasoline	6 cyl	180 hp SAE
280SL	2.8 liter gasoline	6 cyl	180 hp SAE
300SEL	2.8 liter gasoline	6 cyl	180 hp SAE
300SEL 6.3	6.3 liter gasoline	8 cyl	300 hp SAE
600 5 passenger	6.3 liter gasoline	8 cyl	300 hp SAE
600 7 passenger	6.3 liter gasoline	8 cyl	300 hp SAE

For 1976 Daimler-Benz offered for sale:

200D	2.0 liter diesel	4 cyl	55 hp DIN
220D	2.2 liter diesel	4 cyl	60 hp DIN
240D	2.4 liter diesel	4 cyl	65 hp DIN
240D 3.0	3.0 liter diesel	5 cyl	80 hp DIN
200	2.0 liter gasoline	4 cyl	95 hp DIN
230.4	2.3 liter gasoline	4 cyl	110 hp DIN
230.6	2.3 liter gasoline	6 cyl	120 hp DIN
250	2.8 liter gasoline	6 cyl	130 hp DIN
280	2.8 liter gasoline	6 cyl	160 hp DIN
280E	2.8 liter gasoline	6 cyl	185 hp DIN
250C	2.8 liter gasoline	6 cyl	130 hp DIN
280C	2.8 liter gasoline	6 cyl	160 hp DIN
280CE	2.8 liter gasoline	6 cyl	185 hp DIN
280S	2.8 liter gasoline	6 cyl	160 hp DIN
280SE	2.8 liter gasoline	6 cyl	185 hp DIN
280SEL	2.8 liter gasoline	6 cyl	185 hp DIN
350SE	3.5 liter gasoline	8 cyl	200 hp DIN
350SEL	3.5 liter gasoline	8 cyl	200 hp DIN
450SE	4.5 liter gasoline	8 cyl	225 hp DIN
450SEL	4.5 liter gasoline	8 cyl	225 hp DIN
450SEL 6.9	6.9 liter gasoline	8 cyl	286 hp DIN
280SL	2.8 liter gasoline	6 cyl	185 hp DIN
350SL	3.5 liter gasoline	8 cyl	200 hp DIN
450SL	4.5 liter gasoline	8 cyl	225 hp DIN
280SLC	2.8 liter gasoline	6 cyl	185 hp DIN
350SLC	3.5 liter gasoline	8 cyl	200 hp DIN
450SLC	4.5 liter gasoline	8 cyl	225 hp DIN

For 1976 the following models were sold in the U.S.

240D	2.4 liter diesel	4 cyl	62 hp SAE
300D	3.0 liter diesel	5 cyl	77 hp SAE
230	2.3 liter gasoline	4 cyl	93 hp SAE (Cal. 85)
280	2.8 liter gasoline	6 cyl	120 hp SAE
280C	2.8 liter gasoline	6 cyl	120 hp SAE
280S	2.8 liter gasoline	6 cyl	120 hp SAE
450SE	4.5 liter gasoline	8 cyl	180 hp SAE
450SEL	4.5 liter gasoline	8 cyl	180 hp SAE
450SL	4.5 liter gasoline	8 cyl	180 hp SAE
450SLC	4.5 liter gasoline	8 cyl	180 hp SAE

Production Totals and United States Sales

Year	MB Pass. Car Production	MB Pass. Car Sales in US	% of MB Sales to Total Imp. Car Sales	Total Imp. Car Sales in US
1946	214			
1947	1,045			
1948	5,116	1		
1949	17,417	2		
1950	33,906	13		
1951	42,222	18		
1952	36,824	253		
1953	34,975	421		
1954	48,816	636		
1955	63,683	2,041		
1956	69,601	3,101		
1957	80,899	6,039		
1958	99,209	7,404		
1959	108,440	12,071		
1960	122,684	12,254		
1961	137,431	12,625		
1962	146,393	12,947		339,160
1963	153,182	11,688	3.03	385,624
1964	165,532	11,867	2.45	484,131
1965	174,007	12,117	2.13	569,415
1966	191,625	16,162	2.46	658,123
1967	200,470	20,691	2.66	779,220
1968	216,284	24,553	2.49	985,767
1969	256,713	26,193	2.47	1,061,617
1970	280,419	29,108	2.36	1,230,961
1971	284,230	35,192	2.36	1,487,613
1972	323,878	41,556	2.72	1,529,402
1973	331,682	41,865	2.43	1,719,913
1974	340,006	38,170	2.79	1,369,148
1975	350,098	45,159	2.87	1,571,472
1976	370,348	43,205	2.88	1,498,745
1977	401,255	48,872	2.36	2,074,390
1978	393,203	46,695	2.33	2,002,413
1979	422,159	52,820	2.26	2,332,296
1980	429,078	53,790	2.24	2,397,887
1981	440,778	63,059	2.71	2,327,106
1982	458,345	65,963	2.97	2,222,214

Model Designations

Times past were not as complicated as the years are now, and things were not as confusing as they sometimes get in this electronic and computerized age.

Gottlieb Daimler called his first motorized vehicle (1889), which did not resemble a horse carriage, simply the Stahlradwagen, and a steel-wheel car it was. His earlier carriages (1885-1886) were a Motorkutsche, a motorized coach.

Karl Benz named his first four-wheeled car (1893) Viktoria, and subsequent styles were all carriages and had those designations, Landauer, Phaeton, etc. The name Velo was derived from velociped (bicycle), and it looked not like a carriage any more.

To indicate the performance of the vehicles, the horsepower was added to the name and from about 1902 on, the calculated rated output, called nominal output, and the brake horsepower were also given along with the designation, as in 14/18 h.p. Phaeton. After the rating formula was introduced, the first number referred to the taxable horsepower and the second to the effective output, as in 10/30 Benz touring car. Vehicles with superchargers had three numbers: the taxable horsepower, the effective output, and the maximum output with the supercharger engaged.

After the merger of Daimler and Benz in 1926, some models were given specific names, usually the plant where they were manufactured, as Stuttgart and Mannheim. Soon, the designation of the model signified the displacement of the engine, as in 180, which meant a 1.8-liter engine. This nomenclature went on for a long time and is still in effect, at least to some extent. Difficulties were soon encountered, however, and even greater difficulties were experienced with the letters.

The D stood for Diesel. Rear-engined models had the H for Heck, rear end. V indicated front-engined, Vorn. Fuel injection engines had the E for Einspritzung, injection. But the letter S stood for several things, but generally for Super.

The S designation in the 300SL stands for Sport and the L for Leicht, or light. In the 190SL it stood for the same, but that was neither a sports car nor was it light. Weight was 2,596 pounds against the 300SL's 2,849 and half the engine power. However, in sedans the L stands for Lang, or long wheelbase chassis, as in 280SEL.

In the elegant 300S line, the S stood for Super. It was the superior version of the 300 sedan model. But when another S was added, the first S did not stand for Sport, but Super, and the second S was Sport, as in the SS models (1927-1935). The added K meant Kurz, or short chassis, and the L was the model with holes drilled almost everywhere to save weight. The S, incidentally, never stood for supercharger — that was a K, for Kompressor, as in 500K, etc. They were not short wheelbase cars, but large sedans for special bodied roadsters or coupes.

Later C stood for coupe, as in the SLC line, or the 250C, which was actually a 280 in this country, with the 2.8-liter engine instead of the 2,496 cubic centimeter power unit, as elsewhere. Other misnamed cars were the 280 line in 1969, with 3.5-liter engines, as 280SE 3.5, later 4.5. The 300SEL had the same problem, as a 300SEL 4.5, etc. This confusion went on to the 6.3- and 6.9-liter cars, and the 450SLC 5.0, or even the first 300 diesels in Europe, which were the 240D 3.0; here the 300D. The 350SL was actually a 450 in this country, but a 3.5-liter engined car elsewhere, and the 280 or 450 SLs were correctly identified.

Occasionally, a slight difference is made for reasons of simplicity. The 633 Grosser sounded perhaps better as a 600, but the engine was, of course, of 6,332 cc capacity. There were 600, 620, 630, 660 and 680 models, some with K or S from 1924 to 1942, incidentally.

After having built so many different types of cars over the years, a shortage of designations was probably only natural. Thus, when the turbo-charged diesel engined models appeared, the T had already been appropriated elsewhere. That was the T for Touristik and Transport in the station wagon line of cars, as in 230T to 300TD. (On the factory production sheets this turbo station wagon model was shown as TDT, but then the sporty SL line was SLR; for roadster, not Racing, as in former years for the factory 300SLR machines.) Here the station wagon was merely the 300TD turbo.

    The first turbo-charged diesel sedan, at least, got the S designation to differentiate this model from the regularly aspirated diesel sedan, and became the 300SD. When the regular line of five-cylinder diesel models got the turbo-charged engine, nothing but the extra power was added. They simply remained the 300D. This generation, of course, does not remember that an SD sedan in 1953 to 1955 was a diesel version of the 170V series (S for Special) and that a year before that there was a 170DS. That time the S designated really a Special model of the 170V series, because the car incorporated the components of several others, such as the engine and front axle from the V, the chassis from the Sb, and the body from the S model. The smaller letters are sometimes used in the subdivisions of a certain model and they indicate merely a further development, usually in the engine only, as 200, 200b, 200c, etc.

Conversions of Power

Engine output is not only given in horsepower but is also listed as Kw (kilowatt). And torque is not only mkg (meter/kilogram) or lb/ft (pounds/feet), but also Nm (Newton meter). [Conversion factors: 1 hp = 0.736 Kw; 1 mkg = 9.81 Nm].

Herewith are a few examples of the later model 1980 cars (in European trim).

Model	hp (DIN)	Kw	Nm	mkg
200D/TD	60	44	113	11.5
240D/TD	72	53	137	14.0
300D/TD	88	65	172	17.5
300SD/TD turbo	125	92	250	25.5
200/T	109	80	170	17.3
230E/CE/TE	136	100	205	20.9
250	140	103	200	20.4
280/S/SL/SLC	156	115	223	22.7
280E/CE/TE/SE/SEL	185	136	240	24.5
380SE/SEL/SL/SLC	218	160	305	31.1
500SE/SEL/SL/SLC	240	177	404	41.2

and earlier (1975 models had these figures:

Model	hp (DIN)	Kw	Nm	mkg
200D	55	40	113	11.5
220D	60	44	126	12.8
240D	65	48	137	14.0
240D 3.0	80	59	172	17.5
200	95	70	156	15.9
230.4	110	81	186	19.0
230.6	120	88	179	18.2
250/C	130	96	216	22.0
280/C/S	160	118	226	23.0
280/E/CE/SE/SEL/SL/SLC	185	136	238	24.3
350SE/SEL/SL/SLC	200	147	286	29.2
450SE/SEL/SL/SLC	225	165	378	38.5
450SEL 6.9	286	210	550	56.0

Engine and Chassis Codes

To recognize the chassis or the engine numbers is simple because in the chassis numbers the fourth digit always is 0 or 1, while in the engine numbers it is always a 9.

The chassis as well as the engine numbers from 1946 to 1950 always had eleven digits consisting of the basic type, model style, and serial number.

In 1951 and 1952 the production year was added to the serial number, and from 1953 through 1959, while the numbers still consisted of 13 digits, code letters were added for clutch and transmission, and the production year digits were reversed.

From 1960 on, there were 14 digits to the identification numbers. The code letters had been changed to numbers and the production year was eliminated. Each model, regardless of year of manufacture, was numbered consecutively, making for a six-digit serial number.

As an example, a car has the following numbers (my 300CD coupe, 1980):

12315012005611 and 61791212098083

Chassis type 123, model 150, left-hand drive 1, automatic transmission 2, and serial number 005611. Engine type 617, model 912, left-hand drive 1, automatic transmission 2, and serial number 098083.

The Mercedes-Benz STAR

Total Production of Models

(For specific body styles and annual figures, consult the text in this book.)

Model designation		Years built	Total production	Model designation		Years built	Total production
170V	[136]	1949-1953	49,367	220D	[115]	1967-1976	420,273
170S	[136]	1949-1955	34,319	230	[114]	1967-1976	221,783
	[191]	1952-1953	8,094	250	[114]	1967-1972	78,303
170D	[136]	1949-1955	48,710	280S	[108]	1967-1972	93,666
	[191]	1952-1953	12,985	280SE	[108]	1967-1972	99,301
220	[187]	1951-1955	18,514		[111]	1967-1971	5,187
	[180]	1954-1956	25,937	300SEL	[109]	1967-1970	2,519
300	[186]	1951-1956	8,288	250C	[114]	1968-1976	42,379
	[189]	1957-1962	3,142	280SE 3.5	[111]	1969-1971	4,502
300S	[188]	1951-1958	760	300SEL 3.5	[109]	1969-1972	9,483
180	[120]	1953-1962	118,234	250	[114]	1970-1976	34,061
180D	[120]	1953-1962	152,983	280SEL 3.5	[108]	1970-1972	951
300SL	[198]	1954-1963	3,258	280SE 3.5	[108]	1970-1972	11,309
190SL	[121]	1955-1963	25,881	350SL	[107]	1970-1980	15,304
190	[121]	1956-1961	89,808	350SLC	[107]	1971-1980	13,925
	[110]	1961-1965	130,554	280	[114]	1971-1976	44,537
219	[105]	1956-1959	27,845	280E	[114]	1971-1976	22,836
220S	[180]	1956-1959	58,708	280C	[114]	1971-1976	13,151
220SE	[128]	1958-1960	3,916	280CE	[114]	1971-1976	11,518
190D	[121]	1958-1961	81,938	280SE 4.5	[108]	1971-1972	13,527
	[110]	1961-1965	225,645	280SEL 4.5	[108]	1971-1972	8,173
220	[111]	1959-1965	69,691	300SEL 4.5	[109]	1971-1972	2,553
220S	[111]	1959-1965	161,119	450SL	[107]	1971-1980	66,298
220SE	[111]	1959-1965	82,988	450SLC	[107]	1972-1980	31,739
300SE	[112]	1961-1967	9,875	280S	[116]	1972-1980	122,848
230SL	[113]	1963-1967	19,831	280SE	[116]	1972-1980	150,775
250SL	[113]	1966-1968	5,196	350SE	[116]	1972-1980	51,140
280SL	[113]	1967-1971	23,885	230/4	[115]	1972-1976	87,765
600	[100]	1963-1981	2,677	240D	[115]	1973-1976	131,319
200	[110]	1965-1968	70,207	280SEL	[116]	1973-1980	7,032
200D	[110]	1965-1968	161,618	350SEL	[116]	1973-1980	4,266
230	[110]	1965-1968	40,258	450SE	[116]	1972-1980	41,604
230S	[111]	1965-1968	41,107	450SEL	[116]	1972-1980	59,575
250S	[108]	1965-1969	74,677	230/6	[114]	1973-1976	84,590
250SE	[108]	1965-1968	55,181	240D 3.0/300D	[115]	1974-1976	53,690
	[111]	1965-1967	6,213	450SEL 6.9	[116]	1975-1980	7,380
300SE	[108]	1965-1967	2,737	280SL	[107]	1974-	
	[109]	1965-1967	2,369	280SLC	[107-	1974-1981	10,666
300SEL 6.3	[109]	1968-1972	6,526	200	[123]	1975-1980	158,772
200	[115]	1967-1976	288,785	200	[123]	1979-	
200D	[115]	1967-1976	339,927	200D	[123]	1975-	
220	[115]	1967-1973	128,739	220D	[123]	1975-1979	56,736

Model designation		Years built	Total production
230	[123]	1975-1981	196,185
230E	[123]	1979-	
240D	[123]	1975-	
250	[123]	1975-	
280	[123]	1975-1981	33,206
280E	[123]	1975-	
300D	[123]	1975-	
300D (turbo)	[123]	1981-	
240TD	[123]	1978-	
300TD	[123]	1977-	
230T	[123]	1978-1980	6,884
230TE	[123]	1979-	
250T	[123]	1977-	
280TE	[123]	1977-	
450SLC 5.0 /500SLC	[107]	1977-1981	2,769
300SD	[116]	1977-1980	28,634
280CE	[123]	1976-	
280C	[123]	1976-1980	3,704
230C	[123]	1976-1980	18,675
230CE	[123]	1980-	
300CD	[123]	1977-1981	7,502
300CD (turbo)	[123]	1981-	
280S	[126]	1979-	
280SE	[126]	1979-	
280SEL	[126]	1979-	
380SE	[126]	1979-	
380SEL	[126]	1979-	
500SE	[126]	1979-	
500SEL	[126]	1979-	
300TD (turbo)	[123]	1979-	
200T	[123]	1980-	
380SL	[107]	1980-	
380SLC	[107]	1980-1981	3,789
500SL	[107]	1980-	
500SLC	[107]	1980-1981	1,299
300SD	[126]	1979-	
380SEC	[126]	1980-	
500SEC	[126]	1980-	
190	[201]	1982-	
190E	[201]	1982-	

Engine Designations

Gasoline Engines (designated M = Motor)

M136	4 cyl	1.7 and 1.8 liter	carburetor	1946-57
M121	4 cyl	1.9 and 2.0 liter	carburetor	1953-68
M115	4 cyl	2.0 and 2.2 and 2.3 liter	carburetor	1967-
M180	6 cyl	2.2 and 2.3 liter	carburetor	1951-76
M127	6 cyl	2.2 and 2.3 liter	fuel injection	1958-67
M108	6 cyl	2.5 liter	carburetor	1965-69
M129	6 cyl	2.5 liter	fuel injection	1965-68
M114	6 cyl	2.5 liter	carburetor and fuel injection	1967-72
M123	6 cyl	2.5 liter	carburetor	1976-
M130	6 cyl	2.8 liter	carburetor and fuel injection	1967-76
M110	6 cyl	2.8 liter	carburetor and fuel injection	1972-
M186	6 cyl	3.0 liter	carburetor	1951-67
M188	6 cyl	3.0 liter	carburetor	1952-55
M198	6 cyl	3.0 liter	fuel injection	1954-63
M199	6 cyl	3.0 liter	fuel injection	1955-58
M189	6 cyl	3.0 liter	fuel injection	1957-67
M116	8 cyl	3.5 liter	fuel injection	1969-80
M117	8 cyl	4.5 liter	fuel injection	1971-80
M100	8 cyl	6.3 and 6.9 liter	fuel injection	1964-
M116	8 cyl	3.8 liter	fuel injection	1979-
M117	8 cyl	5.0 liter	fuel injection	1979-
M102	4 cyl	2.0 liter	carburetor and fuel injection	1979-
M102	4 cyl	2.3 liter	carburetor and fuel injection	1979-

Diesel Engines (designated Om = Oel Motor)

OM636	4 cyl	1.7 and 1.8 liter	injection	1949-61
OM621	4 cyl	1.9 and 2.9 liter	injection	1958-68
OM615	4 cyl	2.0 and 2.2 liter	injection	1967-
OM616	4 cyl	2.4 liter	injection	1973-
OM617	5 cyl	3.0 liter	injection	1974-
OM617A	5 cyl	3.0 liter	turbo-charged injection	1977-

Engine Production Details

Comments:

lo comp: *lower compression engine*
sedan: *four-door sedan*
cp/con: *coupe and convertible*
roadster: *roadster model*

autom: *for automatic transmission model*
cp/lt met: *light metal coupe*
lt met dif: *light metal differential*
K-Jet: *K-Jetronic fuel injection*

Diesel Engines

Construction Design Number	Cylinders	Bore cc	Stroke cc	Displacement cc	Compression Ratio	Horsepower DIN	Revolutions Per Minute	Model	Manufacturing Designation	Built from - to	Comments
636.915	4	73.5 x 100.0		1,697	19:1	38	3,200	170D	W136	May 1949 to May 1950	
636.916	4	75.0 x 100.0		1,767	19:1	40	3,200	170Da	W136	May 1950 to Apr 1952	
636.916	4	75.0 x 100.0		1,767	19:1	40	3,200	170Dc	W136	May 1952 to Oct 1953	
636.918	4	75.0 x 100.0		1,767	19:1	40	3,200	170D-S	W191	Jan 1952 to Aug 1953	
636.930	4	75.0 x 100.0		1,767	19:1	43	3,500	180D	W120	Oct 1953 to Jul 1959	
636.930	4	75.0 x 100.0		1,767	19:1	43	3,500	180Db	W120	Jul 1959 to Aug 1961	
636.931	4	75.0 x 100.0		1,767	19:1	40	3,200	170S-D	W136	Jul 1953 to Sep 1955	
621.910	4	85.0 x 83.6		1,897	21:1	50	4,000	190D	W121	Aug 1958 to Jul 1959	
621.910	4	85.0 x 83.6		1,897	21:1	50	4,000	190Db	W121	Jun 1959 to Sep 1961	
621.912	4	87.0 x 83.6		1,988	21:1	55	4,200	190Dc	W110	Apr 1961 to Aug 1965	
621.914	4	87.0 x 83.6		1,988	21:1	48	3,800	180Dc	W120	Jun 1961 to Oct 1962	
621.918	4	87.0 x 83.6		1,988	21:1	55	4,200	200D	W110	Jun 1965 to Feb 1968	
615.912	4	87.0 x 92.4		2,197	21:1	60	4,200	220D	W115	Jul 1967 to Dec 1976	
615.913	4	87.0 x 83.6		1,988	21:1	55	4,200	200D	W115	Oct 1967 to Dec 1976	
615.940	4	87.0 x 83.6		1,988	21:1	55	4,200	200D	W123	Jan 1976	
615.941	4	87.0 x 92.4		2,197	21:1	60	4,200	220D	W123	Jan 1976 to Mar 1979	
616.912	4	91.0 x 92.4		2,404	21:1	65	4,200	240D	W123	Jan 1976	
616.916	4	91.0 x 92.4		2,404	21:1	65	4,200	240D	W115	Aug 1973 to Dec 1976	
617.910	5	91.0 x 92.4		3,005	21:1	80	4,000	240D 3.0	W115	Sep 1974 to Nov 1976	
617.911	5	91.0 x 92.4		3,005	21:1	80	4,000	300D	W123	Jan 1976	

Gasoline Engines

Construction Design Number	Cylinders	Bore cc	Stroke cc	Displacement cc	Compression Ratio	Horsepower DIN	Revolutions Per Minute	Model	Manufacturing Designation	Built from - to	Comments
136.920	4	73.5 x 100.0		1,697	6.5:1	38	3,600	170V	W136	Jun 1946 to May 1950	
136.921	4	73.5 x 100.0		1,697	6.5:1	38	3,600	170V	W136	Jun 1946 to May 1950	
136.922	4	75.0 x 100.0		1,767	6.5:1	52	4,000	170S	W136	May 1949 to Feb 1952	
136.922	4	75.0 x 100.0		1,767	6.5:1	52	4,000	170Sb	W191	Feb 1952 to Aug 1953	
136.923	4	75.0 x 100.0		1,767	6.5:1	45	3,600	170Va	W136	May 1950 to Apr 1952	
136.923	4	75.0 x 100.0		1,767	6.5:1	45	3,600	170Vb	W136	May 1952 to Aug 1953	
136.925	4	75.0 x 100.0		1,767	6.7:1	52	4,000	180	W120	Jul 1953 to Jun 1957	
136.926	4	75.0 x 100.0		1,767	6.5:1	45	3.600	170S-V	W136	Jul 1953 to Feb 1955	
121.920	4	85.0 x 83.6		1,897	7.5:1	75	4,600	190	W121	Mar 1956 to Aug 1959	
121.920	4	85.0 x 83.6		1,897	8.5:1	80	4,800	190b	W121	Jun 1959 to Aug 1961	
121.921	4	85.0 x 83.6		1,897	8.8:1	105	5,700	190SL	W121	Jun 1953 to Jul 1961	
121.923	4	85.0 x 83.6		1,897	6.9:1	65	4,500	180a	W120	Jun 1957 to Jul 1959	
121.923	4	85.0 x 83.6		1,897	7.0:1	68	4,400	180b	W120	Jul 1959 to Aug 1961	
121.924	4	85.0 x 83.6		1,897	8.7:1	80	5,000	190c	W110	Apr 1961 to Aug 1965	
121.927	4	85.0 x 83.6		1,897	7.0:1	68	4,400	180c	W120	Jun 1961 to Oct 1962	
121.928	4	85.0 x 83.6		1,897	8.7:1	105	5,700	190SL	W121	May 1961 to Feb 1963	
121.940	4	87.0 x 83.6		1,988	9.0:1	95	5,200	200	W110	Jun 1965 to Feb 1968	
180.920	6	80.0 x 72.8		2,195	6.5:1	80	4,600	220	W187	Apr 1951 to Aug 1955	
180.921	6	80.0 x 72.8		2,195	7.6:1	85	4,800	219	W105	May 1955 to Jul 1959	
180.921	6	80.0 x 72.8		2,195	7.6:1	85	4,800	220a	W180	Jan 1954 to Apr 1956	
180.924	6	80.0 x 72.8		2,195	7.6:1	100	4,800	220S	W180	Apr 1956 to Jul 1959	
180.940	6	80.0 x 72.8		2,195	8.7:1	95	4,800	220b	W111	May 1959 to Aug 1965	
180.941	6	80.0 x 72.8		2,195	8.7:1	110	5,000	220Sb	W111	May 1959 to Jul 1965	
180.945	6	82.0 x 72.8		2,306	9.0:1	105	5,200	230	W110	Jul 1965 to Jun 1966	
180.947	6	82.0 x 72.8		2,306	9.0:1	120	5,400	230S	W111	Jul 1965 to Jan 1968	
180.949	6	82.0 x 72.8		2,306	9.0:1	120	5,200	230	W110	Jul 1966 to Dec 1967	
180.954	6	81.75 x 72.8		2,292	8.7:1	120	5,400	230.6	W114	Sep 1967 to Nov 1976	
180.955	6	81.75 x 72.8		2,292	7.2:1	106	5,300	230.6	W114	Sep 1967 to Nov 1976	lo comp
127.980	6	80.0 x 72.8		2,195	8.7:1	115	4,800	220SE	W128	Apr 1958 to Aug 1959	sedan
127.981	6	82.0 x 72.8		2,195	9.3:1	150	5,500	230SL	W113	Mar 1963 to Jan 1967	
127.982	6	80.0 x 72.8		2,195	8.7:1	120	4,800	220SEb	W111	Aug 1959 to Aug 1965	sedan
127.983	6	80.0 x 72.8		2,195	8.7:1	115	4,800	220SE	W128	Jul 1958 to Nov 1960	cp/con
127.984	6	80.0 x 72.8		2,195	8.7:1	120	4,800	220SEb	W111	Sep 1960 to Oct 1965	cp/con

Gasoline Engines

Construction Design Number	Cylinders	Bore cc	Stroke cc	Displacement	Compression Ratio	Horsepower DIN	Revolutions Per Minute	Model	Manufacturing Designation	Built from - to	Comments
115.920	4	87.0 x 92.4		2,197	9.0:1	105	5,000	220/8	W115	Oct 1967 to Jul 1973	
115.923	4	87.0 x 83.6		1,988	9.0:1	95	4,800	200	W115	Oct 1967 to Dec 1976	
115.924	4	87.0 x 92.4		2,197	7.8:1	90	5,000	220/8	W115	Oct 1967 to Jul 1973	lo comp
115.926	4	87.0 x 83.6		1,988	8.0:1	85	5,000	200	W115	Oct 1967 to Dec 1976	lo comp
115.938	4	87.0 x 83.6		1,987	9.0:1	94	4,800	200	W123	Jan 1976 to Aug 1980	
115.939	4	87.0 x 83.6		1,987	8.0:1	84	4,800	200	W123	Jan 1976 to Aug 1980	lo comp
115.951	4	93.75 x 83.6		2,307	9.0:1	110	4,800	230.4	W115	Aug 1973 to Dec 1976	
115.954	4	93.75 x 83.6		2,307	9.0:1	109	4,800	230	W123	Jan 1976 to Sep 1981	
108.920	6	82.0 x 78.8		2,496	9.0:1	130	5,400	250S	W108	Jul 1965 to Mar 1969	
108.924	6	82.0 x 78.8		2,496	7.7:1	115	5,400	250S	W108	Jul 1965 to Mar 1969	lo comp
129.980	6	82.0 x 78.8		2,496	9.3:1	150	5,500	250SE	W108	Aug 1965 to Jan 1968	
129.980	6	82.0 x 78.8		2,496	9.3:1	150	5,500	250SE	W111	Apr 1966 to Dec 1967	
129.981	6	82.0 x 78.8		2,496	9.3:1	150	5,500	250SE	W111	Aug 1965 to Apr 1966	
129.982	6	82.0 x 78.8		2,496	9.5:1	150	5,500	250SI	W113	Nov 1966 to Jan 1968	
114.920	6	82.0 x 78.8		2,496	9.0:1	130	5,400	250/8	W114	Jul 1967 to Apr 1972	
114.923	6	82.0 x 78.8		2,496	7.7:1	115	5,400	250C/8	W114	Oct 1968 to Apr 1972	lo comp
114.980	6	82.0 x 78.8		2,496	9.5:1	150	5,500	250CE/8	W114	Oct 1968 to Apr 1972	
114.981	6	82.0 x 78.8		2,496	7.1:1	130	5,500	250CE/8	W114	Oct 1968 to Apr 1972	lo comp
123.920	6	86.0 x 72.45		2,525	8.7:1	129	5,500	250	W123	Jan 1976	
130.920	6	86.5 x 78.8		2,778	9.0:1	140	5,200	280S	W108	Nov 1967 to Sep 1972	
130.921	6	86.5 x 78.8		2,778	7.8:1	125	5,200	280S	W108	Nov 1967 to Sep 1972	lo comp
130.923	6	86.5 x 78.8		2,778	9.0:1	140	5,200	250	W114	Jul 1970 to Aug 1972	
130.923	6	86.5 x 78.8		2,778	9.0:1	130	5,000	250C	W114	Jun 1972 to Jun 1976	
130.933	6	86.5 x 78.8		2,778	7.6:1	118	5,000	250C	W114	Jun 1972 to Jun 1976	lo comp
130.980	6	86.5 x 78.8		2,778	9.5:1	160	5,500	280SE	W108	Nov 1967 to Sep 1972	
130.980	6	86.5 x 78.8		2,778	9.5:1	160	5,500	280SEL	W108	Jan 1968 to Mar 1971	
130.980	6	86.5 x 78.8		2,778	9.5:1	160	5,500	280SE	W111	Nov 1967 to Feb 1971	
130.981	6	86.5 x 78.8		2,778	9.5:1	170	5,750	300SEL	W109	Dec 1967 to Jan 1970	
130.983	6	86.5 x 78.8		2,778	9.5:1	170	5,750	280SL	W113	Nov 1967 to Mar 1971	
130.984	6	86.5 x 78.8		2,778	7.8:1	140	5,250	280SE	W108	Nov 1967 to Sep 1972	lo comp
130.984	6	86.5 x 78.8		2,778	7.8:1	140	5,250	280SEL	W108	Jan 1968 to Mar 1971	lo comp
130.984	6	86.5 x 78.8		2,778	7.8:1	140	5,250	280SE	W111	Nov 1967 to Feb 1971	lo comp

Gasoline Engines

Construction Design Number	Cylinders	Bore cc	Stroke cc	Displacement cc	Compression Ratio	Horsepower DIN	Revolutions Per Minute	Model	Manufacturing Designation	Built from - to	Comments
186.920	6	85.0 x 88.0		2,996	6.4:1	115	4,600	300	W186	Nov 1951 to Mar 1954	
186.920	6	85.0 x 88.0		2,996	7.5:1	125	4,500	300b	W186	Mar 1954 to Jul 1955	
186.921	6	85.0 x 88.0		2,996	7.5:1	125	4,500	300c	W186	Jul 1955 to Aug 1967	
188.920	6	85.0 x 88.0		2,996	7.8:1	150	5,000	300S	W188	Jan 1952 to Jul 1955	
199.980	6	85.0 x 88.0		2,996	8.5:1	175	5,300	300Sc	W188	Jul 1955 to Apr 1958	
189.980	6	85.0 x 88.0		2,996	8.5:1	160	5,400	300d	W189	Aug 1957 to Mar 1962	autom
189.981	6	85.0 x 88.0		2,996	8.5:1	160	5,300	300d	W189	Aug 1957 to Mar 1962	autom
189.984	6	85.0 x 88.0		2,996	8.7:1	160	5,000	300SE	W112	Jul 1961 to Nov 1963	sedan
189.985	6	85.0 x 88.0		2,996	8.7:1	160	5,000	300SE	W112	Sep 1961 to Nov 1963	cp/con
189.986	6	85.0 x 88.0		2,996	8.8:1	170	5,400	300SE	W112	Oct 1963 to Jul 1965	sedan
189.987	6	85.0 x 88.0		2,996	8.8:1	170	5,400	300SE	W112	Oct 1963 to Dec 1967	cp/con
189.988	6	85.0 x 88.0		2,996	8.8:1	170	5,400	300SEL	W109	Aug 1965 to Dec 1967	
189.989	6	85.0 x 88.0		2,996	8.8:1	170	5,400	300SEb	W108	Aug 1965 to Dec 1967	
198.980	6	85.0 x 88.0		2,996	8.5:1	215	5,800	300SL	W198	Sep 1954 to May 1957	cp
198.980	6	85.0 x 88.0		2,996	8.5:1	215	5,800	300SL	W198	May 1957 to Mar 1962	roadster
198.981	6	85.0 x 88.0		2,996	8.5:1	215	5,800	300SL	W198	Sep 1954 to May 1957	cp/lt met
198.982	6	85.0 x 88.0		2,996	8.5:1	215	5,800	300SL	W198	Mar 1962 to Feb 1963	roadster lt met dif
116.980	8-V	92.0 x 65.8		3,499	9.5:1	200	5,800	280SE 3.5	W111	Aug 1969 to Jul 1971	
116.980	8-V	92.0 x 65.8		3,499	9.5:1	200	5,800	280SE/SEL 3.5	W108	Mar 1971 to Aug 1972	
116.981	8-V	92.0 x 65.8		3,499	9.5:1	200	5,800	300SEL 3.5	W109	Sep 1969 to Sep 1972	
116.982	8-V	92.0 x 65.8		3,499	9.5:1	200	5,800	350SLC	W107	Aug 1971 to Feb 1976	
116.982	8-V	92.0 x 65.8		3,499	9.5:1	200	5,800	350SL	W107	Feb 1971 to Feb 1976	
116.983	8-V	92.0 x 65.8		3,499	9.5:1	200	5,800	350SE	W116	Sep 1972 to Feb 1976	
116.983	8-V	92.0 x 65.8		3,499	9.5:1	200	5,800	350SEL	W116	Nov 1973 to Feb 1976	
116.984	8-V	92.0 x 65.8		3,499	9.5:1	200	5,800	350SL/SLC	W107	Feb 1976 to Mar 1980	K-Jet
116.985	8-V	92.0 x 65.8		3,499	9.5:1	200	5,800	350SE/SEL	W116	Feb 1976 to Sep 1980	K-Jet
116.990	8-V	92.0 x 65.8		3,499	8.0:1	180	5,500	280SE 3.5	W111	Aug 1969 to Jul 1971	lo comp
116.990	8-V	92.0 x 65.8		3,499	8.0:1	180	5,500	280SE/SEL 3.5	W108	Mar 1971 to Aug 1972	lo comp
116.991	8-V	92.0 x 65.8		3,499	8.0:1	180	5,500	300SEL 3.5	W109	Sep 1969 to Aug 1972	lo comp
116.992	8-V	92.0 x 65.8		3,499	8.0:1	180	5,500	350SL	W107	Feb 1971 to Feb 1976	lo comp
116.992	8-V	92.0 x 65.8		3,499	8.0:1	180	5,500	350SLC	W107	Aug 1971 to Feb 1976	lo comp
116.993	8-V	92.0 x 65.8		3,499	8.0:1	180	5,500	350SE	W116	Sep 1972 to Feb 1976	lo comp
116.993	8-V	92.0 x 65.8		3,499	8.0:1	180	5,500	350SEL	W116	Nov 1973 to Feb 1976	lo comp

Gasoline Engines

Construction Design Number	Cylinders	Bore cc	Stroke cc	Displacement cc	Compression Ratio	Horsepower DIN	Revolutions Per Minute	Model	Manufacturing Designation	Built from - to	Comments
110.921	6	86.0 x 78.8		2,746	9.0:1	160	5,500	280	W114	Apr 1972 to Sep 1976	
110.921	6	86.0 x 78.8		2,746	9.0:1	160	5,500	280C	W114	Jun 1972 to Aug 1975	
110.922	6	86.0 x 78.8		2,746	9.0:1	160	5,500	280S	W116	Aug 1972 to Jul 1977	
110.923	6	86.0 x 78.8		2,746	8.7:1	156	5,500	280	W123	Jan 1976 to Jul 1981	
110.931	6	86.0 x 78.8		2,746	8.0:1	145	5,500	280	W114	Apr 1972 to Sep 1976	
110.931	6	86.0 x 78.8		2,746	8.0:1	145	5,500	280C	W114	Jun 1972 to Aug 1976	lo comp
110.932	6	86.0 x 78.8		2,746	8.0:1	145	5,500	280S	W116	Aug 1972 to Jul 1980	lo comp
110.981	6	86.0 x 78.8		2,746	9.0:1	185	6,000	280E	W114	Mar 1972 to Sep 1976	
110.981	6	86.0 x 78.8		2,746	9.0:1	185	6,000	280CE	W114	Apr 1972 to Jul 1976	
110.982	6	86.0 x 78.8		2,746	9.0:1	185	6,000	280SL/SLC	W107	Sep 1974 to Jul 1975	
110.983	6	86.0 x 78.8		2,746	8.7:1	177	6,000	280SEL	W123	Jan 1974 to Jul 1981	
110.983	6	86.0 x 78.8		2,746	8.7:1	177	6,000	280SE	W116	Aug 1972 Jul 1977	
110.984	6	86.0 x 78.8		2,746	8.7:1	177	6,000	280E	W123	Jan 1976 to Jul 1981	
110.991	6	86.0 x 78.8		2,746	8.0:1	170	6,000	280E	W114	Mar 1972 to Sep 1976	lo comp
110.991	6	86.0 x 78.8		2,746	8.0:1	170	6,000	280CE	W114	Apr 1972 to Jul 1976	lo comp
110.992	6	86.0 x 78.8		2,746	8.0:1	170	6,000	280SL/SLC	W107	Sep 1974 to Jul 1975	lo comp
110.993	6	86.0 x 78.8		2,746	8.0:1	170	6,000	280SEL	W116	Jan 1974 to May 1980	lo comp
110.993	6	86.0 x 78.8		2,746	8.0:1	170	6,000	280SE	W116	Aug 1972 to Jul 1980	lo comp
117.981	8-V	92.0 x 85.0		4,520	8.0:1	195	5,800	300SEL 4.5	W109	Apr 1971 to Oct 1972	
117.982	8-V	92.0 x 85.0		4,520	8.8:1	225	5,000	450SL/SLC	W107	Mar 1973 to Oct 1975	
117.983	8-V	92.0 x 85.0		4,520	8.8:1	225	5,000	450SE	W116	Nov 1972 to Oct 1975	
117.983	8-V	92.0 x 85.0		4,520	8.8:1	225	5,000	450SEL	W116	Mar 1973 to Oct 1975	
117.984	8-V	92.0 x 85.0		4,520	8.0:1	195	5,800	280SE/SEL 4.5	W108	Apr 1971 to Nov 1972	
117.985	8-V	92.0 x 85.0		4,520	8.8:1	217	5,000	450SL/SLC	W107	Oct 1975 to Nov 1980	K-Jet
117.986	8-V	92.0 x 85.0		4,520	8.8:1	217	5,000	450SE/SEL	W116	Oct 1975 to Jun 1980	K-Jet
117.992	8-V	92.0 x 85.0		4,520	7.5:1	210	4,800	450SL/SLC	W107	Mar 1972 to Oct 1975	lo comp
117.993	8-V	92.0 x 85.0		4,520	7.5:1	210	4,800	450SE/SEL	W116	Nov 1972 to Oct 1975	lo comp
100.980	8-V	103.0 x 95.0		6,332	8.8:1	250	4,000	600	W100	Jan 1964 to May 1981	
100.981	8-V	103.0 x 95.0		6,332	8.8:1	250	4,000	300SEL 6.3	W109	Dec 1967 to Aug 1972	
100.982	8-V	103.0 x 95.0		6,332	7.3:1	220	4,000	600	W100	Jan 1964 to Jun 1981	lo comp
100.983	8-V	103.0 x 95.0		6,332	7.3:1	220	4,000	300SEL 6.3	W109	Dec 1967 to Aug 1972	lo comp
100.985	8-V	107.0 x 95.0		6,834	8.8:1	286	4,250	450SEL 6.9	W116	Jun 1975 to May 1980	

Acknowledgments

Without the assistance of many fine people in the Daimler-Benz organization here and in Germany, these compilations of production details would, of course, have been impossible. I wish to express my most sincere thanks for all of the valuable help I received from Untertürkheim and Montvale, and especially to Herrn Claus-Peter Schulze in the Archives department and Frau Ruth Witzel in the Press-Photo section.

The final responsibility of the entire contents of this book is mine alone, however, and any seeming variations in the many detailed specifications, either inch or metric, are due often to the several documents used which did not always agree on every given model. Generally then, I have used what I felt was the most authoritative information available.

The museum at the factory contains almost every model ever built

Even the oldest vehicles are meticulously restored and exhibited

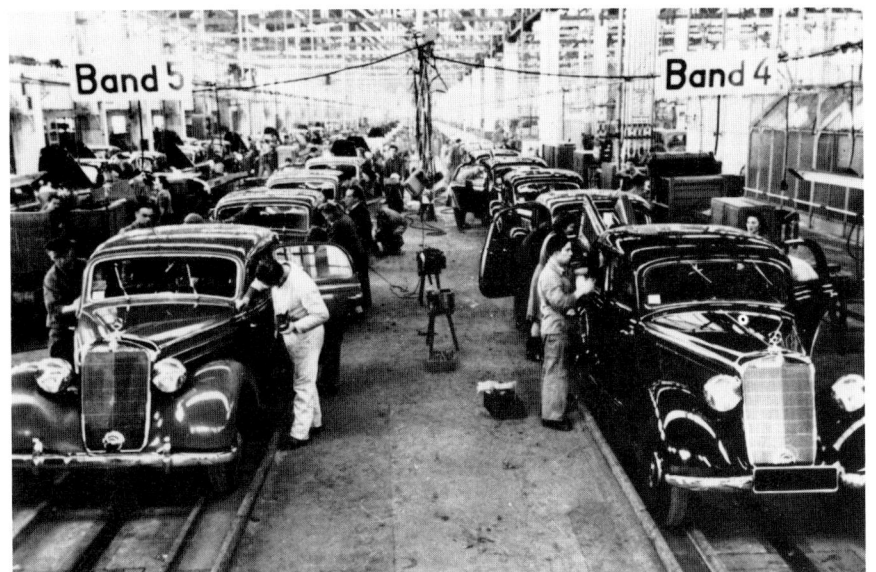
An early production line at Sindelfingen, 1946

Modern, computerized welding of bodies, 1980

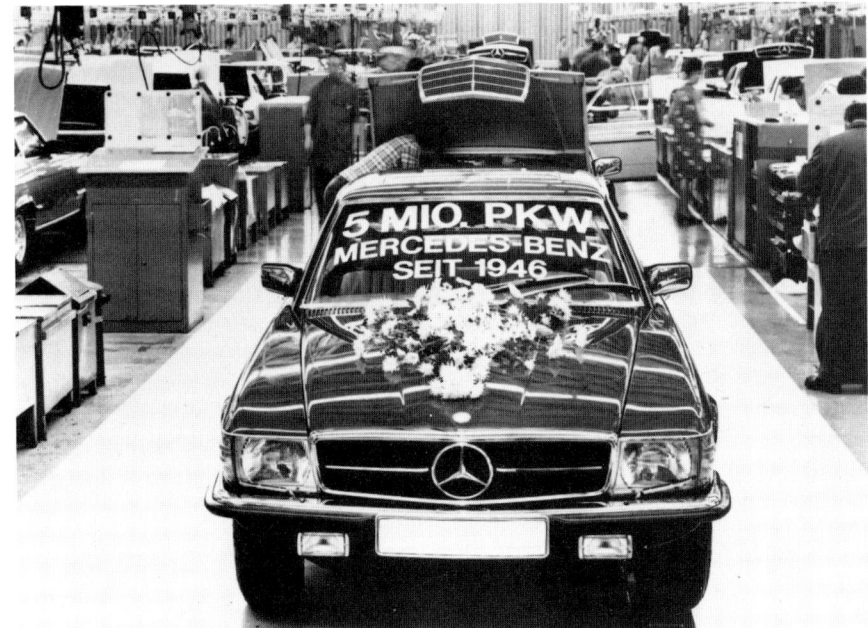
The 5-millionth production, an SLC coupe, 1978

Revolving cradle turns the car around handily, 1980

The experimental C111 in various body styles has served as excellent test vehicle

With different engine types installed, the car has set numerous world speed records

The Daimler-Benz factory at Untertürkheim

The body and assembly plant at Sindelfingen